# Valuing the Unique

————————————————

# Valuing the Unique

THE ECONOMICS
OF SINGULARITIES

*Lucien Karpik*

*Translated by Nora Scott*

PRINCETON UNIVERSITY PRESS

PRINCETON AND OXFORD

Originally published as *L'économie des singularités* by Lucien Karpik,
© Editions Gallimard, Paris, 2007

Cet ouvrage a bénéficié du soutien des Programmes d'aide à la publication de
Culturesfrance/Ministère français des affaires étrangères et européennes
*This work, published as part of a program of aid for publication, received support from
CulturesFrance and the French Ministry of Foreign Affairs*

ISBN: 978-0-691-13584-7
ISBN (pbk.): 978-0-691-13710-0

Library of Congress Control Number: 2010925019

British Library Cataloging-in-Publication Data is available

This book has been composed in Sabon

Printed on acid-free paper ∞

press.princeton.edu

Printed in the United States of America

1  3  5  7  9  10  8  6  4  2

# CONTENTS

## PART FOUR: Finale

# ILLUSTRATIONS AND TABLES

# PREFACE

*Valuing the Unique: The Economics of Singularities* is a translation from the original French *L'Economie des singularités*. In the process the text has been extensively revised, either for clarification or to improve the arguments, and the chapter on prices has been rewritten.

In conjunction with Nora Scott, the translator, and after a number of discussions and consultations, rather than attempt to translate the French notion of *singularités*, I decided to keep the same word in English: *singularities*. It is not often used in this sense in either language, but in both it was the closest to what we were looking for, and it was the means to avoid the notions of quality or qualities, since they have come to carry too many different meanings.

I would like to thank Jean Gadrey (Professor of Economics, University of Lille–1), Catherine Paradeise (Professor of Sociology, University of Marne-la-Vallée), and Philippe Steiner (Professor of Sociology, University of Paris–4) for their readings of a first version of this book. They have been as rigorous in their criticisms as they have been generous with their advice.

# PART ONE

# An Overlooked Reality

*Chapter One*

# THE PROBLEM

NEOCLASSICAL ECONOMICS, even in its latest versions, ignores one particular category of markets. I therefore propose a set of tools and reasonings to describe this reality and to explain its function as well as its evolution.

These overlooked markets are markets of *singular*, incommensurable products. Far from being restricted to marginal realities, they encompass those exchanges governed by the search for a "good" or the "right" . . . fine wine, novel, doctor, lawyer, or consultant. More generally, these markets include works of art, haute cuisine, movies, fine wines, recorded music, luxury goods, literature, tourism, certain handcrafted items, personalized professional services, and particular kinds of expertise.

Neoclassical analysis ignores these singular products as singular products. Not deliberately, of course; this blind spot is the logical consequence of a theoretical framework whose universalism implies a definition of exchange products (goods and services) that, *in the end*, excludes all differential features but price.[1] For example, with the central distinction between standardized and differentiated products, singularities are lost in the mass of differentiated goods and therefore remain invisible. But once defined, they can be separated, and their exchange is regulated by a particular form of economic coordination irreducible to the orthodox market. We must therefore explore the *terra incognita* of the market of singular products, or what I will term the *market of singularities*, and construct the theory that will account for it: namely, the *economics of singularities*.

• • •

This approach is part of a collective history that has spawned a diversification of market analyses over the last thirty or forty years. To neoclassical theory and its offshoots—which include, among others, transaction-cost theory, agency theory, and property-rights theory—must now be added heterodox economics—the theory of regulation, the theory of conventions, and neoinstitutional theory—and the development of the New Economic Sociology. In this book, I will draw some comparisons with these theoretical perspectives.

[1] For the comparison between singularities and differentiated products, subgroups like *experience goods*, *search goods*, and *credence goods*, see chapter 3.

As its position is central, neoclassical theory will be our principal term of reference.[2] Simplified comparison of its concepts and principles remains the easiest way to highlight the differences and bring out the changes in the stakes and arguments associated with singular products. To be sure, neoclassical theory is a vast universe that is both diversified and sophisticated, but as long as our use of the term does not occasion misunderstandings—as long as we do not mistake for a global judgment what is merely a presentation that points out discrepancies and new elements—this rhetorical device can be useful; moreover, it does not exclude, when the occasion arises, a closer, critical look at one or another specific argument.

•  •  •

In the usual interpretation of the changes observed in the economy and society, the apparently irresistible extension of the market can occur only at the expense of all that borders on its sphere. This evolution was clearly outlined by Marx: "Exchange has a history of its own. It has passed through different phases. . . . Finally, there came a time when everything that men had considered as inalienable became an object of exchange, of traffic and could be alienated. This is the time when the very things which till then had been communicated, but never exchanged; given but never sold; acquired but never bought—virtue, love, conviction, knowledge, conscience, etc.—when everything, in short, passed into commerce. It is the time . . . when everything, moral or physical, having become a marketable value, is brought to the market to be assessed at its truest value."[3] And elsewhere he continued, "Objects that in themselves are not commodities, such as conscience, honour, etc., are capable of being offered for sale by their holders, and of thus acquiring, through their price, the form of commodities."[4]

The market encounters its limit, and relentlessly pushes it back, in an exteriority that encompasses mainly—in French law—gifts, inalienable goods, and free things. Though the circulation of objects follows its own specific logic in the first case, it is subject to the prohibition of commerciality in the other two. This common taboo on the "capacity to circulate from one agent or actor to another"[5] should not be allowed to hide the

[2] I will also call neoclassical theory *mainstream economics* or *orthodox economics* and will use the term *standard market* for the homogeneous/differentiated market which corresponds to that theory.

[3] K. Marx, *The Poverty of Philosophy*, trans. Institute of Marxism Leninism (Moscow: Progress Publishers, 1955), *http://www.marxists.org/archive/marx/works/1847/povertyphilosophy/index.htm*, chapter 1.1.

[4] K. Marx, "Money, or the circulation of commodities," chap. 3 in *Capital*, vol. 1, trans. S. Moore and E. Aveling, ed. F. Engels (Moscow: Progress Publishers, n.d.), Marx and Engels Internet Archive, *http://www.marxists.org/archive/marx/works/1867-c1/ch03.htm*.

[5] I. Moine, *Les choses hors commerce* (Paris: LGDJ, 1997), p. 11.

differences: even with the consent of those who control their attribution, unlike free things, inalienable things, whether tangible or intangible, cannot be the object of a commercial transaction that would necessarily downgrade them. This absolute prohibition applies more particularly to the human body and to its detachable parts (organs, gametes), to subjective rights (those applying to the private citizen, such as the right to privacy and image rights), and to cultural creations, language, ideas, and works of art. The unity of this universe, often designated by the generic term *culture*, resides nowhere else than in the human person. This connection singularizes, whereas commerce leads to the system of equivalences. Legal systems vary according to time and place, but the principle of a separation between market and culture is found everywhere, even as past prohibitions are today being called into question.[6] The dividing line is contingent.

The conflict between culture and the market is more alive than ever. Karl Polanyi noticed it.[7] And more recently, the anthropologist Igor Kopytoff gave it a theoretical framework: things and people are not simply physical or biological entities, they are also cultural constructions, and the variations in their status compose veritable biographies. These processes are part of the general opposition between "commodities" and "singularities." The first fall into the category of generalized equivalence; the second, whether they are goods, services, or persons, are "uncommon, incomparable, unique, singular," incommensurable in sum, and consequently excluded from the sphere of exchange. The "career" of these goods is tied to the extension of the market, and singular goods—public monuments, museum art collections, the public patrimony, and a restricted form of exchange of end products such as medical care—can be preserved only by safeguarding them in state-protected "enclaves."[8] In fact, as soon as we concern ourselves with values, a great variety of reasons can be adduced to justify rejecting the market.[9]

The anthropological model, which underpins the antinomy between market and culture, has a long history and is still fully alive in today's social sciences. Because it is binary, it is also radical: *singularity is preserved in culture and lost in the market.* In passing from the former to the latter, it can only be dequalified. This model lends intelligibility to the

---

[6] P. Steiner, *La transplantation d'organes: Un commerce entre les êtres humains* (Paris: Gaillimard, forthcoming).

[7] "What nature makes different, the market makes homogeneous." K. Polanyi, "The economy of instituted process," in K. Polanyi, C. Arensberg, and H. W. Pearson, (eds.), *Trade and Market in the Early Empires* (New York: Free Press, 1957), p. 261.

[8] I. Kopytoff, "The cultural biography of things: Commoditization as process," in A. Appadurai (ed.), *The Social Life of Things: Commodities in Cultural Perspective* (Cambridge: Cambridge University Press, 1986), pp. 64–91.

[9] M. Walzer, *Spheres of Justice: A Defense of Pluralism and Equality* (New York: Basic Books, 1983), p. 97.

longstanding struggle between commoditization and singularization. It favors a representation dominated by the tendency toward the "boundless market"[10] and, by its corollary, the inevitable impoverishment of culture and hence of the world. Nothing seems able to stem this dynamic, since all powers—state, administrative, scientific, and economic—join forces to relentlessly extend the sphere of calculativeness in the name of order, truth, technology, and economic wealth.[11] The market grows unremittingly, driven by the conversion of incommensurabilities into generalized equivalence.

From Max Weber to Oliver Williamson, Alfred Chandler, and Theodore Porter, not forgetting Georg Simmel and many others, the extension of calculativeness goes on unabated. Weber reminds us that this practice has existed since time began and that it is a constituent feature of capitalism, since it makes it possible to assess profitability, is rooted in accounting as well as in the separation between professional and personal patrimony, and becomes generalized with the rational organization of free labor, the progress of science and technology, and the development of rational law.[12]

Simmel advances that money—that "purely arithmetical addition of value units," indifferent to the ends pursued, abstract and capable of unlimited reutilization, "the most terrible destroyer of form"[13]—incessantly expands the space in which quantities circulate. Chandler details the invention and development of the methods and techniques of calculation that, applied to production and sales, have enabled large corporations to calculate their costs, ensure their organizational coordination through budgetary techniques, forecast changing demand, and simulate the likely effects of pricing.[14] Porter enlarges the study of "the culture of objectivity" from the market to science and public life,[15] while Williamson exempts only relations between close relatives and friends from the

---

[10] V. Zelizer, "Beyond the polemics on the market: Establishing a theoretical and empirical agenda," *Sociological Forum* 3–4 (Fall 1988): 620–622.

[11] O. E. Williamson uses the notion of calculativeness in his article "Calculativeness, trust and economic organization" (*Journal of Law & Economics* 36 [April 1993]: 453–486) without formally defining it. Here it designates the constructed qualities that make it possible to bring goods and services within calculation.

[12] M. Weber, *The Protestant Ethic and "The Spirit of Capitalism,"* trans. P. Baehr and G. C. Wells (London: Penguin Books, 2002), pp. 13–31.

[13] G. Simmel, *The Philosophy of Money*, trans. T. Bottomore and D. Frisby (London and New York: Routledge, 2004), p. 272.

[14] A. D. Chandler, *Strategy and Structure* (Cambridge, MA: MIT Press, 1962); and *The Invisible Hand: The Managerial Revolution in American Business* (Cambridge, MA: Harvard University Press, 1977).

[15] T. M. Porter, *Trust in Numbers: The Pursuit of Objectivity in Science and Public Life* (Princeton: Princeton University Press, 1995).

calculativeness of the world that is the basis on which the universality of the economic science is grounded.[16]

This rationalization process has not always been regarded as beneficial. After examining its effects on economic efficiency, Weber voices his fears as to the extent of the accompanying change, which he superbly christens the "disenchantment of the world": the disappearance of magic and religion, the loss of the sacred, the vanishing of the meaning of social existence.[17] Simmel, for his part, depicts the rise of this "measuring, weighing and calculating exactness of modern times," which is the reflection of "one who calculates in an *egoistic* sense,"[18] and he makes it the bearer of impersonal relations dominated by indifference to others. As qualities are gradually converted into quantities, the world becomes more homogeneous, more impersonal, and more of a threat to the aesthetic, sensitive, and moral richness of humankind. And as the density of calculating agents and calculating machines is forever increasing, most of the authors do not conceal their pessimism: the loss of singularities is seen as the consequence of extending the market's purview.

$$\bullet \quad \bullet \quad \bullet$$

But what if this anthropological or historical model is considered to be unacceptable? Why should culture be kept outside the market? Why should we concentrate solely on the passage from the nonmarketable to the marketable? Why should *singularities not be part of the market?*[19] Is it so certain that the contradiction between the two terms is absolute? And that they are so easily separated? After all, the social history of art shows just the opposite, but then it deals with only certain categories of activities, works, and actors. And yet it is from a general perspective that we must inquire into the modes of relation between singularities and the market.

One could be in favor of the exclusion of trade, of the certainties of inalienability, and/or of the ways and means by which the state refuses commercial exchange. But these choices do not justify confusing fiction with reality and, consequently, accepting the generalized and radical metamorphosis of skills and qualities as they enter the market. It is not a matter of denying the transformations associated with the passage of culture to market or of choosing between what should or should not be sold; it is a question of understanding how the market comes to ensure the

[16] Williamson, "Calculativeness."

[17] Weber, *Protestant Ethic*, pp. 13–31.

[18] Simmel, *Philosophy of Money*, p. 444.

[19] The same remark is made by A. Appadurai in the introduction to Appadurai (ed.), *Social Life of Things*, p. 17.

circulation of incommensurable entities and thereby restores a reality that has been overlooked.

If singularities look likely to be swallowed up by the market, independently of any examination of the workings and outcome of the concrete process, that is also, and perhaps above all, the mechanical consequence of a mainstream economics that reasons in terms of homogeneous or differentiated products. Given this dichotomy, singularities can only be engulfed in the sphere of differentiation. And since it is then impossible to identify them as what they are, it is obviously impossible to follow their concrete transformations.

Knowledge of the relationship between singularities and the market will escape us as long as the concept of *singularity* has not been systematically constructed, that is, as long as a theoretical body has not been developed and its relationship with concrete reality been organized. The classical opposition between market and culture is not unjustified, but, far from being confused with the separation between inside and outside the market only, *this opposition is also located within the market*. And at the moment we do not possess the means to observe and explain it. A new analysis is needed, one capable both of recognizing singularities without necessarily disqualifying them and of making sense of a form of economic coordination ignored by neoclassical theory. The market of singular products should be *added to* the markets of homogeneous and differentiated goods. It justifies the elaboration of a specific theory that also entails ethical and political consequences.

Not only must this theory allow us to separate what is presently interwoven, to make visible a reality that is presently concealed in the sphere of differentiation, it must also lead to identifying the diverse causes that affect singularities. By abandoning the conception of a conflict centered solely on the relationship between market and nonmarket spheres and which, for this reason, conjures up such powerful global forces that humans are disarmed, the new theory restores their capacities for action. Internal market transformations are in effect linked to arrangements and actors that belong to ordinary economic and social life; they are no longer beyond the scope of a collective action that would aspire to keep the singularities in the world.

• • •

The following presentation of the economics of singularities includes a construction of the conceptual system adjusted to the economic coordination of singular products and a comparison of the *coordination regimes* supported by studies of concrete markets.

Part 1 introduces the concept of singularity, without which this specific sphere of exchange cannot be delimited, and studies its relations with the old and new versions of neoclassical theory.

Part 2 presents the tools of analysis, which, taken together, describe and explain the economic coordination of singular products.

Part 3 tests a classification of coordination regimes by using it in the study of several concrete markets: fine wines, luxury products, movies, popular music, professional services, and some others. Part 3 also includes a chapter on price theory.

Part 4 is devoted mainly to some sociohistorical processes like desingularization and the relationship between the economics of singularities and democratic individualism.

*Chapter Two*

---

# SINGULARITIES

DELINEATING THE world of singular products does not mean revealing what is hidden but, on the contrary, rediscovering the strangeness of what has become all too familiar. Singularities are everyday goods and services. They are part of our daily life and include movies, popular and classical records, restaurants, novels, doctors, lawyers, and so on. In a word, they embrace at the very least art works, products of the cultural industry,[1] and professional services. To describe and explain the way these markets operate, we need to know what singularities are and how they are exchanged. Although they seem quite heterogeneous, they nevertheless share crucial characteristics, which entail common consequences.

## WHAT ARE SINGULARITIES?

For a long time, I used the term *quality* (or *qualities*) and its derivatives *quality goods* and *economics of quality* or *qualities*.[2] But the word's affinity with a unidimensional reality, its increasingly frequent use, the growing diversity of its meanings, and the misunderstandings it prompted led me to replace it with the notion of *singular products* (goods and services) or, more simply, *singularities*, and its derivatives—*market of singularities*, processes of *singularization*, and *desingularization*. I called the theory of this particular reality the *economics of singularities*. Singularities are goods and services that are *structured, uncertain*, and *incommensurable*. Although a more detailed discussion will be presented below, I would like to briefly consider here the defining features of singularities.

### Multidimensionality

Singularities are multidimensional, but this alone does not fully determine them: they must also be structured, since the significance of each one of the dimensions is inseparable from the significance of all others. A singularity is thus also indivisible.

---

[1] The products of what R. Caves calls "creative industries." *Creative Industries: Contracts between Art and Commerce* (Cambridge, MA: Harvard University Press, 2001).

[2] L. Karpik, "L'économie de la qualité," *Revue française de sociologie* 30, no. 2 (1989): 187–210; and *French Lawyers: A Study in Collective Action 1274–1994*, trans. Nora Scott (Oxford: Oxford University Press, 1999), pp. 157–190.

The configuration of qualities explains the difficulties encountered by singular products in exchange, as everything depends on the *grasps* by which singularities are to be made visible at either close or long range.[3] How are they to be presented and represented? How can they be made visible and meaningful to the consumer? It is not unusual for these deliberate practices to be foiled by the way consumers interpret them.

## Uncertainty

Singularities are characterized by two kinds of uncertainty. First, *strategic uncertainty*, because from an ontological perspective the human person is a mystery. Products are presented to the public from a certain point of view, which is expressed by an arbitrary selection of some dimensions at the expense of others. Nothing guarantees that this display will match up with the clients' point of views. Strategic uncertainty arises from the intersection of two processes of interpretation; it is inherent to the relationship between multidimensional products and customers or clients, and it is all the greater when the pace of product renewal is rapid.

Second, and more important, there is *quality uncertainty*. In the neoclassical market, products are determined: they are knowable and known before purchase. As a consequence, the constraints on the encounter between supply and demand are limited to the information on the product nomenclature and prices. In the singularities market, on the contrary, the final adjustment is uncertain due to the mystery surrounding the product; this means that the purchase must be made even though knowledge of the product remains at least partially imperfect. After the transaction, the *evaluation lag* measures the time it takes to arrive at a realistic judgment concerning the quality of the product. But when quality uncertainty is *radical*, when it excludes any probabilistic calculation, even the long term is no guarantee of the relevance of the evaluation, not only because the consumer does not know the pertinent signs that would enable him to make a valid judgment, but also because reality can remain ambiguous to the very end, even for experts. This is the prosaic experience of anyone having to choose a new doctor or lawyer or having to buy a ticket for a new play or to purchase a trip in an unknown country. It explains why professionals selling these services are held responsible for the means but not for the end results.

This conception of quality uncertainty is by no means obvious. It is in line with Frank Knight's and George Akerlof's conceptions,[4] and it entails

[3] C. Bessy and F. Chateaureynaud, *Experts et faussaires* (Paris: Métailié, 1995). "The 'grasp' results from the meeting of a device embodied in the person or persons involved in the ordeal with a network of bodies which provide protrusions, folds, interstices" (p. 239).

[4] F. H. Knight, *Risk, Uncertainty and Profit* (Boston: Houghton Mifflin, 1921, 1956); G. A. Akerlof, "The market for lemons: Qualitative uncertainty and the market mechanism," *Quarterly Journal of Economics* 84 (1970): 488–500.

four major consequences: (1) it turns the exchange of products into an exchange of promises; (2) it cannot simply be conflated with information asymmetry; (3) it cannot be eliminated by the sole extension of information or of calculation; and (4) in association with free competition, it leads to "market failure." The two forms of uncertainty reinforce each other, even if quality uncertainty wields the more radical influence in creating an unpredictable market.

### Incommensurability

How can *incommensurability* be compatible with the market since it excludes comparison? How is it possible to choose between "realities that have nothing to do with each other"? For Kopytoff this contradiction is absolute. When culture is "uncommon, unique, singular," when it is located in state-protected enclaves, it becomes just another commodity, and thus subject to generalized equivalence, when it is traded.[5] Comparison in that case implies dequalification.[6] But if we do not accept the idea of discontinuity between culture and the market, we have to recognize that under certain conditions incommensurability and commensurability can be mutually convertible within the market.[7]

Incommensurability is the basis on which a shared culture has been built and maintained over time: it allows us to recognize the equal dignity and value of different artistic worlds. No *general* hierarchy can be justified between Rembrandt and Mondrian, between Mozart and Wagner, or between the Beatles and the Rolling Stones. It has taken centuries of commentaries by and debates between artists, historians, and philosophers to establish this now commonly accepted worldview. Nevertheless I can recognize the equal artistic worth of a great diversity of works while legitimately affirming that I prefer Vermeer to Mondrian and the Beatles to the Rolling Stones. As long as it is pluralist and reversible, commensurability is no threat to incommensurability, and vice versa.

[5] I. Kopytoff, "The cultural biography of things: Commoditization as process," in A. Appadurai, (ed.), *The Social Life of Things: Commodities in Cultural Perspective* (Cambridge: Cambridge University Press, 1986), pp. 64–91.

[6] *Dequalification (dequalify)* means "a loss of qualities." That process may apply to all types of products, but in the case of singularities, it may take the extreme meaning of "losing uniqueness, of becoming a banal good or service." In that case, the word *desingularization* is also sometimes used.

[7] There is little agreement as to the various meanings of the notion of incommensurability, a situation that has given rise to a very open debate. See, for example, E. R. Chang (ed.), *Incommensurability, Incomparability, and Practical Reason* (Cambridge, MA: Harvard University Press 1997); W. N. Espeland and M. L. Stevens, "Commensuration as a social process," *Annual Review of Sociology* 24 (1998): 313–343; and E. A. Povinelli, "Radical worlds: The anthropology of incommensurability and inconceivability," *Annual Review Anthropology* 30 (2001): 319–334.

The two perspectives exist all the more easily side by side in that each one corresponds to a different situation. On the one hand, incommensurability orders a collective representation of the products that eschews the idea of progress and assimilates historical diversity. On the other hand, commensurability is a modality of action that expresses the actor's autonomy and plurality of preferences. The oscillation between a relatively stable common reality and the multiplicity of the constructions associated with individual and collective points of view is constitutive of markets of singularities. It authorizes equivalence without calling incommensurability into doubt.

Singularities are thus defined by qualities (structured multiple dimensions), quality uncertainty, and incommensurability—*by all three together*.

## A Preliminary Journey

This journey proposes a preliminary schematic view of the relationship between producers and consumers as it is articulated around the markets of singularities. It presents the main notions and arguments that will be developed and illustrates them by a short interpretation of the market of psychoanalysis.

> *Singular products are characterized by quality*
> *uncertainty, which creates two threats for*
> *market continuity: opacity and opportunism.*

On its own or in association with asymmetry of information, quality uncertainty increases the probability of breach of trust. From this standpoint, human malice is the main danger, and as a consequence, the issue of opportunism comes to dominate mainstream economics. The singularities market, too, is threatened by opportunism, but it is *opacity* that is the principal menace. It is just as impossible to compare without knowing as to rely on an experience that intervenes only after the transaction. If all choices are random, then there is no choice at all. Reciprocal commitments cannot be made, and if they are made, they cannot be kept. The very existence of the market is therefore at stake.

The issue is all the more central because in order to achieve reasonable action, the market of singularities requires knowledge of the product that far exceeds anything necessary for the standard market. The consequences of this quasi-structural gap between the knowledge needed and the customers' usual competences directly threatens the continuity of the market. Faced with imperfect information, mainstream economics concentrates on price formation, whereas in the same situation, the economics

of singularities will be concerned less with prices than with choice of the
"good" or "right" products. Too many errors over a long period can only
bring about "market failure."

> *The market of singularities requires coordination*
> *devices to help the consumer make decisions.*
> *The market is "equipped" or it does not exist.*

With the multiplicity of singularities and the diversity of preferences, the
spontaneous and happy encounter between supply and demand must of
necessity be rare. The knowledge requirements are so extensive and varied that it is not enough for consumers to be active, curious, intelligent,
and motivated; they also need outside help, which comes from *personal*
and *impersonal judgment devices*. Together, these two categories of devices make up a varied and crowded world that is supposed to provide
consumers with enough knowledge about singularities to help them make
reasonable choices. The effectiveness of these devices varies with the credibility of the information furnished, which in turn depends on the trust
placed in the judgment devices. Thus the adjustment between clients seeking "good" singularities and the multitude of singular products can only
come about through a third party whose information and advice ensures
the buyer's greater or lesser happiness.

> *Quality competition prevails over price competition.*

The search for a "good" or the "right" singular product, whatever the
meanings assigned to these words by different consumers, is the activat-
ing principle of the singularities market. The requirement is more or less
stringent, but it is always present. It is expressed by the need for detailed
knowledge collected through a sometimes long search for the desirable
object, and it explains why quality competition prevails over price competition: choosing a "good" film rarely boils down to choosing the cheapest theater. And the same is true for a novel—or for a doctor.

> *Since quality competition prevails, the adjustment between*
> *products and consumers is achieved by seeking concordance*
> *between the evaluation criteria of the two sides.*

Two conditions must be met for there to be an adjustment: one concerns
qualities and the other prices. Since the bulk of my analysis is devoted to
quality adjustment, I will simply call it *adjustment;* otherwise, a qualification will be added: adjustment by quantities (volumes) or by prices. In

order for the exchange to occur, the representation of the product must be "known" in a way that corresponds sufficiently to the consumer's representation. In theory it is preferable for the qualifications of the singularities to be shared by producers and buyers, but despite the existence of judgment devices, this is rarely the case. For there to be a good adjustment—that is, the "good" or "right" encounter between product and buyer—the evaluation criteria governing both singularities and consumers presuppose exacting knowledge, complicated pathways, and sometimes a stroke of luck as well. Because ignorance and ambiguity are inherent to the commerce of incommensurable products, they explain the greater number of errors and disappointments here than in the neoclassical market.

> *Since quality competition is the more influential, prices*
> *can no longer be explained by supply and demand alone.*
> *Nevertheless, they still have to be explained.*

The subordinate position of prices implies that they are no longer determined solely by the relations between supply and demand, as in the standard market. One therefore has to discover the concrete procedures for setting prices in the market of singularities, to identify the causes that determine economic value, and to assess the effects of these heterodox practices on rational resource allocation within the market.

## THE MARKET OF PSYCHOANALYSIS

The psychoanalysis market shows that what appears to be an opaque market can be relatively efficient. For any ordinary patient, choosing a psychoanalyst is a difficult task. Generally speaking, those engaged in the search for a "good" psychoanalyst suffer from psychic disorders and share the belief that the probability of "improvement" or "cure" rises with the practitioner's skills. In view of what is at stake, price is usually a secondary consideration: it does not act as a choice criterion but as a more or less strong constraint on the patient's range of choices.

The definition of a "good" practitioner varies from one patient to the next and is represented by different configurations of characteristics from a long list that contains, among others, age, sex, open or reserved manner, address, office hours, office setting, length of session, price, reputation via publications, and membership in this or that psychoanalytic association. Not only are psychoanalysts not interchangeable, but the diversity of the demands heightens the heterogeneity of the professional world. And yet, in France, nowhere can one find lists of psychoanalysts classified according to most of these criteria. Furthermore, the absence of official training excludes reference to diplomas, and advertising is more or less restricted. The information available to the general public is sparse, dispersed in books, television programs, or often picturesque classified ads. Thus no systematic information is available to prospective patients that might enable them to identify competencies and fees: the market looks opaque. The minimum conditions for making a rational choice are lacking.

The meeting between supply and demand is brought about in most cases by a network acting as a third party. It is the informal practice of looking for information through personal relations—friends, acquaintances, family, one's general practitioner, and so on—that makes it possible to gather knowledge about the names and qualities of one or several practitioners. Of course this knowledge is limited, and its quality varies with the competences of the network members. But in exchange it is free and disinterested, the stories of personal experiences are rare and valuable, and a reasoned relationship can be constructed between what one is seeking and the information provided. The use of social relations is not the exception but the rule. The intermediary creates the condition for making a more or less relevant choice.

The psychoanalysis market carries the restriction of public information to the extreme; it operates exclusively on *personalized relations*. Its opacity is not a pathology, however, but a professional collective choice. This particular definition of the profession affects competition, relations between practitioners, relations between practitioners and their patients, and the search for a "good" practitioner.

The economics of singularities explains the workings of the psychoanalysis market insofar as the search for a "good" psychoanalyst is not separated from the patient's interpersonal relations. The network is an invisible judgment device that transmits individual and collective experience to whoever inquires, and the psychoanalysis market could not exist without it. But this originality is not peculiar to psychoanalysis; it is true of many other singularities as well.

## Two Models of Singularity

Can incommensurable products be put into categories? The distinction between goods and services is hardly pertinent, for, while the bulk of singularities are probably services, a great number of singular products combine goods and services; in other words, they are hybrids. The useful distinction is more specific: it separates devices and practices according to whether they refer to evaluation criteria pertaining to the *originality model* or to the *personalization model*.

## The Originality Model

The pure form of the originality model is the work of art; it acts as a model for a whole set of products and is their common reference through multiple real or imaginary lineages. However, it does not follow that the singularities that come under this model need, like the work of art, embody the qualities of originality, incomparability, and uniqueness simultaneously.

In a work written before the Second World War, Walter Benjamin developed the idea that even the most perfect technical reproductions inevitably undergo an irremediable loss. This, he argued, is because the meaning of the work is connected to the initial conditions of its appearance, to its original function, usually ritual, to the *hic et nunc* of the work; in other words, to the uniqueness of its existence where it happens to be, to everything that participates in its authenticity—which Benjamin summed up by the term *aura*. That is what is unavoidably lost even with the most perfect reproduction of works of art from the past. To reproduce is to draw closer to the present-day public and, at the same time, to move away from tradition, from authenticity, from the "power of historical testimony." By losing its uniqueness, the work of art reaches the "masses," but at the cost of an irreversible downgrading.[8]

Confronted with a form of production like the movie industry, Benjamin admitted that it is not confined to the function of reproduction: movies are works in their own right. And yet, even though some of his formulations seem to show the contrary, he nevertheless insisted that, in the main, the cinema, which owes its existence to the technical reproduction of film copies, cannot keep the *aura* of the work intact. In the final analysis, he denied that movies have any artistic value. Such an absolute criticism raises the question of the relationship between scarcity and the artistic value of singularities in the originality model.

Today it is for paintings that Walter Benjamin's thesis is the most pertinent, since the requirements have never been so stringent: the painting must be unique, original, and authentic. Unique: there is only one exemplar, though sometimes rarity is acceptable. Original: there is no other like it. Authentic: it must be signed or at the very least the artist must be identified. Thus its artistic value does not rest on aesthetic judgment alone, since absence of the signature banishes the work to obscurity and oblivion. The sacralization of the unique work, which has been largely unchallenged by the few attempts at producing multiple copies, is experiencing a fundamentalist comeback, which finds expression in the growing numbers of deattributions as well as in the collective strategies aimed

---

[8] W. Benjamin, "The work of art in the age of mechanical reproduction," UCLA School of Theater, Film, and Television; transcribed by Andy Blunden 1998; proofed and corrected Feb. 2005, http://www.marxists.org/reference/subject/philosophy/works/ge/benjamin.htm.

at reinforcing scarcity.[9] The unique and the multiple may therefore be viewed as incompatible for the artistic model.

In that regard, there have been numerous variations. For example, the individuality of the work and the individuality of the artist assert themselves strongly for the first time with Rembrandt, as Svetlana Alpers' interpretation shows. How is it that Rembrandt's work can be considered as the prime form of individuality when the number of his paintings undergoing deattribution—including of some of the most famous—is still on the rise? How can singularity be embodied simultaneously in the artist responsible for unique works and, without any objection on Rembrandt's part, in the many paintings, copies, or new subjects that—although they have been attributed to him—were painted by his assistants, disciples, or epigones? How can individuality be compatible with multiplicity?

The answer is based on the twin rupture that the painter created between home and the workshop, between patronage and the market. The workshop had become the place where those who came to learn from the master were trained and where they produced—combining both copies of the master's works and original subjects, many of which would be signed by Rembrandt himself; and these disciples would then take away with them the art of painting "in the manner of Rembrandt." The market became the acting space for a free and active "entrepreneur" who sold "Rembrandts."[10] These practices can be explained by the large number of paintings hanging in Dutch interiors at that time.

It was for this "mass market" that Rembrandt "invented the work of art most characteristic of our culture—a commodity distinguished by among others not being factory produced, but produced in limited numbers."[11] The initial paradox is thus dissipated. The conception that played a founding role in the West teaches us that the relationship between individuality and number can vary and that singularity can be based on limited series as well as on unique works. With the novel or the cinema, mass production reigns to an even greater extent. Here, once again, the singularity is not threatened by the production process, because the similarity of the material medium does not jeopardize the arbitrariness of the content and therefore the unlimited number of its meanings. The product of the cultural industry does not destroy the notion of singularity as long as it safeguards the diversity of personal interpretations.

To sum up: the originality model defines a diversified sphere of singular products whose legacy implies the use of *aesthetic criteria*. Further-

---

[9] R. Moulin, *The French Art Market: A Sociological Perspective* (New Brunswick, NJ: Rutgers University Press, 1988).

[10] S. Alpers, *Rembrandt's Enterprise: The Studio and the Market* (Chicago: University of Chicago Press, 1988), pp. 86–87, 101, 102.

[11] Ibid., p. 102.

more, singularities may be unique or multiple, and their material medium may be industrially produced whenever their symbolic power—and therefore their capacity to accommodate an indefinite number of particular interpretations—is maintained.

## The Personalization Model

The term *personalized product* more often designates a service than a good, but the two can be variously combined. Keeping to personalized services for the moment, I will call upon the notion of *service relations* as used by sociologists and economists. For the sociologist, a service relation is a personalized service; it is an activity characterized by uncertainty about both quality and results. It defines the modes of action of the *professions*, that is to say, those organized groups that associate an area of expertise with a collective ethic and (at least officially) demand that their members put the client's interests ahead of their own and place the service rendered ahead of profit-seeking.[12] For heterodox economists, the service relation replaces *services* as a privileged object of study. This shift indicates the key position occupied by the "co-production of services," in other words, by the cooperation between practitioners and clients. The service relation is diversified, then, "according to the intensity of the relations and interactions between the actors of the supply and the demand,"[13] and the differences are accentuated by the degree of uncertainty and irreversibility of the results they produce.

These twin roots make it possible to conceive of the *personalized* product as a pure form of singularity and to define it as being the intervention best suited to the specific problems of persons and collectivities. This is shown clearly by the comparison between *occupational physicians*, who work with companies or the state (*médecins du travail*) and use an administrative frame to regulate their intervention on patients, and clinical practitioners, who regard each patient as unique and use a clinical frame to fit their interventions to the patient's idiosyncratic particularism.[14]

The personalized product should not be confused with the *customized product*, which is gaining ground with the growing flexibility and so-

[12] The notion of *profession* covers a multitude of definitions, which have sparked numerous controversies. I will content myself with a simplified conception pending the analysis devoted to professional services later in this volume.

[13] J. Gadrey and J. De Bandt, "De l'économie des services à l'économie des relations de service," and J. Gadrey, "Les relations de service dans le secteur marchande," in J. De Bandt and J. Gadrey (eds.), *Relations de service, marches de services* (Paris: Editions du CNRS, 1994), pp. 17 and 11–41.

[14] N. Dodier, *L'expertise médicale: Essai de sociologie sur l'exercice du jugement*, (Paris: Métailié, 1993); and "Expert medical decision in occupational medicine: A sociological analysis of medical judgment," *Sociology of Health and Illness* 16, no. 4 (1994): 489–514.

phistication of industrial production.[15] The post-Fordism era no longer suffers from the monotony of mass production and can reconcile individualized supply and demand. Such *customization* finds expression, for example, in an automobile industry now capable of turning out a variety of combinations of parts or of basic functions within preset technical limits. But these variants are still part of the same sphere of equivalences: they simply enhance the differentiation. It is the *tailor-made* service provided by a vast number of professions and trades—doctors, dentists, oral surgeons, pharmacists, lawyers and attorneys, corporate consultants, etc.—that gives access to personalization based on professional *criteria of excellence.*

The originality model and the personalization model are by far the most important models today, but others exist and new ones may develop. These two models apply to two distinct sets of singular products, though this does not mean they are foreign to each other; hybrid products exist. Above all, the two models share an implicit or explicit common reference: they are inseparable from that which is the most radically opposed to interchangeability: the *human person.* As a result, producers, consumers, original goods, and personalized services are incommensurable entities. This circularity is not a spontaneous reality, however: it is a collective construction without which the market of singularities could not exist.

The same representation is found in the world of products characterized by reference to aesthetic value or professional excellence. And by no means does it exclude autonomous individual judgment.

· · ·

Singularities are multidimensional, uncertain, and incommensurable; the consumer is searching for the "right" or a "good" singularity; quality competition prevails over price competition; and the market is opaque. These and other features are foreign to the neoclassical theory; therefore, another theory is needed to explain the functioning and evolution of singularities markets. But before beginning that task, we should try to explain why singularities have been overlooked.

[15] M. Piore and C.F. Sabel, *The Second Industrial Divide: Possibilities for Prosperity* (New York: Basic Books, 1984); W. Streeck, "On the institutional conditions of diversified quality production," in E. Matzner and W. Streeck (eds.), *Beyond Keynesianism: The Socio-economics of Production and Full Employment* (Brookfield, VT: Edward Elgar, 1991).

# Chapter Three

# DO WE NEED ANOTHER MARKET THEORY?

THERE IS NOTHING new about questioning the limits of the neoclassical theory, although doing so has been and still is usually regarded by mainstream economics as a sign of ignorance or naivety. Two counter-arguments are regularly advanced by orthodox economists to dismiss the charges that critics confuse the model with reality and overuse the term *neoclassical theory*, thereby demonstrating their ignorance of a complex and evolving body of knowledge.

In some cases these reactions are justified, but that should not prevent us asking the following question: what discrepancy would make the concrete, peculiar marketplace unfit for neoclassical analysis? For orthodox economists, the question is literally meaningless, since every marketplace, however "impure" and "imperfect" its information or competition may be, can only belong to the same theoretical framework. Distance and strangeness can never be transformed into exteriority.[1]

Such a proposition stems from an operation that is striking not so much for its complexity as for its simplicity. Far from being the result of a demonstration, the inseparable relationship between the unity of theory and the unity of reality is the product of a postulate: that there is only one market model and, as a result, no market reality, however peculiar, can be external to it.

Can this theoretical perspective account for singularities? A reasoned answer must break down the overly general term *neoclassical theory* into two categories: *mainstream economics* and the *new economics*, as it was called when it appeared in the 1970s. The general question remains the same, but for each form of economics, the discussion is different.

## WHAT MAINSTREAM ECONOMICS COULD ONLY IGNORE

The countless definitions of the neoclassical theory differ only by a few, usually minor, stylistic features. The constitutive elements are always the same: a rational actor endowed with stable, ordered preferences and exclusively

---

[1] "Of course, our theory should cover all such special cases. The general laws of the market should apply to the diamond market, the market for Raphael's paintings and to the market for tenors and sopranos. These laws should even apply to a market like the one Mr. De Quincey imagines, in which there is a single buyer, a single seller, one commodity and only one minute in which to make the exchange." L. Walras, *Elements of Pure Economics: Or, the Theory of Social Wealth* (London: Routledge, 1988, 2003), p. 86.

oriented toward profit or utility maximization; the regulation of supply
and demand by price variations; and market equilibrium states that are
determined by the conditions of competition.

The generality of the theory implies that the conditions of pure and
perfect competition vary along a continuum: however far they may de-
part from the model, market realities can never escape it altogether. Since
the theoretical model requires goods to be homogeneous, their choice
by the consumers is based exclusively on one differential feature: price.[2]
Thus, this reasoning finds an exception in the products, as they may or
may not be homogeneous.

What happens when the goods are not homogeneous? This issue was
addressed by Edward Chamberlin in a book published in 1933, *The Theory of Monopolistic Competition*, in which he demonstrates that, for
differentiated goods—goods particularized by any difference that represents a competitive advantage on the market—as well as for homogeneous goods, price theory retains its unity and its universal validity.[3]

Chamberlin was not the first to have noticed the extension of a new
form of competition that expresses the relative capacity of firms to produce, in advance of their competitors, new commodities that are the
source of monopolistic rents. But he was the first to resolve the problem
he had raised: how can we explain a form of economic struggle that calls
on both competition and monopoly?

The solution was to consider each differentiated product as a homogeneous product associated with a specific market (thus there are as many
markets as there are differentiated goods[4]), to analyze pricesetting for
each homogeneous market, to link markets through price relations, and
to identify the effects of the variety of products on prices. The theoretical
difficulty was thus resolved by converting differentiated goods into homogeneous goods. And the use of Hotelling's model, which transforms
the degree of substitutability of differentiated goods into a more or less

[2] "Conventional competitive economic theory begins with the hypothesis of price-taking
firms and consumers buying and selling homogeneous commodities at well-defined marketplaces. . . . This is the condition of 'the Law of Single Price.'" J. Stiglitz, "The cause and
consequence of the dependence of quality on price," *Journal of Economic Literature* 25
(1987): 2.

[3] "A general class of product is differentiated if any significant basis exists for distin-
guishing the goods (or services) of one seller's merchandise (or services) from those of another. Such a basis may be real or fancied, so long as it is of any importance whatever to
buyers, and leads to a preference for one variety of the product over another." E. H. Chamberlin, *The Theory of Monopolistic Competition: A Re-orientation of the Theory of Value*
(Cambridge, MA: Harvard University Press, 1933, 1969), p. 56.

[4] "Now it is to be recognized that each is in some measure isolated, so that the whole is
not a single large market of many sellers, but a network of related markets, one for each
seller"; hence the technical complexity Chamberlin complains about further on, since there
would have to be as many diagrams as there are varieties of "products." Ibid., p. 69.

distant continuous line, confirmed that these goods belonged to a system of equivalences.[5] Moreover, since differentiated and standardized goods alike are delineated, knowable, and known before purchase, the issue of product heterogeneity disappeared and market theory could continue to coincide with price theory.

Although the theory of monopolistic competition was often assimilated to a revolution because it combined two terms that had previously been not only separate but also opposed, and although the author himself regarded his approach as a new perspective—a new "economic view," a new *Weltanschauung*—the change, prompted by differentiation, took place without any major clashes in the already existing body of knowledge and so became an integral part of a neoclassical theory which, after having included differentiated goods, recovered its universal validity.

*In this theory, singularities cannot exist as singularities.* To be taken into account, they must give up qualities, uncertainty, and incommensurability, and doing so amounts to a systematic process of dequalification that will transform them into differentiated goods; or else they must remain unexplained. The economics of singularities cannot be confused in any way with mainstream economics.

## WHAT THE "NEW ECONOMICS" CHOSE TO IGNORE

In the 1970s, uncertainty appeared in economic theory, where it progressively came to occupy a central position and to exert a major influence on the analysis of prices, products, economic coordination, and market equilibrium. Imperfect information replaced perfect information and bounded rationality supplanted omniscient rationality. Products characterized by quality uncertainty became promises, their evaluation was deferred until after purchase, and price-setting, as well as the credibility of commitments, became problematic.[6]

The term *new economics* was applied to the new analysis, which was built around "information" and based on a particular view of uncertainty that applied to strategic uncertainty as well as to quality uncertainty.[7]

[5] H. Hotelling, "Stability in competition," *Economic Journal* 39(1929): 41–57. Before its publication in 1933, economists had been acquainted with Chamberlin's doctoral dissertation (1927).

[6] "Much of what economists believed that they thought to be true on the basis of research and analysis over almost a century turned out not to be robust to considerations of even slight imperfections of information." J. Stiglitz, "The contributions of the economics of information to twentieth century economics," *The Quarterly Journal of Economics* 115, no. 4 (Nov. 2000): 1461.

[7] Williamson developed the most detailed interpretation of the conditions and effects of strategic uncertainty: (1) The greater the uncertainty (when rationality is bounded), the

During the same period, the question of quality was also resolved by a theory of multidimensionality. The new economics thus integrated multidimensionality, quality uncertainty, and even (to a lesser degree) incommensurability.

This achievement raises two questions, which in reality are but one: Might not singularities belong to one of the new categories of products constructed by the new economics, even if the term *singularity* was not used? And if this is not the case, how do we explain that singular products were overlooked? The first question justifies a comparative study of the use of the three terms—*multidimensionality, quality uncertainty,* and *incommensurability*—while the second finds its answer in the analysis of a conflict that was present within the new economics from the beginning.

### *Multidimensionality*

To explain the relationship between the differences in prices and the quality of the goods, the usual solution was (and still is) to select a quality as a single dimension that would then become the common term of a ranking system. Different dimensions were usually chosen—such as reliability, warranties, price as an index of quality, and most often, reputation. This procedure brought multidimensional products into the sphere of generalized equivalences and thus into the neoclassical framework. But in the end, none of these methods met with general intersubjective agreement; none could lay claim to general validity.

The solution came from Kelvin Lancaster. His theory rests on the general assumption that consumers are not interested in the goods but in their elementary components: their "characteristics." These are the sources of utility and, moreover, they are immutable, independent of each other, and can be combined with each other. They are the targets of individual ordered preferences, and, because everyone shares this intersubjective agreement, they are "objective." The list of characteristics for each

---

more incomplete the contract will be, because the contracting parties are unable to foresee all future contingencies and are therefore unable to imagine all the legal clauses that would ensure the predictability of each side's behavior and therefore the security of the contract. (2) The more incomplete the contract and the more specific the assets—whether they are territorial, technical, or human—the higher the probability of opportunism and the higher the probabilities of a market failure. (3) The more opportunism threatens the interests of the contracting parties, the more tempted they are to complete their contracts, which as a result become ever more complex and costly. (4) The higher the "transaction costs," the more they favor the shifting of the "same" transaction toward a firm, whose transaction costs are theoretically lower. However, market "failure" is counteracted by "protective mechanisms" such as networks, regulation, company culture, codes of ethics. O. E. Williamson, "The economics of organization: The transaction cost approach," *American Journal of Sociology* 87 (1981): 548–577.

good has to be exhaustive, but it could be simplified. Their relative value is set by the perfect competitive market and remains the same whatever the goods in which this characteristic is embodied. Thus, a product is a "bundle of characteristics," and its global price is the sum of the prices of all its characteristics. The theory is general; moreover, it can be easily applied to reality through the hedonic method. Lancaster seems to have succeeded in squaring the circle: he transformed the unidimensional good into a multidimensional one and he explained its global price by the sum of the prices of its "characteristics." Subsequently, concrete studies have proliferated, but none has set any limits to the theory's validity. They exist, however, and it is crucial to identify them for the economics of singularities.[8]

I will compare two hedonic studies: one on housing and the other on fine wines. Using econometric methods, the studies calculate the *shadow prices* (the hedonic prices of the characteristics), that is to say, the relative contribution of each characteristic to the total price of the product. The two studies yield analogous formal results but their meanings are completely different.

The housing study uses a large database combining seventeen different characteristics that enables the user to know the contribution of different elements—an additional room, a garage, a furnished kitchen, a balcony, or a garden—to the global price.[9] Formally, the findings of the study on fine wines are no different. The wine characteristics include sensory qualities and the objective qualities printed on the bottle labels: classification, appellation (protected geographic designation), and year. If the classification and year come first for the relative contributions to the global price, "taken alone, each sensory characteristic has very little effect on price."[10] Thus the taste characteristics have only a slight impact on the global price, while the inverse holds for the information on the labels. The consequences of this observation are crucial because information labels are not taste characteristics: they are indicators of quality, which is an altogether different reality. The difference could easily be explained by the fact that a large majority of nonprofessional buyers are too ignorant in wine matters to recognize the sensory dimensions. But it is not really

[8] K. Lancaster, "A new approach to consumer theory," *Journal of Political Economy* 74 (1966): 132–157; K. Lancaster (ed.), *Modern Consumer Theory* (Aldershot, UK: Edward Elgar, 1990).

[9] N. Gravel, M. Martinez, and A. Trannoy, "Une approche hédonique du marché des logements," *Études foncières* 74 (1997): 16–20; and "L'approche hédonique du marché immobilier," *Études foncières* 78 (1998): 14–18.

[10] P. Combris, S. Lecocq, and M. Visser, "Estimation of a hedonic price equation for Bordeaux wine: Does quality matter?" *Economic Journal* 107 (1997): 390–402; and "Estimation of a hedonic price equation for Burgundy wine," *Applied Economics* 32 (2000): 961–967.

ignorance that explains why one sensory quality cannot be distinguished from another; it is the fact that sensory qualities are interdependent: each one depends on all the others and cannot be separated from them. Consequently, the hedonic study of the wines does not explain anything. And the distinction between houses and fine wines is a distinction between divisible and nondivisible goods. In an inconspicuous remark, Lancaster foresaw the limits of his theory when he pointed out that, for indivisible and noncombinable products, "we are in real trouble because the true shadow price may not become manifest in any form at all."[11]

The difference between houses and fine wines is the same as that found, for example, between cars and movies, and, more generally, between differentiated goods and singular goods: all of them are multidimensional but the first are *aggregates* of characteristics and the second are *structures* of characteristics. Multidimensionality does not have the same meaning for all goods and services. Thus, despite its true ingenuity, Lancaster's theory is not general: *it is not valid for singularities.*

### Uncertainty

Sometime in the 1970s, quality uncertainty became the criterion for a new classification of products. This was a major change, but to give a realistic glimpse of its scale, we should consider some of the terms that are part of what has sometimes been called a revolutionary history: the consumers' ignorance becomes an explanatory variable of their behavior, their actions are considered as a more or less costly "search," and heterogeneous entities such as friends and advertising can be combined to explain the variations in the available information.[12] Consumer practices become a central object of study.

The central issue was the notion of quality uncertainty. Different conceptions of it have arisen and may still arise; the debate has been, and still is, complicated. The presentation of the arguments will be limited to what seems necessary to identify the two general opposing conceptions, to explain how they have created a tension within the new economics, and to the consequences that have followed the victory of one side over the other. The easiest way to draw this picture is to compare the two conceptions as they have been expressed, on one hand, by Phillip Nelson, Michael Darby, and Edi Karni and, on the other, by Knight and Akerlof.

Nelson makes a distinction between *search goods* and *experience goods*, to which Darby and Karni add *credence goods* and present a general definition of these terms: "Search qualities . . . are known before purchase, experience qualities . . . are known costlessly only after purchase,

---

[11] Lancaster, *Modern Consumer Theory*, p. 97.
[12] G. Stigler, "The economics of information," *Journal of Political Economy* 69 (1961): 213–225.

and credence qualities . . . are expensive to judge even after purchase."[13] Their studies are guided by two main questions: How can consumers make reasonable choices when their information is uncertain? How can consumers protect themselves against seller fraud when the exchange entails experience goods, or when uncertainty is even higher, as in the case of credence goods?

Nelson opened the way for consumer studies with his comparisons between different combinations of goods (experience goods and search goods), of information origins (friends or personal experience), and of types of advertisement.[14] Darby and Karni used the example of a repair service to show that in the case of credence goods, sellers have many ways of increasing their profit while decreasing the quality of the service.[15] That sounds like the end of the age of innocence. Williamson would soon show that *opportunism,* "self-interest seeking with guile," is the omnipresent threat hovering over uncertain markets and would study the means that may be mobilized to prevent "market failure."[16] Numerous economists would assess the relative effectiveness of the available means of protection: contracts, warranties, brands, advertising, public standards, repeat purchases, and seller reputation.[17]

All these issues, notions, and analysis were based on the same conception of uncertainty. Another conception found expression when Akerlof published the most famous article of the period. Taking the example of the "lemon" market—the used-car market—he demonstrated that quality uncertainty combined with information asymmetry necessarily leads to market self-destruction.[18] The only way to prevent this outcome is to rely on the action of "counter-institutions": guarantees, brands, certifications, diplomas, professional licensing, intervention of the state and

---

[13]M. Darby and E. Karni, "Free competition and the optimal amount of fraud," *Journal of Law and Economics* 16 (1973): 69.

[14]P. Nelson, "Information and consumer behaviour," *Journal of Political Economy* 78, no. 2 (1970): 311–329; "Advertising as information," *Journal of Political Economy* 81 (1974): 729–754; and "Comments on 'The economics of consumer information acquisition,'" *The Journal of Business* 53 (1980): 164–165.

[15]Darby and Karni, "Free competition," 69.

[16]O. E. Williamson, "The economics of organization: The transaction cost approach," *American Journal of Sociology* 87 (1981): 554.

[17]J. Tirole, *The Theory of Industrial Organization* (Cambridge, MA: MIT Press, 1988, pp. 106–113.

[18]G. A. Akerlof, "The market for lemons: Quality uncertainty and the market mechanism," *Quarterly Journal of Economics* 84 (1970): 488–500. In the used-car market, certain vehicles (*lemons*) have hidden defects that are known to the seller but not to the buyer. Therefore the average price, which expresses this socially known risk, is relatively low because it is impossible to tell the lemons from all the others. The owners of good cars, who would normally have put them up for sale, refuse to do so because they consider that prices are too low. From here on out, risks for potential clients rise and, therefore, prices fall. The owners of less-good used cars in turn do not put them up for sale, and so on. Bad cars drive out good ones. When only bad cars are left to fight it out, no one is willing to buy and the market "collapses."

private institutions, and, of course, trust. In the absence of such mediations, the market collapses. Thus, under certain conditions, free competition leads to market self-destruction, while market continuity requires
the regulation of competition. In sum, with quality uncertainty, continuity of the market and free competition are at cross-purposes: *the very
foundations of neoclassical theory are undermined.*[19]

Here we have two opposing conceptions of uncertainty. For Nelson,
Darby, and Karni, and a large majority of economists, uncertainty is moderate (more or less so according to whether we are dealing with experience
goods or credence goods), while for Akerloff it is *radical*. Concrete expressions of this difference can be found in the consequences of uncertainty—
less efficient market equilibrium versus market self-destruction—and in
the means used to avoid them—the various measures compatible with
free competition versus the arrangements which, like professional licensing or state intervention, not to mention the reference to trust, can only
reduce free competition.

What is ruled out in one conception becomes necessary in the other. A
prohibition respected by the first is lifted by the second. Although Akerlof does not explicitly refer to it, he is close to Knight's conception, formulated twenty years before, in which a distinction is made between
probabilizable, and therefore calculable, uncertainty and nonprobabiliz-
able, or radical uncertainty, the first being called *risk* and the second,
*uncertainty*.[20] The prevailing conception in the new economics is that of
a continuous and moderate uncertainty that entails risk and maintains
the possibility of calculating the most rational decision. This possibility
no longer exists with radical uncertainty. In this sense, singularities are an
inheritance from Knight and Akerlof.

Risk and uncertainty are not only two different conceptions, they are
also two competing conceptions. In the past, a large majority of economists were busy excluding the radical conception of quality uncertainty.[21]
I will present briefly three operations that have led to this exclusion.

First, repeated critiques of Knight's theory made it possible to end the
distinction between risk and uncertainty, so that the world of the new

---

[19] See below re. game theory, which cannot resolve such a crisis single handedly.

[20] F. H. Knight makes a distinction between uncertainty associated with repeated operations and uncertainty associated with unique, incomparable operations. In the case of risk,
the probability of the event happening can be calculated, which is not the case for "uncertainty." This second kind of uncertainty is sometimes called "radical uncertainty." *Risk,
Uncertainty and Profit* (Boston: Houghton Mifflin, 1921, 1956).

[21] "While the distinction between risk and uncertainty so defined is often encountered in
the literature, its role until recently has been reduced to the ceremonial: economists, especially those working in the neoclassical tradition, invoke the distinction only in order to rule
out uncertainty." S. LeRoy, D. Larry, and J. Singell, "Knight on risk and uncertainty," *The
Journal of Political Economy* 95, no. 2 (1987): 394–406.

economics has turned into the empire of risk.[22] Second, a generalized re-interpretation of Akerlof's article resulted in the replacement of quality uncertainty by information asymmetry. The latter notion, linked to *moral hazard* and *adverse selection*, applies to risk and thus comes to occupy a core theoretical position. But information asymmetry is not indispensible for quality uncertainty to produce its effects. And Akerlof's demonstration of the inverse relationship between market continuity and free competition remains embarrassing. Third, rejection of quality uncertainty can take the extreme form of dissimulation. In certain presentations of Akerlof's article, the notion is purely and simply passed over in silence. The reader of these articles must wonder what aberration led the future Nobel laureate to include the word in his title. The fact remains that, with this discarding-disappearance practice, *the reality characterized by this form of uncertainty becomes invisible. In other words, singularities could not and still cannot exist.*[23]

No history is without surprises. What happened with quality uncertainty explained three mutually reinforcing consequences. First, a few economists among Knight's and Keynes's descendants have clung to the conception of radical uncertainty.[24] Second, the revival of radical uncertainty came, unexpectedly, from heterodox economics, particularly the economics of conventions,[25] and from a few sociologists.[26] Third, some of the economists and sociologists who have conducted empirical research have justified the notion of radical uncertainty. This is the case of Caves, who organized his study around the "nobody knows" property rule, by which he meant that there was no means of predicting the success of a product of the culture industry. As a result, he considered creative

[22] J. Hirshleifer and J. G. Riley, "The analytics of uncertainty and information: An expository survey," *Journal of Economic Literature* 17, no. 4 (1979): 1375–1421.

[23] The spontaneous interpretations of the familiar decisions we make about singularities are usually largely divorced from reality. We have so strongly incorporated the major neoclassical framework and principles that they have become constitutive of our ways of thinking and therefore the interpretation of the real world becomes problematic. The blind spot exists, even for those who have a direct knowledge of the real logic that governs their choices Although we observe and understand quite well how competition between movies or novels works, nevertheless it seems difficult to accept the idea that quality competition prevails over price competition.

[24] "The distinction Knight makes between risk . . . and radical uncertainty . . . still has a bright future." N. Moureau and D. Rivaud-Danset, *L'incertitude dans les théories économiques* (Paris: La Découverte, 2004), p. 112.

[25] J-P. Dupuy, F. Eymard-Duvernay, O. Favereau, A. Orléan, R. Salais, and L. Thévenot, "L'économie des conventions," *Revue économique* (2 May 1989); J. Gadrey, "Dix thèses pour une socio-économie de la qualité des produits," *Sociologie du travail* 44 (2002): 272–277.

[26] J. Beckert, "What is sociological about economic sociology? Uncertainty and the embeddedness of economic action," *Theory and Society* 25 (1996): 803–840; L. Karpik, "L'économie de la qualité," *Revue française de sociologie* 30, no. 2 (1989): 187–210; H. C. White, *Markets from Networks* (Princeton: Princeton University Press, 2001), pp. 6–9.

products as "experience goods" that depend not on the asymmetry of information but on "the symmetry of ignorance."[27] Writing on the movie industry, De Vany is even more adamant: "There really is nothing that is predictable, not costs, not performance value and certainly not revenue"; and again: "Movies, hurricanes, earthquakes, floods, stock market returns, innovations and patents, and just about any really important phenomenon in human affairs are almost completely unpredictable. . . . Just as there [are] no typical hurricanes, or earthquakes there is no typical movie."[28] The same observation holds for French lawyers.[29]

The exchange of singularities is linked to radical uncertainty; as a result, no knowledge, calculation, or contract can dissipate it: something more has to be added, which is trust. *Because the universe of singularities is defined by radical uncertainty, the complete notion will be recalled from time to time but usually the term "uncertainty" alone will be employed.*

## Incommensurability

Although incommensurability could not logically exist in a universe of generalized equivalences, it is by no means absent from the new economics. It features, for example, in Williamson's theory, in the form of the *asset specificity idiosyncrasy*. More generally, nothing forbids adding it to "subjective preferences." It thus partakes of the "magical" operation by which, although present at the level of individual behaviors, it disappears in the supply-and-demand formation processes (which appear at the collective level) in the full objectivity of price formation. To avoid such obliteration, the economics of singularities has to show, for example, how pricing is related to the primacy of quality competition.

• • •

Comparison of the three notions shows that neither multidimensionality nor quality uncertainty nor incommensurability has the same meaning in the new economics and in the economics of singularities. *Singular products cannot be confused with experience goods, credence goods, or differentiated goods.* Singular products are an irreducible reality.

Singularity is not a strange meteor fallen to earth by accident. The interpretation I propose shows that the history of the new economics has

---

    [27] R. Caves, *Creative Industries: Contracts between Art and Commerce* (Cambridge, MA: Harvard University Press, 2001), p. 3.

    [28] A. De Vany, *Hollywood Economics: How Extreme Uncertainty Shapes the Film Industry* (London: Routledge, 2004), p. 206.

    [29] L. Karpik, *French Lawyers. A Study in Collective Action, 1274–1994*, trans. Nora Scott (Oxford: Oxford University Press, 1999), pp. 157–179.

been built on the tension between creations and exclusions, with the latter probably being necessary to the former. *Those who rejected the radical version of quality uncertainty also eliminated singularities.* Only a different point of view could "discover" them, name them, and subject them to analysis. If we add that Lancaster's conception of product does not apply to singular goods, we must conclude that some goods and services which share common features are not amenable to neoclassical theory. Two examples—paintings and movies—confirm this.

Comparison of paintings shows that even the few that have long been the object of a collective and universal worship which should have exempted them from subjectivity conserve the quality uncertainty that might jeopardize their artistic value either in the event of a deattribution or when there has been a change in the public's taste. Comparison shows, too, that their incommensurability cannot be reduced to the objective determination of shared or different characteristics and that these paintings are unique totalities which elude all attempts at objective classification. But this impossibility disappears when it comes to classifications drawn up by people sharing the same point of view. Incommensurabilities thus prohibit neither reasoning nor acting, but they cannot furnish the bases of a general theory whose first requirement would be to make them equivalent entities, that is, to require them to give up precisely that which makes them desirable. Comparison shows, last of all, that competition bears fundamentally on "aesthetic qualities" because buyers are looking for a "beautiful" picture, whatever concrete meaning they may put on the term. Speculators aside, price is not the fundamental criterion of choice for lovers of art.

The same analysis applies to widely shared, ordinary experiences—movies, for instance. First of all, each movie represents a particular configuration of "qualities" that includes actors, script, music, construction of the work, rhythm, character development, entertainment value, metaphysical depth, seat comfort, quality of the copy, admission price, and cinematographic style. The configurations are incommensurable. They are worlds of meanings that are constantly being rated by moviegoers and which nevertheless constantly resist an objective classification whose validity would be indisputably obvious to all. Viewers go to see a "good" movie, whatever they mean by the term, usually without even knowing the admission prices in the different theaters. As a result, quality competition prevails over price competition. And promotion notwithstanding, the success or failure of movies remains unpredictable.

# PART TWO

# Tools for Analysis

The analysis of the economy of singularities rests on six main notions: judgment, judgment devices, trust devices, Homo singularis, qualification, and economic coordination.

Chapter 4 presents the notion of judgment particularly by comparing it to another modality of economic choice: decision.

In chapter 5, judgment devices in their capacity as knowledge "producers" are studied successively as representatives of the consumer, as cognitive supports for consumers' action, and as powers facing off in competitive struggles.

Chapter 6 develops an approach to trust and applies it to judgment devices.

Chapter 7 deals with the two principles linked to the action of Homo singularis—*value orientation* and *instrumental orientation*—and shows that the adjustment between singularities and clients can take many forms, as demonstrated by the study of the Michelin Guide and by the convoluted search for a CD of Beethoven's Ninth Symphony by a young man named Recordo.

Chapter 8 analyzes the qualification of singular products and some of the many paradoxes it engenders. It will be shown for example that identical products can be considered as incommensurable products as well.

Chapter 9 presents the way these elements are put together in order to explain the economic coordination of singularities. A classification of coordination regimes is proposed, based on a combination of categories of judgment devices that involves a corresponding typology of qualified singularities.

*Chapter Four*

# JUDGMENT

LET US FOR THE MOMENT agree that *decision* and *judgment* are two distinct modalities of economic choice, that the first is based primarily on calculation, and the second, primarily on qualitative criteria (which does not mean that calculation does not come into the picture). Let us for the moment agree, too, that with decision go differentiated/homogeneous goods, a single criterion of evaluation (profit or utility), information, and universal truth, while with judgment are associated singular goods, plurality of evaluation criteria, knowledge, and general truth.

This contrast expresses the presence of two frames of action for economic choices. It does not follow, however, that one is general and the other specific, or that one is rational and the other irrational. Although they are the results of two different ways of going about it, these choices are nevertheless equally rational or, rather, equally reasonable.[1]

### CAN ECONOMIC ANALYSIS IGNORE INFORMATION?

In neoclassical theory, exchange exists only thanks to a medium endowed with exceptional properties: everything it touches becomes instantly visible, free of cost, and ubiquitous. It establishes a single world that is home to all humankind. This natural entity, called *information*, is immaterial and homogeneous; it creates objective knowledge about reality and, thereby, the universality of rational choices.

The exact nature of information remains mysterious, though. Those who attempt to define it waver between news, "data," "natural states," or technical units of transmission. This vagueness does not, however, keep us from imagining this intermediary as a "sort of fluid injected into the motor to keep it running smoothly,"[2] from observing that the quantity of information needed for the contracting parties to reach an

---

[1] I prefer *reasonable* to *satisficing* because the second term is linked exclusively to bounded rationality, while the first indicates the difficulties of dealing with rationality when not only is rationality limited but also quality competition prevails over price competition. This issue will be addressed later.

[2] P. Chaskiel, "Commentaires et débat," in P. Petit (ed.), *L'économie de l'information: Les enseignements des theories économiques* (Paris: Editions La Découverte, 1998), p. 69.

agreement is limited,[3] and from noting that both economists and actors are looking at reality from above: a position that guarantees a universal perspective.

The market of singularities ignores information, because both the products and the actors belong to several worlds. Information, as a "natural" reality, spontaneously suited to the demands of its function, cannot overcome this constraint; it is replaced by *knowledge*. That term designates everyday, as well as academic, knowledge, and in both cases, it is the result of a particular construction.[4] Knowledge has to be produced. It demands skills and time. It is costly. It is an interpretation and is itself subject to interpretation.[5] The limits of its validity vary, and it can deceive us. Knowledge is therefore a far cry from information.

In a heterogeneous world, the plurality of sources of knowledge dissipates opacity. With them, we do not stand outside the world nor are we confined to mentalism; we work with varied combinations of interpretations and logistics, of value and cognition. In the market of singularities, knowledge is the necessary resource for reasonable action.

## DECISION AND JUDGMENT

As the canonical expression of the construction and comparison of costs and prices, economic decision usually means calculation. When things are taken for granted, it is not easy to acknowledge that another form of choice exists, one that is just as rational, although it does not rely exclusively or even primarily on calculation; this other choice is *judgment*. The argument calls on two authors, one of whom shows, although unwittingly, that the domain of economic calculation has its limits, and the other, that judgment can take the form of general, reasonable propositions.

In a text dealing with trust, but which goes even further, Williamson asserts that the explanation of the world—with the exception of relations between "family, friends, lovers"—is strictly a matter of economics.[6] The demonstration rests on a reasoning close to a syllogism: since the social

---

[3] A. Kirman, "Information and price," in P. Petit (ed.), *Economics and Information* (Dordrecht : Kluwer Academic Publishers, 2001), pp. 61–82.

[4] D. Foray, *The Economics of Knowledge* (Cambridge, MA: MIT Press, 2001), pp. 3–5; A. Hatchuel, "De l'information à la connaissance," in P. Petit (ed.), *L'économie de l'information*, pp. 396–400.

[5] J. Beckert, "Economic sociology and embeddedness: How shall we conceptualize economic action?" *Journal of Economic Issues* 37, no. 3 (2003): 769–787.

[6] O. E. Williamson, "Calculativeness, trust and economic organization," *Journal of Law & Economics* 36 (1993): 453–486; p. 474. For a fuller presentation of the following argument see L. Karpik, "La confiance: réalité ou illusion. Examen critique d'une analyse de Williamson," *Revue économique* 1 (1997): 1043–1056.

and economic world is qualified by calculativeness, and since the actors are rational and self-interested and use calculating machines for making choices, economics, which is a science of calculation, is the only social science that can achieve universal truths.

To prove this thesis, to show that explanation by trust should be replaced by calculative reasoning, the author examines a number of fables purported to offer a simplified but nevertheless accurate representation of reality. For the discussion I retain only the strangest case: that of "the assaulted girl." Let there be a girl who is rarely asked out, although she is pretty. One afternoon, a young man she hardly knows, but who seems interested in her, offers to walk her home. She accepts. While they are walking along chatting, he suggests they take a shortcut through the woods, where he suddenly declares that he would like to make love. She refuses and tries to run away; as he runs after her, she falls and hurts her leg; he then attacks her, rapes her, and runs off. She tells her story much later.[7]

How do we explain the young woman's decision to let the man walk her home? For the interpretation founded on misplaced trust, Williamson substitutes other scenarios, all of which ultimately posit that the wrong decision was the result of a miscalculation. Carrying his argument to its extreme, he advances that, had the choice been submitted to the girl beforehand, economic calculation would have unfailingly demonstrated that such a walk could yield nothing but negative gains. In such a situation, the only rational solution would have been: "Do not walk in the woods with strangers." Thus even for the choice of a walking companion, it would be possible to calculate the most rational solution, while the constraints of the real world would account for the "wrong" decision.

"Do not walk in the woods with strangers": this rational maxim is inseparable from some specific indisputable social knowledge. However, the news quite often reminds us that, for children and young people, it is not strangers who are the most dangerous, but friends, and even members of their own family. This observation reveals that, far from being unified and indisputable, social knowledge is multiple and debatable. And every interpretative version linked with a different viewpoint can be used to construct the "most rational" maxim, for example: "do not walk in the woods," "do not walk with men," "do not walk without a weapon," "do not walk with members of the family," "do not walk with close friends." Each of these maxims prevents the "wrong" decision, each combines evaluation criteria and facts, and each involves a different conception of society. With such a plurality, calculation of the "most rational" decision is meaningless. The relative value of the maxims depends on a comparison that cannot be decided by calculation, but only by a process of discussion and persuasion.

[7] Williamson, "Calculativeness," p. 464.

Williamson's demonstration has failed. But a contrario, it shows the condition under which his thesis would be correct: general calculativeness, which means a unique evaluation criterion and generalized equivalence. For the claim of economics to be justified, actors must not only be rational and self-interested, they must also share the same world. This is brought about by information but is excluded by knowledge. Yet does a plurality of worlds mean that solipsism is inevitable?

This is the issue Hannah Arendt addressed when she examined the theoretical status of judgment. Taste is the starting point. It defines the sphere of beauty and ugliness, of good and bad. And it lies outside calculation. Yet it is a universal mode of thought: "everyone seems to be able to discriminate between right and wrong in matters of art."[8] Anyone can decide that they like or do not like something. This capacity for discernment is specific; it applies to particular cases and is carried by particular viewpoints. Confronted with the spectacle of the stage or the world, as well as with works of genius, "spectators" become particular entities "by the simple fact that each person occupies a place of his own from which he looks upon and judges the world,"[9] "by the simple fact" that they observe and evaluate particular events and objects. Together they make up the "plurality" of worlds.

Taste and smell stand apart from the three other senses because they "give inner sensations that are entirely private and incommunicable,"[10] because they refer to particulars in their particularity, and because they are unique and thereby immediately and irresistibly fall into the category that seems to render any discussion pointless: "*to each his own.*" The truth of the saying seems self-evident: taste is idiosyncratic, and therefore no argument can prove any overall superiority, just as no argument can make someone like something they do not. On this point, the subjectivity seems irreducible.

It is this inner sanctum that Hannah Arendt used as her springboard to assert that *judgment comes from taste.* However, it differs from taste by the distance it takes with regard to the object and by its reference to other judgments. Like taste, judgment *chooses*; but unlike taste, choice is grounded not only on "I like" or "I don't like," but also and especially on the construction of a time interval between immediate and deferred pleasure by thinking about the representation of particular objects. Judgment is *reflexive.*

Judgment is also inseparable from other characteristics. It is not the same thing as either the subjectivity enclosed within bodily sensations or the particularity of a solitary actor: it is totally in the world. Because it

---

[8]H. Arendt, *Lectures on Kant's Political Philosophy*, ed. Ronald Beiner (Chicago: University of Chicago Press, 1982), p. 65.

[9]Ibid., p. 105.

[10]Ibid., p. 64.

embodies a norm, it is inseparable from all other judgments; because it is rooted in sociability, it partakes of relationship and, therefore, "communicability"; it is part of the public space. Judgment is both particular and public.

By allowing me to say at the very least "I like" or "I don't like," judgment gives me the means to choose between two incomparable entities. Since judgment is reflexive, the choice can be reasonable and therefore satisficing. And while its validity cannot help falling short of universality, it can be more or less *general*, according to whether the judgment is more or less shared.

When products are singularities, when the actors give more weight to qualities than to price, when their choices are oriented by heterogeneous criteria of evaluation, when, in sum, the market encompasses the qualitative diversity of human works and the qualitative diversity of evaluation criteria, *choice takes the form of judgment.*

## What Is Judgment?

In a society characterized by a pluralism of tastes, no "decision" proceeding from a unidimensional calculation can help discern a good restaurant, a fine wine, a good doctor, a good corporate consultant, a good hi-fi system, a good interpretation of a classical music recording, and so on. Judgment can. How do we define this general operator of the market of singularities?

For the judicial system, judgment has long been defined—at least in France—by the syllogism that links the individual decision with the general law: all thieves must go to jail; you are a thief; therefore you must go to jail. To the demonstrative rigor of calculation corresponds the no less demonstrative rigor of logic. Beyond the rare formalized arguments that depict a world of objective and necessary relations, reality in no way fits and never has fitted this model, as one judge who spoke from experience described it: "The judge must adopt a teleological attitude, must direct his decision toward a certain end. . . . This policy should not exclude from among his preoccupations the demands of equity, but these will be tempered by considerations of legal security and of citizens' equality before the courts, which will lead him to take precedents carefully into consideration. Lastly, he will have to evaluate the actual economic and social 'practicability' of the solution that appears to him as being ideally fair."[11]

[11] P. Souleau, *La logique judiciaire* (Paris: Presses Universitaires de France, 1969), p. 60. Concerning the pluralism of judgment criteria among clinical practitioners, see K. M. Hunter, *Doctors' Stories* (Princeton: Princeton University Press, 1991). For a general reflection, see S. Dubuisson-Quellier and J.-P. Neuville (eds.), *Juger pour échanger: La construction sociale de l'accord sur la qualité dans une économie des jugements individuals* (Paris: Editions de la Maison des Sciences de l'Homme & INRA, 2003), pp. 9–26.

Ends, legal certainty, equality before the courts, equality of citizens, case law, "practicability": all these heterogeneous evaluation criteria need to be taken into account together, and no a priori formula should guide their selection and relative weighting. These two operations shape the judicial decision. Viewed from above, the multiplicity of incommensurable evaluation criteria cannot be converted into one hierarchy; commitments on the ground, on the contrary, necessarily imply different orders of preference, which govern different configurations of criteria and, correlatively, different forms of action. Each particular viewpoint overcomes the heterogeneity of judgment criteria and thus ensures the conversion of incommensurable into equivalent entities. Through this operation, incomparables are compared, and the individual choice becomes reasonable.

The numerous possibilities of judgment criteria that characterize complex judicial affairs do not disappear with misdemeanor trials, even when the time comes to decide on a sentence. Although the legal qualification of the act is already established and time constraints weigh heavily in favor of the application of a sentencing schedule, ethnographic observation still uncovers an oscillation between several constellations of evaluation criteria and their accompanying relevant facts: Should the past be taken into account or not? The context? The victim? The conceptions of social order? Should the judge stick to the act itself or look at the personality of the defendant? Legal, managerial, moral, and political criteria are not lacking; there are even too many for all of them to be taken into account, and their composition varies with the situation: "In principle several logics attend the choice of a sentence, and they are rarely mutually exclusive."[12] Each viewpoint carries its own criteria of evaluation, which express a principle for organizing the world.

Compared with the administrative decision, which relies on a general rule to produce individualized decisions, the legal judgment intervenes on a case-by-case basis through *personalized* solutions. Yet its scope can vary: we therefore need to distinguish the art of forming a judgment from the mechanisms whereby this choice takes on a more or less general scope. In the case of the judicial system, generality is the result of deliberation by a collegial court or even of the private deliberation of one judge,[13] of the appeal mechanism, and of shared references to case law and to the law as a whole. The generality of the judgment rests on a symbolic and social organization that brings into play, for example, authority and intellectual

---

[12] D. Drai, *Une nouvelle figure de la pénalité: La décision correctionelle en temps réelle* (Paris: Mission de la recherche ["Droit et justice"], 2000), p. 231.

[13] "Deliberation on one's own takes the form of a reconstitution of the trial *in petto*, with the judge alternating between the roles of prosecution and defense, before going back to being a judge." A. Garapon, *Bien juger: Essai sur le rituel judiciaire* (Paris: Odile Jacob, 1997), p. 312.

persuasion in order to ensure the construction and validity of the judicial judgment. So fragile are the composition and relative weights of its constitutive criteria, however, that the outcome of the trial remains largely uncertain.

Judgment is therefore primarily a qualitative choice, whereas decision is based on logic and calculation. This is confirmed by the philosophy of argumentation: "The person in charge of coming to a legal decision—whether lawmaker, judge or administrator—must shoulder his responsibilities. He cannot avoid personal involvement, whatever good reasons he may allege for his thesis. For there are few situations in which good reasons which plead in favor of one solution are not balanced out by more or less good reasons for a different solution: it is the appreciation of the value of these reasons—which is only rarely a matter of simple calculation, weighting or measuring—that can differ from one individual to the next, which underscores the personal character of the decision taken."[14] The author associates the "legal decision," which means in this case a ruling and designates what we call judgment, with the lawmaker, the judge, or the administrator; the list could be extended to include seller and buyer in the market of singularities.

Whether local or general, unusual or routine, the judgment expresses a particular point of view. It constructs the appropriate relationship between criteria of evaluation whose relative composition and weighting are variable and the way the situation is framed,[15] in other words, the organization of the facts. *Judgment combines value and knowledge.* It integrates the heterogeneity of the criteria and of the worlds into an arbitrary synthetic decision. Judgment grounds the comparison of incommensurabilities.

Decision and judgment are therefore two different modalities of choice and two different frames of action. Whereas the decision is taken by economic agents who possess objective information and share the same world, the judgment is formed by particular actors whose knowledge is common only to those who share the same point of view. Whereas the decision is lodged in a system of equivalences and, for this reason, can avail itself of the powers of calculation to arrive at objective or universal solutions, judgment generality is limited by the multiplicity of particular points of view.

The same comparison can be made in another form. First, whereas in the case of the decision, preferences apply to the products and price is the unique or predominant criterion (the lowest price or the best quality-price ratio), in the case of judgment, preferences are criteria of judgment. Second, whereas for decision the choice of alternative means dictated by

[14] C. Perleman, *Logique juridique: Nouvelle rhétorique* (Paris: Dalloz, 1976), p. 6.

[15] E. Goffman, *Frame Analysis: An Essay on the Organization of Experience* (New York: Harper & Row, 1974).

profit or utility maximization liberates the space of calculation and makes it possible to establish the degree of rationality of the action, for judgment the goals are unstable, so that their relation with the means cannot qualify a general form of action. And calculation can be used only within the boundaries of the domains governed by the same judgment criterion or the same configuration of judgment criteria. Finally, whereas for decision there is in principle no difficulty in applying the notion of rationality, with judgment it becomes problematic. What allows us to establish the degree of rationality of the forms of action dictated by different evaluation criteria?

Whatever the difference between "decision" and judgment, it does not take the form of an opposition between calculation and no calculation. Calculation impinges on each judgment or each evaluation criterion. Thus the so-called opposition between qualitative analysis and quantitative analysis, one of the favorite topics of discussion and sometimes of dispute, is absurd. *The real difference lies in the conditions that govern the use of calculation.* Whenever only one evaluation criterion is used, the market is based on a generalized-equivalence system and the world is homogeneous. As a result, the calculation modalities are countless, and the calculation domain is without limits. But when the evaluation criteria are multiple, the systems of equivalence are numerous and the world becomes heterogeneous: as a result calculation works within each domain defined by shared evaluation criteria. In other words, where *mainstream economics* is defined by a general calculation space, the *economics of singularities* is defined by a plurality of (more or less) restricted calculation spaces. One should add that this perspective opens the possibility to move from less to more general analyses, since the number and content of the multiple-judgment criteria vary with the multiple peculiar points of view.

To sum up: Judging is a synthetic act that integrates a plurality of heterogeneous and variably weighted criteria. It is the particular viewpoint that allows unification of heterogeneous criteria and thus comparison of incommensurable products. It permits a choice based on direct comparison of singular products, on comparison of knowledge provided by judgment devices, and on interaction between the comparison of knowledge and the interpretations stemming from a direct contact appreciative of the products themselves. It may be based on calculations whose extension is limited to the relevance domains of the logics of action.

---

[16]M. de Certeau, *L'invention au quotidien*, vol. 1, *Arts de faire*, Series 10/18 (Paris: Union Générale d'Éditions, c1980), p. 15. For the author, the term gets around representations and theorizations and makes it possible to look at practices assimilated to "a way of thinking involved in a way of doing."

Judgment looks complicated. But before anything else, it is an *art of doing*, a practice.[16] As such, it is the basis of the economics of singularities. But for a judgment to be valid, it must marshal sufficient knowledge of reality. Left to themselves, whatever their personal competences, the actors could generally not satisfy this requirement. The relevance of the judgment therefore cannot be separated from external entities—the judgment devices—without which the market of singularities could not exist.

• • •

Replacement of *information* by *knowledge* and replacement of *decision* by *judgment* are the conditions for making reasonable choices in the market of singularities. But the relationship between judgment and knowledge requires an "equipped" market.

## Chapter Five

# JUDGMENT DEVICES

JUDGMENT DEVICES are used to dissipate the opacity of the market. They offer buyers the knowledge that should enable them to make reasonable choices. Whatever the specific causes of their presence, whatever their specific aim—to promote products, give disinterested information, propose advice, protect consumers, and so on—globally, even though or perhaps because competition for visibility and influence is stiff, judgment devices reduce the *cognitive deficit* that characterizes consumers in the market of singularities. By decreasing the ignorance associated with multidimensional singularities and removing the uncertainties that dog their trajectories in the market place, they authorize the comparisons without which consumers would be limited to random choices. Without judgment devices, the market of singularities could not function.

Borrowed from Michel Foucault, the notion of *device* (he used the term *dispositif*) is made ample use of in the social sciences. It partially replaces the notion of institution, whose global, vertical nature, and relative coherence remain entirely relevant for designating a whole category of phenomena, but not the hodgepodge of texts, images, sounds, signs, knowledge, advertisements, ideologies, objects, and persons, as well as their partial and varied grouping into symbolic and material configurations used to ensure the workings of the market of singularities. Besides the sometimes illusory greatness attached to the institutions, it is very often the discreet, visible or invisible arrangements that work to influence the action.

Judgment devices act as guideposts for individual and collective action. Unlike the rules designed to build the "architecture of the market,"[1] and therefore—among other things—to set the conditions for market access and establish the exchange rules, judgment devices exclude relations of authority and obedience. Typically, they do not enter into a command chain; they are foreign to proscription or prescription; they are alien to the semantic field that contains these notions. The aid consumers expect of them must therefore be part of the diversified range of practices that combine, among others, teaching, persuasion, and seduction.

[1] See N. Fligstein, *The Architecture of Markets: An Economic Sociology of Twenty-first Century Capitalist Societies* (Princeton: Princeton University Press, 2001). It includes primarily the rules attached to property rights, to structure of governance, to forms of exchange and modes of state control of the market.

Because they are freely chosen and rejected, devices cannot go too far in their modes and degrees of intervention for fear of displeasing consumers. In this vast, heterogeneous universe, a few exceptions do not invalidate the general observation that their mode of action is organized around a consumer who, though not sovereign, is free, much freer than he has ever been, and much freer than in many other spheres of social life. Of course, the absence of orders, proscriptions, and prescriptions does not necessarily equate with lack of constraint. Relations between judgment devices and consumers are not always irenic; but to become more than optional, they must take such byroads as the use of monopolistic power.

These devices are built by a great number of actors: producers, sellers, marketers, mass media, and public authorities. They are ever more numerous, ever more diversified, and ever more visible in the public space. They can be divided into five broad categories: networks, appellations, cicerones, rankings, and confluences.

The relationship between the composition of the networks and the way it helps the market operate leads to a distinction between three categories: personal networks, trade networks, and practitioner networks.

The *personal* network is composed of interpersonal relations—family members, friends, work colleagues, and contacts. It emerges spontaneously, is socially invisible, and operates by *circulation of the spoken word*. The personal network provides its users with credible information about products. It affords every actor the possibility of accessing any point of the social relationship to avail themselves—via one or several persons—of personal experience and capitalized knowledge while on the whole remaining protected from the dangers of opportunism. The *trade* network is made up of sellers or their delegates and of buyers; in situations of uncertainty it spontaneously produces the trust indispensable to relations of exchange. The *practitioner* network is composed of professionals: it ensures the circulation of knowledge about nonobservable activities between practitioners. Although they may appear modest, especially because they are invisible, networks, particularly the personal ones, are very hardy and effective social structures.

*Appellations* are names associated with the attributes and meanings that define singular products or families of singular products. They include quality labels, registered designations of origin, certifications, professional titles, product brands, and umbrella brands. For instance, registered designations of origin are labels guaranteeing the public that the singularity of the goods or of services is rooted in the mandatory use of specific means of production and/or of particular *terroirs*, certified by an administrative authority. And the brand concentrates a meaning supposed to maintain its identity and that of the products it represents over time and through space. Together, appellations structure the sphere of singularities by structuring the designations that populate the shared imaginary space.

The term *cicerones* comprises the critics and guides that offer specific evaluations of singularities. They embody a soft, symbolic form of authority whose influence, when it intersects with user consent, reduces or dispenses with the distress of individual choice. The ambiguity of the terms must be retained: critics and guides designate not only the people—critics, experts, prophets—who pronounce judgments concerning literature, music, gastronomy, cinema, and so on, but also products that can be reproduced, mobilized, and transported—books, CDs, and now the Internet—which are devoted to choices in the domains of gastronomy, tourism, wines, recordings, not to mention the comparative reviews published in specialized journals and consumer reports.

*Rankings* are hierarchical arrangements of singularities according to one or several criteria. Two categories must be distinguished. First, *expert rankings* include diverse realities like the hierarchy of diplomas, prizes periodically awarded by juries (literary prizes or film festival winners), and the public rankings of universities, hospitals, and so on. Second, *buyers' rankings*, which are governed by the selling of singular products: the top-ten songs, best-seller lists, box-office hits, and so forth.

Finally, *confluences* designate the numerous techniques used to channel buyers, whether in shopping malls or luxury shops, and range from territorial location, spatial organization, and displays to selling skills.

Judgment devices are defined by three distinct and interlinked functions: they act as *representatives* of the producers and/or consumers, as *knowledge operators* in charge of reducing the cognitive deficit, and as competing *forces* striving to become more visible and more desirable than their competitors.

## Devices Are Representatives

The relationship between judgment devices and consumers is a particular form of social relation: it is a *delegation*. In order to act, whatever the nature of the goal, I voluntarily decide to rely on a device, even though I neither understand nor control the way it works;[2] I renounce direct exercise of my freedom on behalf of a representative whose action I hope, think, or am certain will not disappoint me. Thus I act through the intermediary of some entity that will make a commitment on my behalf. The advantages of delegation are valuable, as they combine extreme diversity of ends with unconstrained cooperation.

[2] P. Dasgupta, "Trust as a commodity," in D. Gambetta (ed.), *Trust: Making and Breaking Cooperative Relations* (Oxford: Blackwell, 1988), pp. 49–72.

Delegation is intimately bound up with trust. For Emile Benveniste, *fides* is part of the general figure of personal loyalty; in other words, it is "the bond established between a man who possesses authority and the man who is subjected to him by a personal pledge." To trust is to "plac[e] one's *fides* in somebody [which] secure[s] in return his guarantee and his support";[3] and the voluntary relation of dependence is the way to recognize the authority of the person who has received the trust. However unequal and indeterminate it may appear, reciprocity is nevertheless not left to individual good will: it is an obligation that, as the proximity of the term *credo* indicates, is rooted in a belief that is founded in the certainty of recovering that which was entrusted. The relation of delegation is founded on *voluntary dependence*, by which the person who gives his trust establishes or confirms the authority of the person who receives it,[4] and on a temporally deferred reciprocity that moral obligation obliges the representative to respect. It is no accident that the meaning of *trust*, and more generally of the relation of delegation—which may seem odd— is nevertheless as generously defined in English as in French.[5] It is anything but obedience.

Not all forms of delegation are socially valid: when delegation is based on "blind trust," it is in principle unacceptable. Excessive credulity is, in fact, the sign of a diminished humanity; incapable of respecting the social norm recognized by everyone and sanctioned by law: the individual must be capable of defining and defending his interests.[6] And the law ensures protection by forbidding some individuals the right to enter into a relation of delegation.[7] Over time, however, the line demarcating "blind

[3] Emile Benveniste, *Indo-European Language and Society*, trans. Elizabeth Palmer (Miami: University of Miami Press, 1973), p. 97.

[4] "Confidence always pleases those who receive it. It is a tribute we pay to their merit, a deposit we commit to their trust, a pledge which gives them a claim upon us, a kind of dependence to which we voluntarily submit." François Duc de La Rochefoucauld, *Reflections; Or Sentences and Moral Maxims*, available at http://www.fullbooks.com/Reflections-Or-Sentences-and-Moral-Maxims3.html.

[5] In English: "believe in, have faith in, depend on, count on, bank on, lean on, rely on, swear by, take at face value, take as gospel, place reliance on, pin your faith on, place or have confidence in." *The Free Dictionary*, *http://www.thefreedictionary.com* . In French: "s'abandonner à, compter sur, se confier à, se fier à, se livrer à, s'en rapporter à, s'en remettre à, se reposer sur." P. Robert, vol. 1, *Dictionnaire alphabétique et analogique de la langue française*, 6 vols. (Paris: Société du nouveau Littré, 1965).

[6] Ordinary law and neoclassical economic law agree on this principle, since both consider, implicitly or explicitly, that both the possessor of a right and economic agents are sovereign, rational, and self-interested and that they therefore have the "natural" capacity to take decisions of their own free will. The contract draws its strength from the meeting of two "free and enlightened" wills, and its protection is ensured by the legal sanction of defect of consent.

[7] This is the traditional solution, which was partially abandoned with the creation of the function of *personne de confiance* (person worthy of trust) to represent patients (Law of 4 March 2002).

trust" has shifted as the opportunistic practices of producers and sellers have come to affect wider and wider segments of the population. General and specific laws of protection have become more numerous.[8] Neverthe-less, this intervention is powerless when the party represented refuses all aid in the name of freedom. Thus protection of the personal property of members of sects runs into nearly insurmountable difficulties: it is par-ticularly hard legally to break the link between autonomous decision and loss of self.

The representative can be human or nonhuman: he can claim to per-form his function by explicit mandate or as a spokesperson whose action will or will not be confirmed by those he claims to represent. Whatever its modalities, the relation of delegation is built around *discretionary power*. The term designates the usual situation in which it is the represen-tative that has a large autonomy to define the scope of his mandate and the obligation he must fulfill. With the increase of costs and financial in-vestments, with the capacities for providing knowledge and for persuad-ing and influencing, and with the changes in the scale of action, the issue of judgment devices as a discretionary power has become all the more crucial. This evolution is due to the well-known paradox of an asym-metrical relation exclusively founded on the actor's free choice: the con-ditions favoring the representative's effectiveness are the same as those favoring his capacity to deceive those he represents.[9]

The risks run by those who use devices linked to discretionary power are formally limited by three means: control, rule, and the extent of del-egation. Control by the party represented is difficult not only because the representative's action is usually not observable, but also, and especially, because, if carried too far, it turns the relation of delegation into a relation of authority. Public authority rules formally delimit, forbid, or restrict—more or less severely—the representative's commitment. Lastly, consum-ers may alter the extent of delegation depending on whether the devices chosen are more or less "extensive" or "restricted," depending on whether they retain a large degree of autonomy or whether their possibilities of choice are narrowed down to a few and even one single solution; in the latter cases, the device tends toward prescription.[10]

---

[8] The law forbidding misleading advertising (2 July 1963, amended 27 December 1973), the law on consumer credit (10 January 1978), the law on home mortgages (13 July 1979), the law prohibiting *abus de faiblesse* (exploitation of a vulnerable person) (16 December 1992).

[9] M. Granovetter, "Economic action and social structure: The problem of embedded-ness," *American Journal of Sociology* 3 (1985): 491–492.

[10] A. Hatchuel, "Les Marchés à prescripteurs: Crise de l'échange et genèse sociale," in A. Jacob and H. Verin (eds.), *L'inscription sociale du marché* (Paris: L'Harmattan, 1995), pp. 205–225.

Discretionary power thus defines a form of social relation that combines the free initiative of the representative with the consent of the represented. It carries eminent advantages. In a situation of uncertainty, the representative is not only someone who has knowledge, he or she also possesses broad initiative and great flexibility of action. In principle, the effectiveness varies with the discretionary power: the greater the power, the more latitude the representative has to marshal knowledge and skills to specific ends, and the greater the room for maneuver to seek the solutions best suited to the particular demands. These flexible, inventive, and rapid forms of commitment are not found in hierarchical organizations or in the standard market.

Representatives are not only instruments of action. When their particular points of view are shared by those they represent, they can benefit from strong identifications and thus receive a surplus of authority and capacity to act. The support of those represented culminates when they feel they are members of the collectivity on behalf of which the representative acts or when they participate in the desirable venture he proposes. When the support becomes unconditional and unlimited, the represented party lapses into a state of symbolic adherence.

In spite of the dangers it entails, the relation of delegation is a social mechanism that is frequently used because the association of the representative's autonomy with the consent of the represented creates a form of social organization that is all the more effective for its aim being particular, its situation uncertain, and the appropriate means to be used problematic.

## DEVICES ARE COGNITIVE SUPPORTS

If they are to reduce their ignorance, actors must have access to credible knowledge that can be added to their own store of knowledge. *Perfect information* would be of no help, but *knowledge, even imperfect,* will overcome the incommensurability of the singularities if it is presented in a way suited to making a choice. In other words, knowledge must bend to the requirements that enable its use. Speech, writing, images, or sound must not only make the products known, they must do so by satisfying the demands of a *content* and a *format* that are adjusted to the way the consumer forms his judgments. Knowledge thus presents itself in the form of implicit or explicit evaluations—"this is the right one," "this is the best"—which must be able to confront other evaluations, so that mechanically or with reflection, the consumer can finally adopt one of these judgments.

As guides to consumer action, devices do not aim to reconstruct the
full scope and richness of the world, but exactly the opposite: they aim to
produce and to show a selection of data governed by a particular criterion of evaluation. The consumer chooses the device freely, but, unless he
is an expert, he cannot attain his ends without the device. Actor and device, whose respective contributions are variable, thus form a composite
entity that intervenes through *joint action*.

The support given for the formation of the judgment can be compared
with *situated* analysis.[11] This theoretical perspective appeared in the
1980s, under the twin influences of artificial intelligence and the social
sciences. It considers that the interpretation of action, far from concerning only individual dispositions, should call on the cognitive resources
situated in the "environment." The refusal to add up human cognitive
faculties indefinitely in order to account for action in complex situations[12] explains why studies have dealt with forms of cooperation between actors and *cognitive artifacts,*[13] or *informational supports*, whose
help increases the actors' cognitive capacity. The studies have also dealt
with *distributed cognition*, the effects of distributing knowledge between
a plurality of artifacts and a plurality of individuals.

The studies on cognitive artifacts have essentially highlighted the contribution of computational, representational, and above all, memory
resources. They show, for example, the cognitive interaction between
navigation instruments and pilot knowledge, and as a result, the pilot's
coordination with all of the instruments at his disposal.[14] They show,
too, that the artifact not only increases the actor's cognitive capacities, it
also changes the nature of the task.[15]

---

[11] "Action is situated when the environment's resources increase the agents' cognitive
capacities." F. Laville, "La cognition située: Une nouvelle approche de la rationalité limi-
tée," *Revue économique* 6 (November 2000): 1311.

[12] This refusal is widely shared: L. Boltanski and L. Thévenot, *On Justification: Economies of Worth*, trans. Catherine Porter (Princeton: Princeton University Press, 2006); B. Co-
nein and E. Jacopin, "Action située et cognition, le savoir en place," *Sociologie du travail* 4
(1994): 475–500; N. Dodier, "The conventional foundations of action: Elements of a sociological pragmatics," *Réseaux* 3, no. 2 (1995): 145–166; B. Latour, "On interobjectivity,"
*Mind, Culture, and Activity* 3, no. 4 (1996): 228–245; L. Suchman, *Plans and Situated Actions* (Cambridge: Cambridge University Press, 1987).

[13] "A cognitive artifact is an artificial device designed to maintain, display, or operate
upon information in order to serve a representational function. . . . The speed, power and
intelligence of human beings are dramatically enhanced by the intervention of artificial devices." D. A. Norman, "Cognitive artifacts," in J. M. Carroll (ed.), *Designing Interaction:
Psychology at the Human-Computer Interface* (Cambridge: Cambridge University Press,
1991), p. 1.

[14] E. Hutchins, "How a cockpit remembers its speeds," *Cognitive Science* 19 (1995):
265–288.

[15] Norman, "Cognitive artifacts," pp. 1–18.

When we compare cognitive artifacts and judgment devices, we may notice the same instrumental characteristics in guides and stored-information supports, or in rewards and the logos directly affixed to the objects, which act as *affordances,*[16] or grasps, by which things are made visible for action. Yet the degree of convergence is hard to establish for two reasons. First, the status of the knowledge carried by the artifacts is uncertain: we do not know whether the information is or may not be "objective." In all events, the issue of credibility is not raised, whereas it is inseparable from the knowledge procured by the judgment devices. And second, the position of the cognitive resources situated in the environment seems far from the instability connected with the competition between judgment devices.

Judgment devices are not engines for producing transparency between products and consumers, whose qualities and preferences preexist their intervention. Judgment devices offer *oriented knowledge,* and, implicitly or explicitly, they set the conditions the consumer must respect in order for an adjustment between the product and the consumer to be satisfying. *They qualify simultaneously both product and client*—which means that the third party literally constructs the exchange relationship. Buying a "good" novel can be based on a critique, on the best-seller list, or on friends' recommendations: in each of these cases the title proposed will be different, just as the reader's disposition would be expected to be. If product qualities change with the type of device, it follows that the notions of supply and demand, which presuppose commodity objectivity, become misleading, because the mediation of the judgment devices forbids reasoning on the basis of general categories of products. The same category of goods or services loses its unity when it is subject to a plurality of devices, a plurality of qualifications and, thereby, a plurality of adjustment modalities.

Because they are the support of singularities markets, judgment devices are associated with a diversified set of problems: the struggle to win a clientele (see the following section), trust as a condition for their credibility (Chapter 6), their influence on the products' and actors' qualifications (Chapter 8), and lastly, their positions in the construction of coordination regimes (Chapter 9).

## Devices Are Active Forces

Judgment devices are points of view: they can only offer consumers an oriented knowledge. The meaning of this assistance changes depending on whether the devices are *commercial* or *critical*. The first are committed

---

[16] J. J. Gibson, *The Ecological Approach to Visual Perception* (Boston: Houghton Mifflin, 1979).

to the conquest and the keeping of customers: they compete among themselves to make the products more visible and more desirable. Backed by sometimes huge financial resources, they circulate speech, writing, images, and sound; they employ every means and mobilize all mechanisms in order to make public in every available form the "right" or the "best," so as to catch the consumer and thus increase their share of the market.

The *critical* devices comprise mainly the cicerones, with the diversity of their stances and evaluations; the networks; and the administrative authorities, who, using control or specific devices, make more or less visible a logic of protection and guarantee on behalf of the public. All three inform, advise, teach, and protect, acting more or less as counterpowers.

The relationship between devices oriented by different and sometimes complementary, though usually opposing, ends takes the form of a *battle of judgments*, with each device attempting to win out over the others. But in each of the markets, a principle unifies the judgment devices: this is none other than the economic struggle itself, which operates such that products and judgment devices form an interdependent whole. In the last decades, these struggles have been affected —unequally, depending on the markets—by two developments: the rise of barriers to entry and the increased action of professionals. First, the price of the entry has increased under the double influence of the intensification of the use of advertising and the territorial extension of the market. And second, with the growing intervention of market professionals, the economic struggle has progressively shifted from comparison of products to comparison of judgment devices, and now under some conditions concerns brands more than the products themselves. The Internet only reinforces the process of dematerialization.

How can we obtain the desired behavior from the consumer while appearing to respect his freedom of choice? And, to begin with, how can we get his attention? How can we seduce or persuade him? How can we ensure customer loyalty? Two main categories of strategies are used by producers/sellers: *captation*, meaning channeling, and *capture*, meaning lock-in. They are defined by the same aim—to conquer customers—but they differ by the means used. Whereas the captation, or channeling, model formally preserves the consumer's freedom while mobilizing the resources designed to exert influence from nearby or at a remove, the capture model is organized around immobilizing the consumer by a belief or by a physical enclosure.

Captation predominates and favors competitive struggles: it aims to win out over the opposing devices by being more informative or more persuasive or by any other means. Its cognitive constructions are therefore associated with the countless human drives—curiosity, self-interest, pleasure, passion, distinction, persuasion, seduction, ethics. Its means of influence are increasingly diversified because its targets are increasingly different, and its forms of action operate over increasingly greater distances: brands, promotion, and advertising are supposed to reach the consumers whatever the size of the market. Moreover, marketing is coming to replace segmentation into broad sociodemographic categories by ever more fine-grained, detailed consumer profiles, which increasingly resemble the "unique person." There is no need to peer into the soul to do this: all that has to be done is to construct personalized configurations of action by tracking people's purchases. To these known practices must be added other, more discreet ones, which are trying to get closer to the customer by the rationalization of supply, the codification of relational work, or practices designed to ensure customer loyalty.[17]

Capture, on the contrary, aims to replace choice by lock-in, by enclosure. This may be the result of monopolistic situations using material or immaterial barriers. For instance, in France, some undertakers manage to squeeze out their competitors and establish durable local monopolies by investing in a funeral parlor adjoining the hospital, by channeling the removal of bodies, and in addition, by controlling the hospital's network of professionals and administrative staff.[18] In situations in which logistical and temporal constraints are mutually reinforcing, what could have been a singular service finds itself all the more effectively stripped of its particularisms as the client, relegated to his emotions and caught within a framed decision, is deprived of the possibilities of choice without which the singularity cannot exist. Capture can also be the consequence, as we will discuss later, of such immaterial barriers as beliefs, when they take the modality of adherence, as opposed to attachment.

The diversity of strategies and the diversity of consumers explain the heterogeneity of judgment devices, the complexity of the struggles, and for the winner, the building of a *symbolic authority* that yields the greatest influence. Over the last thirty or forty years, the development of judgment devices has sparked a far-reaching change within the forms of economic struggles: under specific conditions, *competition between*

[17] F. Cochoy (ed.), *La captation des publics: C'est pour mieux te séduire, mon client . . .* , (Toulouse: PUM, 2004); S. Dubuisson-Quellier, "Le prestataire, le client et le consommateur: Sociologie d'une relation marchande," *Revue française de sociologie* 40, no. 4 (1999): 671–688; S. Barrey, F. Cochoy, and S. Dubuisson-Quellier, "Designer, packager et merchandiser: Trois professionnels pour une même scène marchande," *Sociologie du travail* 3 (2000) 457–482; A. Mallard, "Les nouvelles technologies dans le travail relationnel: Vers un traitement plus personnalisé de la figure du client?" *Sciences de la société* 56 (May 2002): 62–77.

[18] P. Trompette, "Customer channeling in the funeral business in France," *Revue française de sociologie* 48, Supplement: An Annual English Selection (2007): 3–34; and *Le Marché des défunts* (Paris: Presses de Sciences Po, 2008).

*products has been increasingly replaced by competition between judgment devices.*

• • •

For Karl Polanyi, the market is embedded in social and cultural organizations; for Harrison White it is embedded in the environment; for Mark Granovetter, it is embedded in networks; and for the economics of singularities, it is embedded in judgment devices.

These devices are at one and the same time representatives, cognitive supports, and mutually opposing forces. All are bearers of oriented knowledge; all claim to represent the client; all are fighting to increase their hold on customers; and all, more or less actively and more or less effectively, ensure economic coordination, as we will see by their link with trust as a condition for their credibility (Chapter 6), by their influence on the qualifications of the products and actors (Chapter 8), and, lastly, by their positions in the construction of coordination regimes (Chapter 9). Finally, all give a central place to the relative symbolic value of singularities: *quality competition prevails over price competition*

Although they are numerous, diversified, and fast changing, and although, with the exception of networks, they are perfectly visible, the devices of the singularities markets have not inspired any global studies.[19] And yet their position in the working of these markets is central. This situation explains the twofold restriction of the analysis.

Ideally, we should have studied the relationship between production, exchange, and consumption, but the emphasis on judgment devices needed to be compensated by a simplified conception of the production sphere. If firms seem to be absent as specific economic powers, they are nevertheless present through the products, a large share of the judgment devices, and the professionals of the market. For the same reason, the state is missing, too, but it is represented by judgment devices in charge of evaluation and control. In both cases, it has seemed preferable to confine the analysis to the mechanisms closest to the concrete exchange. Thus, the analysis concentrates particularly on *the relationship between singularities, judgment devices, and consumers*. These restrictions are purely pragmatic and no theoretical conclusions should be drawn from them.

[19] P. Chantelat, "La nouvelle sociologie économique et le lien marchand: Les relations personnelles à l'impersonnalité des relations," *Revue française de sociologie* 42, no. 3 (July–September 2002): 521–556.

## Chapter Six

# TRUST DEVICES

To be effective, the device must be credible. And to be credible, it must be trusted by those who use it. *Judgment devices are also trust devices.* Or to put it another way, judgment and trust are the two sides of the same reality. But in spite of the studies devoted to it, trust, by and large, keeps its secrets.[1]

"I trust" or "I do not trust" my colleague's loyalty, politicians' honesty, the quality of this brand of fruit juice, the union's effectiveness, the truth of the information published in my newspapers, the punctuality of the national railroad system, the honest fulfillment of this contract, my doctor's dedication, the satisfaction of my Internet order. As this linguistic proliferation shows, trust—which usually designates a mental state, a judgment, or an action—is both multiform and omnipresent. There seems to be no limit to its use except for "natural" or "naturalized" phenomena.[2] I would not say that I trust the sun will rise tomorrow, nor would I say that I trust an institution whose overall logic is beyond my ken.

The notion of trust is polysemic—to such a degree even that it would be exhausting to draw up a list of all of the explicit and implicit definitions that abound in everyday, as well as in learned, practices. Yet in spite of this dispersion, there is one common and literally fundamental meaning, and it is revealed by a tragedy. When Lear, the old authoritarian king, decides to hand over his power and divide his kingdom among his three daughters in proportion to their love for him, it is the two daughters who have multiplied their ostentatious demonstrations of affection who come away with the whole inheritance, but on two conditions: that they take

---

[1] C. Lane, "Introduction: Theories and issues in the study of trust," in C. Lane and R. Bachmann (eds.), *Trust within and between Organizations* (Oxford: Oxford University Press, 1998), pp. 1–31; V. Mangematin and C. Thuderoz (eds.), *Des mondes de confiance: Un concept a l'épreuve de la réalité sociale* (Paris: Editions du CNRS, 2003), pp. 19–29, 249–258.

[2] English, but not French, makes a distinction between *confidence* and *trust*. In the case of confidence, the actor realizes he does not control the reality that imposes itself on him, which can be described as "natural" or "naturalized," whereas trust implies awareness of a capacity for action or a prior personal commitment. See N. Luhman, "Familiarity, confidence, trust: Problems and alternatives," in D. Gambetta (ed.), *Trust: Making and Breaking Cooperative Relations* (Oxford: Blackwell, 1988), pp. 94–107.

turns receiving him at their castle and that each places a hundred knights at his disposal. Once they have the inheritance, however, the promises are forgotten. The illusions vanish. The former king, now a pauper, wanders the heath, and as the tempest winds rise to a howl, he is overcome with madness. Not because of his lost wealth or the injustice he has suffered, nor even because of the life of hardship he now leads, but because a world without trust is a world without meaning, a world of chaos.

Trust is a principle of order. Without it, nothing can be considered acquired, nothing can be predicted. With it the world finds its foundation and its continuity. Beyond the diversity of actions, actors, situations, and historical periods, trust grounds its social value in the exceptional effect it produces: *it removes, dissipates, or suspends uncertainty.*

And yet, with the exception of the long-overlooked interpretations that Simmel presented in the early twentieth century, the social sciences have ignored the question of trust. Its sociological history begins with Talcott Parsons, followed by Harold Garfinkel, Niklas Luhman, and Anthony Giddens. It is largely the product of a functionalism that logically had no need of it. In economics, its history began in the 1970s–80s, following a few remarks made by Kenneth Arrow: "It has at least one very important pragmatic value. Trust is an important lubricant of the social system. It is extremely efficient; it saves a lot of trouble to have a fair degree of reliance on other people's word."[3] Owing to the authority of their author, these few lines lifted a taboo and, as a result, outlined a paradoxical program of research: how can trust be used to restore the universality of the neoclassical theory?

The standard market relies on trust only in one exceptional case: when there is uncertainty. The market of singularities cannot do without it. It is therefore necessary to construct this reality, for while there is no intersubjective agreement on its nature, forms, or causes, everyone agrees on its effects: in the face of uncertainty, trust creates predictability and therefore the possibility of a continuing exchange.

The study of trust can be approached from two different perspectives, here designated as *formalism* and *substantivism*. The first embraces studies that assimilate trust to an "invisible institution," to a calculated bet, a cultural value, a subjective probability, an expectation, a quasi relation of delegation, all these differences having not the slightest consequences for the effects of the phenomenon. Trust designates an indeterminate entity, and the studies focus exclusively on the causes or the conditions, since these are what dictate the strength of its effects. The second perspective implies a relationship between the composition of trust and its effectiveness. These two viewpoints reveal two different conceptions not only of trust but also of the market.

[3] K. J. Arrow, *The Limits of Organization* (New York: Norton, 1974), p. 23.

## FORMAL ANALYSIS

In the last twenty years, trust has become an economic concept.[4] A sign of the gravity of a crisis that threatens the very foundations of neoclassical theory, universal validity made a comeback at the expense of conceptual unity. True, the consequences were slight, since formal analysis presupposes that trust exerts no particular constraints—it is neutral, transparent, without consistency—and that it is legitimate to restrict its study to the relations between the causes and the effects of the phenomenon.

In the main, two general models were developed to restore the overall validity of neoclassical theory: James Coleman's *calculation trust* and *reputation trust*, which was set out principally in a text by David Kreps. For Coleman, when the exchange is oriented toward profit and when it entails time lags between the commitments of the contracting parties, there is a risk, which can be neutralized only by trust. Trust is thus assimilated to a bet or investment. And the trustor must repeatedly collect information on the representative who acts in his name.[5] There is no trust without control and without assessment of the representative's action.

The difficulty encountered by this conception comes not from profit seeking—trust is indifferent to the aims pursued—or from the calculation of advantages and disadvantages, which remains unspecified; it comes from an implicit definition of trust that directly contradicts the classical conception according to which trust leads to "surrendering oneself." If trust is to rely on, if it is to rest on, the voluntary dependence of the represented party, the calculation-trust model is a contradiction in terms: it cannot be about trust.

The reputation-trust model restores the representative's power to act: he is the one doing the choosing, the calculating, the profit seeking; and he is the one who, in order to do this, shows his clients he can be trusted and in return receives their trust and their loyalty. The model ingeniously reestablishes the continuity of the standard market, since profit seeking necessarily maintains trust and in so doing drives out uncertainty.

The validity of this model rests on three propositions: the past guarantees the future (those who were trustworthy yesterday will be trustworthy tomorrow); reputation is a faithful measure of the firm's trustworthiness;

---

[4] P. Billand, "Rationalité et coopération: Le rôle de la confiance en économie," *Revue d'économie industrielle* 84 (1998): 67–84.

[5] "The trustor must use information, and perhaps search for more information and revise his views over time as in an adaptive control system"; "The potential trustor decides at any point whether or not to engage in a further search for information and, once the information search is finished, whether or not to place trust in the other party by engaging in a transaction. . . . The trustor may then revise his estimate of the trustee's trustworthiness, using information from the trustee's actions." J. S. Coleman, *Foundations of Social Theory* (Cambridge, MA: Belknap Press of Harvard University Press, 1990), pp. 111, 114.

and repeated games really do repeat. Nothing should disturb the automatic and general nature of these relations. But these propositions follow from three empirical inductions whose justification is hard to see. We know full well, for example, that the past is not always a reliable guarantee of the future; that reputation acts all the less automatically because it can be manipulated; that not all games are repeated and that those that are, are not indefinitely; and, furthermore, that the alternative between future gains—higher and honest—and present gains—lower and dishonest—is fallacious, because quite often opportunism manages to procure the one without forfeiting the other. The formal model turns out to be fragile, and it takes some good will to believe that trust can be the solution to the crisis of mainstream economics.

## SUBSTANTIVE ANALYSIS

Substantive analysis investigates the nature of trust in order to identify its causes and explain its effects. I will present two already formulated interpretations—the *interaction model* and the *domestic model*—which are part of this general perspective, and then develop a personal view of trust as a symbolic and social reality.

When the interactions between buyer and seller are intense, the resulting mutual trust enables them to surmount the incompleteness of the contracts and to safely engage in economic transactions. Whatever the actors' goals, the network, spontaneously, by the mere repetition of the interactions whereby it exists, usually suffices in all generality to establish trust and, at the same time, to eliminate the effects of ignorance and uncertainty. According to substantive analysis, opportunism would subsist only in markets devoid of networks.

And yet trust is not based on social interaction alone: it also presupposes motives for acting that cannot be reduced to interests. Not only is the help given within the network disinterested, but, moreover, only those who put their own interests second are deemed trustworthy. "The commonsense meaning of 'trust' is that we expect good behavior of others *in spite* of their incentives."[6] As a result, behavior guided by trust follows its own logic, which is expressed by moderation in the pursuit of one's own interests.

The domestic model[7] is indistinguishable from familiarity and is characterized—and this is its originality—by the relationship between, on the

---

[6] M. Granovetter, "A theoretical agenda for economic sociology," in M. Guillén, R. Collins, P. England, and M. Meyer (eds.), *The New Economic Sociology: Developments in an Emerging Field* (New York: Russell Sage Foundation, 2002), p. 40.

[7] F. Eymard-Duvernay, "Conventions de qualité et formes de coordination," *Revue économique* 2 (1989): 329–359; L. Thévenot, "Equilibe et rationalité dans un univers complexe," *Revue économique* 2 (March 1989): 147–197.

one hand, "lasting interpersonal ties," "grounding in traditions," "and considerations of reputation" and, on the other hand, a modality of production/sales based on products sharing the same origin. In that case, trust organizes a particular form of economic coordination.

In both cases, trust is rooted in the network and cannot be reduced to profit seeking. We are a long way from formal analysis. Nevertheless, two difficulties remain. How are we to explain that trust can win out over a passion as strong as interest?[8] That is the enigma the Chancelier d'Aguesseau tried to resolve in a famous *Discours* addressed to a body of seventeenth-century French lawyers.[9] And also, how are we to explain that persons at a distance, that impersonal judgment devices, and that institutions can all enjoy trust, even though they are not involved in networks?

We still do not have a definition. Must we resign ourselves to reiterating: "There must be some basic principle on which we accord credence, but what can such a principle accomplish? Is it more than a natural law of 'taking for true'?"[10] Nevertheless, our side trip is far from having been a waste of time. We now know that trust suspends uncertainty, that it implies that the represented person surrenders him- or herself, that it is indifferent to aims, that it is linked to social interaction without this being the only cause, and that it is present in all spheres of social life. We do not yet know what it is, but we do know that it must be everywhere the same. Here we must step away from the market before we can return to it with a definition of the phenomenon.

How could we bypass the history of the twentieth-century crowds that surrendered themselves to leaders, trusting them absolutely? How can we forget that—at least in several European countries—despite regular evidence to the contrary, the loss of trust in the communist cause was so long in coming?[11] Why do members of sects have such trust in their gurus that nothing their families and friends say can reach them? How can we explain the fact that some people can continue—in spite of the apparent evidence, in spite of the demonstrative strength of the judgments pronounced, in spite of the indifference or the opposition of public opinion—to claim miscarriage of justice in the name of an absolute trust in the person who has been convicted? The list of the forms of trust that do not fall into the categories of wager, or risk, or calculation of advantages or disadvantages, or reputation is long and varied. A definition of trust cannot ignore them.

[8] On the question of interest, see R. Swedberg, *Principles of Economic Sociology* (Princeton: Princeton University Press, 2003), pp.1–52.

[9] L. Karpik, *French Lawyers: A Study in Collective Action, 1274–1994*, trans. Nora Scott, (Oxford: Oxford University Press, 1999), pp. 51–58.

[10] L. Wittgenstein, *On Certainty* (Oxford: Blackwell, 1975), p. 179.

[11] F. Furet, *The Passing of an Illusion: The Idea of Communism in the Twentieth Century*, trans. Deborah Furet (Chicago: University of Chicago Press, 1999), pp. 123–124.

Trust is not merely a mental state; it is also an institution. In this perspective, it must be seen as a *relation of delegation embedded in the symbolic*. It combines a particular social morphology, the relation of delegation (see Chapter 5), with a symbolic system to which the rest of this analysis is devoted. The reasoning is built up in six arguments: (1) The symbolic system of trust is composed of knowledge and beliefs. (2) Belief combines "belief" statements and forms of social interaction. (3) The intensity of belief varies. (4) Trust varies with belief. (5) Trust obeys a symbolic logic of its own. (6) Trust and distrust have a dynamic relationship.

## The Symbolic System of Trust Is Composed of Knowledge and Beliefs

If we are to study trust, we can find no shrewder a guide than Simmel, who first conceptualized trust with originality and with profound insight, who expressed astonishment at the depth of the enigma, who connected social interaction in general and exchange in particular with trust "as far as it is a hypothesis of future conduct, which is sure enough to become the basis of practical action,"[12] and who showed that knowledge is never nor can ever be a sufficient basis for trust, that something else must be added to arrive at the equivalent of total knowledge. And he came to the logical conclusion that the "cognitive leap" which makes the uncertain certain, the unpredictable predictable, could only be taken with the support of a force different from knowledge, for which he used on several occasions, for lack of a better word, the notion of faith; not religious faith, but a secular transcendence: a higher authority, capable of granting that which knowledge alone cannot deliver. And that is *belief*. [13]

If social knowledge were comprehensive, belief would not be needed. Since it is not and, furthermore, can never be, another support is indispensable. To place one's trust in someone or something, to entrust oneself to an outside authority can never be justified by knowledge alone: one must also believe, and that takes a particular form. "To believe in . . ."[14] is to hold it to be true or certain that the representative, as a consequence of the particular qualities one ascribes to him, will prove faithful to the implicit or explicit promise that constitutes the delegation.

Trust is rooted in a symbolic system that combines knowledge and belief. One may think that knowledge is more open to rectification by reality than belief is, that belief makes excessive claims as to the surety it

[12]L. Pouillon, "Remarks on the verb 'to believe,'" in M. Izzard and P. Smith (eds.), *Between Belief and Transgression* (Chicago: University of Chicago Press, 1982), pp. 1–8.

[13]G. Simmel, "The secret and the secret society," *The Sociology of Georg Simmel* (Glencoe, IL: Free Press, 1908, 1950), pp. 305–376.

[14]"The degree of subjective certainty is very strong, even though the degree of objective guarantee may be very weak." P. Engel, "Les croyances," in D. Kambouchner (ed.), *Les Notions philosophiques* (Paris: Gallimard, 1995), vol. 2, p. 11.

offers,[15] but the essential point is to posit that changes in these two realities are independent of each other: they are not engaged in a zero-sum game. Knowledge and belief belong respectively to the two categories of truth and action,[16] each of which has its own dynamics and between which any and all relations are possible. Trust turns the world into a predictable reality; it turns uncertainty into certainty because knowledge receives the support of the belief that, inevitably, inhabits us.

## Belief Combines "Belief" Statements and Forms of Social Interaction

Beliefs come in many forms. Some are modest, some are grandiose, some specific and some general, some shifting and some immutable, some rough-hewn and some sophisticated. The hardest to spot are the most obvious: rituals, habits, sayings, conventional wisdom. . . . Beyond this empirical diversity, can we identify belief's characteristics and effects? How are we to go about studying it?

Although the impasses and pitfalls are many, advance we must, and in order to do so, we need tools. We have found some help in the perspective adopted by Jean-Toussaint Desanti, one of the brightest mathematical philosophers of his generation, in a book whose explicit goal is to explain the meanings and effects of the author's and others' longstanding Stalinist experience in the French Communist Party. This is of course an extreme reality, distant in time and far removed from the market. But these conditions make it easier to illuminate that which is usually so hard to perceive and to pinpoint. We are less interested in Desanti's specific interpretation than in the approach adopted by someone trying to construct an intelligible account of a personal (and collective) enigmatic experience. At least at the outset, such a viewpoint, with of course some modifications, could help us discern how beliefs, in their various guises, work in the world.[17]

## The Intensity of Belief Varies

For Desanti, trust expresses a certainty that is shown in extreme risk taking (not experienced as such) and that is rooted in a shared belief. For him, belief makes it possible to believe the unbelievable. To believe is to

[15] M. de Certeau, "Croire: Une pratique de la différence" (working paper, Centro Internazionale di Semiotica e di Linguistica, Università di Urbino, 2 September 1981, no. 106, series A); P. Engel, "Croyances collectives et acceptations collectives," in R. Boudon, A. Bouvier, and F. Chazel (eds.), *Cognition et sciences sociales* (Paris: Presses Universitaires de France, 1997), pp. 155–173.

[16] G. Lenclud, "Vues de l'esprit, art de l'autre: L'ethnologie et les croyances en pays de savoir," *Terrain* 14 (March 1990): 5–19.

[17] J-T. Desanti, *Un destin philosophique* (Paris: Grasset, 1982).

inhabit a quasi world richer than the real world, a quasi world protected from the world, whose presence nothing either shows or demonstrates and which, silently, governs action. In its extreme form, the believer is bound by an *adherence tie*, an "essential" and "substantial" belonging to this symbolic space. Adherence means that it is no longer in the sole power of the individual to regain his freedom and that it is not even in his power to make the question meaningful. Belief does not designate a mystery, a secret, or an interiority, but a set of statements—spoken words, writings, and practices—which testify that adherence to a quasi world estranges people from freely consented connection to the benefit of a relationship in which they are more or less immobilized, tied up, pinned down.

The solidity of this symbolic world depends on the intervention of three interlinking social bodies. If we alter and generalize the terms used by Desanti, these bodies are defined respectively by the three functions of *representation*, *guarantee*, and *ultimate referee*. The adherence relationship is maintained by relations between spokespersons—when the belief is solid, all believers are spokespersons—organized powers, and those ultimate warranties that are the "laws of history," justice, or God.

When the belief is intense, it is defined by a relationship of adherence protected by a social organization. Reflexivity—understood as the actors' capacity to step back from their decisions and commitments, to assess them, and when necessary, to make changes—withdraws. The certainties have to be shaken in order for self-reflection to set in. Before that, one adheres to what one is. This extreme form helps to define its opposite: moderate belief is founded on *attachment*, with a whole range of intensity separating the two.

### Trust Varies with Belief

Although things are not so simple, we can provisionally posit that trust varies: it can be weak or strong. The market by no means excludes strong beliefs, as is shown, for example, by the ties certain brands have established with consumers. When the brand succeeds in constructing a meaningful world assimilated to an imaginary and desirable quasi-world, which commands faithfulness and loyalty, it then profits not only from favorable judgments about its products and from an economic rent, but also benefits from the commitment of individual identities which transform purchase into

[18] "Brands cohere into systems that consumers create not only to aid in living but also to give meaning to their lives. Put simply, consumers do not choose brands, they choose ways of living." S. Fournier, "Consumers and their brands: Developing relationship theory in consumer research," in D. Miller (ed.), *Consumption: Critical Concepts in the Social Sciences* (London: Routledge, 2001), p. 107. See also Pierre Lascoumes, *Elites irrégulières: Essai sur la délinquance d'affaires* (Paris: Gallimard, 1997). In this book, the author pre-

identification.[18] Usually, however, the trust that accompanies ordinary marketing practices is moderate, and with it come the questions of attachment—more or less fragile—and of the tactics used to maintain customer loyalty.

Swindlers and con men have no doubt as to the existence of beliefs. If the latter were not so strong and numerous, there would be fewer financial scams. These offer an inexhaustible collection of hijacked beliefs, from exceptional affairs to the more run-of-the-mill repeated breaches of trust that are characteristic of petty swindles.[19]

## Trust Obeys a Symbolic Logic of Its Own

When it concerns itself exclusively with the causes and effects of trust, formal analysis and any analogous approach cannot help associating the presuppositions that go with everyday sentiments. Yet the nature of trust opens the way to understanding unexpected practices—sometimes noted but rarely inventoried—whether they are the *adherence relation*, the *disproportion of causes and effects*, a *disconcerting causality*, or a *concentration of energy* that is far from ordinary action.

To illustrate the trust relationship, Desanti proposes two stories about the French Resistance during the Second World War. The head of one network learns that his subordinate has just been arrested, but he refuses to change his hiding place: "If I had, I would have felt I had betrayed her. I trusted her." And in fact, she did not "talk" under torture. The second story concerns the transmission of instructions in the course of fugitive meetings that required strangers to place total trust in each other. In both cases, this trust was based on an absolute shared belief that defined the world of those communists who regarded other communists as totally trustworthy and therefore entirely predictable when it came to acting. The adherence relation corresponds to certainty.[20]

The principle of disproportion replaces the linear relation between causes and effects. We know that, while trust is won slowly, it may be lost quickly. The second part of this aphorism was strikingly illustrated in 2002 by the rapidity with which, starting with the Enron scandal, eighty-nine years of trust vested in the multinational accounting firm Arthur Andersen (number five among the "Big Five" and employing at the time twenty-eight thousand

---

sents a famous case of a very strong belief held collectively by scientists, by the director of a big corporation, and by several high civil servants, all highly intelligent and highly qualified, that lasted around four years and cost a huge sum of money. The story is that of the "sniffer" planes, which were supposed to be able to detect the presence of oil reserves located deep within the earth. The "invention" was in fact an enormous scam.

[19] "When there is the need to believe, all information that might destroy or tarnish faith may be rejected." D. Desanti, *Les Staliniens* (Paris: Arthème Fayard, 1975), p. 9.

[20] M. Piaget and C. Baumann, *La chute de l'empire Andersen* (Paris: Dunod, 2003).

people throughout the world) was inexorably withdrawn. In less than two months the firm had entirely disappeared.[21] Three years later, the judgment that had detonated the fiduciary cataclysm was unanimously overturned by the Supreme Court on the grounds, among others, that the acts of which the firm was accused were not necessarily unlawful.

Desanti observes that, while, for a very long time, the French communists obstinately refused to accept the reality of statements that apparently could not be more convincing, at a given point, a benign remark that was out of phase with the subject was often enough to destroy a trust that had seemed unshakable. This disconcerting causality explains why the phenomenon is hard to control. Lastly, the concentrated energy of the action often characterizes those driven by a strong belief/trust. It has often been observed, and it represents the most astonishing characteristic and the hardest to understand.

The four characteristics associated with practices based on strong belief/trust have in common exaggeration or *excess*. Though it is still difficult to discern the conditions that favor them, they nevertheless challenge the theories of trust that posit a linear relation between causes and effects. The particular *symbolic logic* that governs trust often asserts itself unexpectedly; but surprise is merely the expression of an overly conventional conception of the phenomenon.

### Trust and Distrust Have a Dynamic Relationship

Trust does not depend solely on causes and conditions, it also varies according to adversary forces, as is shown by a study of the partnership between the operators of two large industrial firms, a parts company and an automotive assembly line.[22]

Whereas the official contract was organized around the common goals of *zero defects* and *just-in-time*, the informal exchange that governed

[21] Reading the English translation of this book a few months after the international financial and economic crisis of autumn 2008, one would find it easy to add numerous and high-scale examples. This is true for the suddenness and the scope of the loss of trust in some judgment devices and in some institutions. It is even truer for the numerous financial experts (though not for all of them) who, on the basis of personal relations, gave their money to a crook whose promises should have been unbelievable for them. But when we want to believe, we believe; and when we believe strongly, we "adhere"; knowledge and advice do not.

[22] E. Friedberg and J-P. Neuville, "Inside partnership: Trust, opportunism and cooperation in the European automobile industry," in A. Anna Grandori (ed.), *Interfirm Networks: Organization and Industrial Competitiveness* (London: Routledge, 1999), pp. 67–90; J.-P. Neuville, "La stratégie de la confiance: Le partenariat industriel observé depuis le fournisseur," *Sociologie du travail* 3 (1997): 297–319; J-P. Neuville, "La coopération interindividuelle dans le partenariat industriel," *Revue française de sociologie* 39, no. 1 (Jan.–March 1998): 71–103.

the relationships between the parts suppliers and the assembly-line operators of a large carmaker obeyed a heterodox logic. One side wanted to off-load a maximum of defective parts, while the other side wanted to receive repaired or supplementary parts and to profit from quick supplier-responsiveness in order to keep the assembly line going. Quasi prices were negotiated by the informal representatives of the two groups and they regulated these exchanges. When mutual trust prevailed, this informal exchange was automatic. After a while, opportunistic practices crept in and built up, distrust grew, and the agreement broke down. After a time of crisis, new quasi prices were negotiated and established, mutual trust between the operators returned, and the quasi market worked again.

These alternating periods of trust and distrust were the result of the dynamic articulation of three forms of trust: the strong trust of the operators in their representative, the fragile trust between the operators from each industrial firm, and the strong mutual trust between the operators' representatives from both firms. The first form explains the initial respect the operators showed for the negotiated agreement; the second form accounts for the fact that the operators gave way, after a time, in the face of opportunistic practices; and the third form explains why, even after a serious crisis, new negotiations and a new quasi market could be restored.

Although these large firms were governed by rules, it was nevertheless a quasi market, which periodically broke down and was reconstructed, that ensured the everyday workings of the partnership and determined how realistic the official goal was. This informal reality was both a way of managing uncertainty and the expression of a desire for collective autonomy. The conditions of its possibility were rooted in the diversity of the relations between cooperative and antagonistic groups, and its long-term continuance was determined by a particular configuration of forms of trust that, depending on the moment, established or undid cooperation through exchange. Without the focus on trust, and more specifically on a conception of relational trust, the quasi market could be observed but not explained.

•   •   •

We would have preferred to simplify reality, to stick to the objective character of judgment devices, and to abstain from bringing in trust and belief. However, human actors are troublesome because they themselves are singularities that make judgments about realities. And no metadevice exists that might guarantee the judgment devices. Only trust, whatever its origins and modalities, can create the credibility of judgment devices and thereby bring about the continuity of markets of singularities. Let us be more precise. Following Knight's distinction, we distinguish the market whose risk can be eliminated by information, calculation, contract, or one or another, or some combination of them, from the market whose (radical) uncertainty can never be dissipated by knowledge, calculation, or contract, alone or together: there must be trust as well.

## Chapter Seven

# HOMO SINGULARIS

HOMO SINGULARIS is to the economics of singularities what Homo economicus is to neoclassical economics: a being of Reason whose behavior explains the functioning of economic coordination. The actor of the standard market is rational and self-interested: he seeks to maximize profit or
utility by the optimal combination of means with ends. The actor of the
singularities market is also rational and self-interested. But his action is
determined by the combined effects of two orientations: the search for a
"good" or the "right" product and the best means-end alternative. Homo
singularis approaches the choice of the good product with countless criteria of judgment; he is also oriented toward efficiency. But in an uncertain and complex world where the ends often change, the degree of efficiency is impossible to measure. Whereas Homo economicus uses a single
criterion of judgment and moves in a single world, Homo singularis is
not only the bearer of a plurality of evaluative criteria and the member of
a plurality of worlds, he is also a figure who embodies an unlimited potential for actualizing forms of action.

In his search for singularities, Homo singularis must juggle the discovery, interpretation, and evaluation of judgment of devices; the discovery,
interpretation, and evaluation of singularities; sometimes the discovery,
interpretation, and evaluation of his own tastes; and a reasonable use of
scarce resources. Driven by desires and tastes, subjected to more or fewer
constraints—especially money and time—and confronted with countless
temptations, Homo singularis could easily lose his way. But he maintains
his identity and his coherence through an interpretative frame that expresses a particular viewpoint and ensures the regulation of beliefs, representations, evaluation criteria, and forms of action. It is the *person's* psychic "jurisdiction" that constructs the representation of reality and imposes
the coherence of behavior. The more strongly a guiding principle structures the interpretive frame, the more strongly the frame reinforces the
unity and coherence of the actor's individual form of action;[1] and the better
it explains the existence of relations of homology between concrete mar-

---

[1] Experiences shows this a contrario: "When, for whatever reason, the individual breaks
frame and perceives he has done so, the nature of his engrossment and belief suddenly
changes." E. Goffman, *Frame Analysis: An Essay on the Organization of Experience* (New
York: Harper & Row, 1974), p. 378.

kets, as the same persons move the same interpretive frames from one place to another, and from the past to the present and thence to the future.

The tension between the search for a "good" singularity and the choice of the most effective purchase strategy organizes the analysis in the same way as it organizes the action. It leads the analyst to identify and study two guiding principles of action—value and goal, their interactions, and their relative influence, and then to present the different notions that are useful for describing and explaining purchases on the market. Two concrete analyses will serve as illustrations: one of the Michelin Guide and the other of the different steps a consumer, whom we will call Recordo, goes through in looking for the "right" version of Beethoven's Ninth Symphony.

## VALUE AND INSTRUMENTALITY

In the market of singularities, the structure of the action combines *value orientation* and *instrumental (means-end) orientation*.[2] Even if the two orientations can be separated in the analysis, the same is not possible in the real world. The consumer's behavior can therefore never be reduced to the choice of either the desirable product or the best means of finding and buying it: his behavior depends at one and the same time on both categories of criteria, which, nevertheless, must be analyzed independently before being brought together.

The distinction between the two orientations comes directly from Max Weber's four classes of action, of which only two are retained here: *value commitment* and *goal commitment*. The first is multiple because values are multiple, and it finds its justification in action itself, independent of the consequences of this action; the second, on the contrary, is defined by the adequacy of the means to the given ends; it is unitary and is usually measured by the results of the action.[3] Our analysis focuses on the differences between these two orientations and on the conditions governing their relative influence on individual behaviors.

[2] The notion of *orientation* is used by A. M. Henderson and T. Parsons in their translation of Max Weber, *The Theory of Social and Economic Organization* (Glencoe, IL: The Free Press, 1947).

[3] Value-rational social action is "determined by a conscious belief in the value for its own sake of some ethical, aesthetic, religious, or other form of behaviour, independently of its prospects of success"; "Action is instrumentally rational when the end, the means, and the secondary results are all rationally taken into account and weighed. This involves rational consideration of alternative means to the end, of the relations of the end to the secondary consequences, and finally of the relative importance of different possible ends." M. Weber, *Economy and Society: An Outline of Interpretive Sociology* (Berkeley: University of California Press, 1978), vol. 1, pp. 24–25, 26.

## *Value Orientation*

Action is oriented by operational values that take the modalities of criteria of judgment. The direct connection between value systems and individual criteria logically would imply a deterministic cultural interpretation and the loss of individual autonomy. But the relation is indirect: it necessitates the mediation of the "person," defined by a specific *frame of interpretation*, and that means a particular way of "organizing experience."[4] To analyze action requires understanding the way the logics of action are regulated in the market of singularities and examining the relationship between the criteria of judgment and the purchase aims.

For Weber, criteria of evaluation are numerous in the market as well as in society: "ethical, political, utilitarian, hedonistic, class based, . . . or egalitarian," or again, "duty, dignity, beauty, religious guidelines, piety or the nobility of a [cause]." Multivocal, countless, aesthetic, professional, ethical, and political conceptions intervene in the form of criteria of *judgment*, of criteria of *evaluation*, or of *logics of action* (the terms are interchangeable).[5] They are the visible sign of the irreducible plurality of values and gods. It is these criteria that channel practices and which, over time, leave their imprint in the form of social regularities. The logic of action does not place the consumer above other people; it does not provide him with a universal yardstick. The consumer is one of many, and one who should not be confused with anyone else. The difference with Homo economicus is not that criteria exist, but that they are particular.

Whether the goal pursued is initially vague, whether it is redefined in the course of action, or whether it changes sequentially or appears in new situations, the criterion of judgment generally endures. Moreover, it runs through and links the decisions the consumer makes in different domains, or in the same domain but at different times, whether or not he is aware of it. With this criterion, the buyer in search of a singular product makes his way among the many possibilities and temptations without getting lost. The criterion of judgment should not be confused with either the ends or the conditions of action. It is internal, individual, and relatively stable: it is the compass that guides individuals' actions.

The market of tourist guidebooks, which sell several millions of copies every year in France, provides a simple example of the existence and influence of logics of action. Each of the collections is characterized by an original editorial policy and, therefore, by a different selection of sights,

---

[4] "My phrase 'frame analysis' is a slogan to refer to the examination in these terms of the organization of experience." Goffman, *Frame Analysis*, p. 11.

[5] "There is not one form of rationality but several, which we call logics of action . . . , we are therefore talking about evaluation criteria." L. Karpik, "Les politiques et les logiques d'action de la grande entreprise industrielle," *Sociologie du travail* 1(1972): 87–88.

itineraries, accommodations, and restaurants. The only way to ascertain the meaning of this variety is to compare the collections. The Lonely Planet series is encyclopedic in scope, practical, puts everything on the same footing, and supposes autonomous users. The Literary Guides for Travellers and the Hachette Guides choose and rank cultural curiosities, the Routard Guides and the Knopf Guides mark trails for exploration, while Michelin's Green Guides ensure the transmission of knowledge about history and civilization.

In one swoop, the guide qualifies the trip and the traveler. By the selection and the elaboration of knowledge, it implicitly determines the dispositions necessary for a successful trip. The four logics of action entailed in the guides are matched by four logics of action specific to those who buy them. Planning a successful trip means, in part, using the "right" guide, the one that suits the buyer's form of curiosity and pleasure and also offers the desired degree of autonomy. However, many future tourists are not only ignorant of the differences between the collections, they are also only vaguely conscious of their own tastes. They choose their guide more or less at random when time is short. Once in the foreign country, either the traveler's point of view coincides sufficiently with that of the guide for him to feel at ease, or the contrary is the case, and each stage of the trip risks being marked by disappointments.

When it comes to judgment criteria, the analyst is torn between two radically opposed methods: using an ideal-type approach that imposes a priori an extreme restriction on the number of criteria combined with authoritarian labeling[6] or, on the contrary, keeping the disorderly reality. The first solution is convenient but runs the danger of being arbitrary; the second is faithful but runs the risk of being impotent. Nevertheless, we have chosen the second method, for using the ideal-type method, however justified it may be, would in the present case prevent discovering the ways real actors facing the same constraints go about finding more or less effective solutions. The theoretical problem is constantly resolved in practice by a double movement of *proliferation* and *rarefaction*.

The market of singularities involves an indefinite number of logics of action; competition constantly adds even more; and consumers insist on proving their inventive capacities.[7] In sum, the principle of proliferation is at work. The market must therefore also contain a powerful mechanism for increasing scarcity, without which it could not work. To identify this mechanism, we must take a side trip.

Brand publicity, film trailers, and critical reviews in the press of a novel or a CD are all judgment devices. Each expresses an oriented knowledge,

---

[6] For instance T. Parsons' "pattern variables." *The Social System* (Glencoe, IL: The Free Press, 1951).

[7] This is why firms the world over use specialists to scour the streets for "fashion setters."

and ideally, each is chosen or followed by clients with identical logics of action. Yet on the whole, the world of consumer logics of action is much more diversified than that of product logics of action. Hence, the mechanism of rarefaction.

Each judgment device is linked to a judgment criterion or to a configuration of such criteria and serves as a guidepost for heterogeneous bodies of consumers: those who are guided by the search for absolute concordance between logics of action; those who consider that, of all the devices available, this one best suits their taste; those who have made a mistake and who stand behind their choice; those who have made a mistake and have not yet realized it; those who find their feet after some slipping and sliding; and many more. Each of the devices aggregates a more or less diversified set of logics of action and therefore a more or less diversified group of persons. Those consumers who do not recognize themselves in any device and those who refuse to convert to one of them have no other choice but to exit the market.

*To choose a device is to choose a logic of action*, or a particular configuration of logics of action. Whether they are similar or different, once they have been collapsed onto a single device, all these logics of action merge into one. The actor selects the device according to the way he interprets it, but once this is done, it is the device that interprets the actor in accordance with the logic it imposes. This process of subjectivation/objectivation goes on indefinitely. Judgment devices are therefore not only cognitive aids, they are also mechanisms for aggregating and objectivating logics of action: they are *axiological operators*. In the economics of singularities, the multiplicity of judgment criteria is not abnormal, but no system of production, no market, can tolerate an actor whose *proliferating actualizations* threaten to overwhelm the real possibilities of production and of exchange. It is the judgment devices that curb Homo singularis, and as these operate on a large scale, they also mechanically reduce the variety of preferences.[8]

## Instrumental Orientation

The presentation of instrumental orientation will be brief, since in principle, it comes down to the common conception of rationality. But in the market of singularities, two reasons forbid recognizing this similitude. First, whereas rationality is defined as the combination of means and ends, in the singularities market, the goals cannot be set in advance: the

[8]A sufficient concentration of buyers on a logic of action and therefore on a judgment device is also the condition for realizing economies of scale and therefore lowering prices.

consumer constructs them along with his commitment. Far from being defined beforehand, the purchase of a singularity, very generally speaking, is the product of the journey itself, since the singularity changes as the actor moves from one device to the next and acquires more knowledge, which each time redefines the conditions and the target of his choice. In this situation, the goals are unstable, and the result of the action cannot serve as a term of comparison for the different forms of action.

Moreover, comparison of the degrees of rationality presupposes calculation of the economic value of the means. But in the market of singularities, not all of the scarce resources marshaled by the actor have a price: this is the case, among others, of the *time available*, which can have a crucial influence on choices. This nonequivalence can be overcome by some arbitrary equivalences that are necessarily fragile. Under these conditions, instrumental orientation is guided by the *economizing principle*. And since action requires us to deal simultaneously with logics of action and economizing principles, the notion of rationality becomes problematic.

## The Relative Strength of Value Orientation

In the market of singularities, the consumer gives more importance to qualities than to prices.[9] For the moment, this is simply an observation; the general explanation will be given below. Here we merely intend to indicate how the *cultural complex*, a new notion for a new reality in the study of the market's functioning, influences the relative weight of the two orientations of action. Cultural complexes are loosely structured wholes that develop and maintain beliefs, knowledge, and judgment around the collective activity of producing and selling specific singularities. Such complexes bring together experts, journalists, producers, associations, and organizations, all of which intervene not only in the professional, but also in the public sphere by way of networks, newspapers, magazines, books, guides, TV, radio, and the Internet. They produce knowledge, know-how, and advice. They initiate discussions and conflicts and construct the relationship between the specific collective activity and the various forms of culture. One has only to think of the writings, discussions, and celebrations that accompany the market of movies or of fine wines.

Cultural complexes vary in their make-up, their workings, their visibility, their forms of action, and their effectiveness. They devote themselves to the symbolic production necessary to connect singularities to culture, root them in history, and as a corollary, raise the dignity of all those who take part in their production, sale, and consumption. *They are the bearers, the guardians, and the evangelists of qualities.* Their relative strengths

---

[9]"Even in economic life there are ideals whose force prevails over that of 'material' interests." Max Weber quoted in J.-P. Grossein, introduction to M. Weber, *L'éthique protestante et l'esprit du capitalisme*, trans. J.-P. Grossein (Paris: Gallimard, 2004), p. xviii.

are unequal and therefore they contribute unequally to the *salience* of the logics of action.

## Shopping

The word *shopping* entered the French language long ago: it is defined as the act of "going from store to store to window shop, look over the merchandise, compare and buy."[10] Its meaning thus has three components: search, evaluation, and purchase. If Homo economicus had to do his shopping in the markets of singularities, he would be sentenced to behave erratically unless he were to resort to a generalized dequalification of the products. He is lacking the faculties that Homo singularis possesses.

Shopping must bring together what is desired with what is proposed. The consumer must find his way, choose the right forks in the path, make provisional evaluations, and thus set out on a continuous or discontinuous sequential process that culminates in the purchase. The *purchase path* would be simpler if the goal were known at the outset. This is not the case, though. The initial aim is usually vague; the judgment criteria are less so—they are preferences. Preferences make it possible to confront reality, to return to the action and thereby simultaneously to accumulate knowledge and an increasingly clearer vision of what is sought.[11] Homo singularis's path of action is complicated. Several notions will be used in its analysis: junction and adjustment, deliberation and competence, relevance and efficiency, and disappointment.

### *Junction and Adjustment*

Junction designates the encounter between the actor and the judgment device(s), while adjustment applies to the encounter between the consumer and the product. Logically, the client attempts first of all to single out the judgment devices that will help him learn more about the desired product and how to go about locating it. Selection of the judgment device is something of a hit-or-miss process, since there are no meta-devices that might help. In this phase, the prospective buyer can only rely on personal infor-

---

[10] *Trésor de la Langue Française*, Dictionnaire du XIXe & XXe siècle : définition, étymologie, citations, synonymes, antonymes, 16 vols., online, http://atilf.atilf.fr/tlf.htm .

[11] A. Dubuisson-Quellier, "De la routine à la délibération: Les arbitrages des consommateurs en situarion d'achat," *Réseaux* 135–136 (2006): 78–97; D. Miller, *A Theory of Shopping* (Ithaca, NY: Cornell University Press, 1998). When the options are limited, the purchase itinerary is not far from the dynamics of decision making found in academic juries charged with hiring the "right" or the "best" candidates. See J. Guetzkow, M. Lamont, and G. Mallard, "What is originality in the humanities and the social sciences?" *American Sociological Review* 69, no. 2 (April 2004): 190–212; C. Musselin, *Le marché des universitaires: France, Allemagne, Etats-Unis* (Paris: Presses de Sciences Po, 2005), pp. 139–221.

mation, on his own competence, and eventually on help from the network. The next step depends largely on the quality of the junction. The more "satisfactory" it is, the more satisficing, or reasonable, the adjustment should be. In the meantime, however, anything can happen.

Adjustment—"matching"—indicates the degree of agreement between the qualities proposed and those required, between the product judgment criteria and the consumer judgment criteria. The adjustment can be evaluated in terms of happiness/disappointment or of efficiency.

### Deliberation and Competence

How does the consumer move from junction to adjustment? Indecision, redefinition of the desired product, and error can always lead the consumer to start over again. This is all the more likely because the reasonable purchase, as its name does not indicate, can involve a greater or lesser proportion of fantasy, new curiosities, and accepted side trips. The notion of *deliberation* is useful for understanding the purchase path, because it emphases the individual or collective active reflexivity entailed in making choices. Deliberation implies hesitation, collected knowledge, right choice of judgment devices, reflection, comparison, and so on. It is the central means to achieve the highest degree of rationality.

*Competence* should make a difference in deliberation. The notion combines the mastery of a codified, rationalized, and transmissible body of knowledge and the know-how suited to the concrete circumstances, contexts, and power relations. In the market of singularities, the useful distinction is between *device competence* and *product competence*. One concerns knowledge about judgment devices; it extends the map of the various possibilities. The other concentrates knowledge about the products and, in this sense, is more operational, more limited, and carries more risk of becoming obsolete. In both cases, competence or expertise includes formal learning and/or know-how based on practical experience and ordinary reflexivity.[12] In principle, the efficacy of the consumer's deliberation varies with his degree of competence. But in the market of singularities, a third constraint comes into play: knowledge and know-how cannot be too general because their relevance depends on the consumer's logic of action.

Deliberation has its drawbacks as well. Finding the relevant knowledge is not easy and it is costly in terms of time. Some people can find it hard to tolerate indecision, and no one is competent in all domains. There are several ways of dealing with such a situation. The first is to reduce the consumer's burden through judgment devices, which allow him every degree of autonomy—from complete to very limited—when a device proposes only the "best" choice. Consumers can see this as more or less convenient.

[12] J. Lave, *Cognition in Practice* (Cambridge: Cambridge University Press, 1988).

The second example is impulse buying, which is beyond speech and argumentation; it saves on time, deliberation, and reasoning, even if it is considered to be irrational, which remains to be proven. The third example is routine. In all cases, the time-savings is considerable, but the degree of pertinence is undetermined.

### Relevance and Efficiency

Logic of action and economizing principles, although inseparable, belong nevertheless to two worlds in which rationality does not have the same meaning. The *relevance* of the action is all the greater when the product logic of action and the consumer logic of action are close; the *efficiency* of the action is all the greater when the buyer manages to make his purchase while having economized on scarce resources. This dualistic conception of action is difficult to fit into the frame of classical, and even procedural, rationality. Nevertheless, one may consider that the reasonable choice will be a trade-off, varying, with each consumer or each category of consumer, in its degrees of relevance and efficiency.

### Disappointment

Happiness rewards the satisficing intersection of the product trajectories and the purchase trajectories. It means that the consumer was not mistaken in his tastes, that he chose the pertinent judgment devices, and that—at the end of a journey which was long or short, circuitous or direct, but in any event well adjusted—he successfully discerned and purchased the desired singularity. There is no specific word for the sentiment that accompanies this success, given the degree to which it varies with the consumer and the singularity. The notion of *satisfaction*, after having been largely used in industrial sociology, has been eliminated because of its ambiguity. This is not the case when it comes to disappointment. *Disappointment* is the hallmark of failure. The varying degrees of intensity measure the different significant gaps between explicit or implicit expectations and reality. Hirschman, one of the few authors to have taken an interest in this phenomenon, observes that, far from being marginal, "disappointment is a central element of the human experience." And he shows that it has serious repercussions for both the client and the market.[13]

The economics of singularities, with its uncertainty and complexity and with its stringent selection of the product, cannot help leading to some unsatisfactory purchases—probably more often than in other markets. Habitual consumers are familiar with such experiences and, to a certain extent, include them among the unavoidable risks.

[13] A. Hirschman, *Shifting Involvement: Private Interest and Public Action* (Princeton: Princeton University Press, 1982), p. 11.

Disappointment stems not only from exceptional human slip-ups, it is an integral part of the way the market works. Hirschman proposes an explanation of the probabilities of being disappointed in terms of product category that is hardly convincing. It seems more useful to look to opportunism or to error to explain the causes: opportunism on the part of the seller, or error on the part of the consumer owing to lack of competence and/or ineffective judgment devices. In either case, the result is the same. To be deceived or to be mistaken, sometimes after having invested a great deal of knowledge and time, are the risks the consumer faces.

Disappointment must be broken down into the probabilities of its appearance and the magnitude of its repercussions. The first arise with the general causes that favor opportunism and ignorance; the second increase with the amount of personal investment and the actor's pride. Disappointment has a strange effect when a person cannot tell whether he has been deceived or has deceived himself. Because it does not rely on impersonal measurement or comparison but involves an experience about which it is not always easy to say whether it should be ascribed to a failure of the judgment device, to a failure on the part of the consumer, or both, and because the source of error is not obvious, disappointment entails ill-known causes—and consequences.

For Hirschman, widespread disappointment could be the source of a political movement that could travel from the market to the public sphere. If one combines globalization with the market of singularities—in which, to a greater extent than in the standard market, products are associated with individual identifications and with collective meanings and involve a conception of social life—one can imagine that collective action could become more influential and general, providing one accepts—which is by no means evident—that in this event, consumption has overtaken production as the principal site of political mobilization.

In fact, the issue of political consumerism is broader than the question of disappointment with the market. It asserts itself through specific stakes, movements, and conflicts; through the expansion of hedonism, now a key word in contemporary analysis; or through "consumption" as "a form of drudgery, part of the capitalist civilizing process."[14] But uncertainty remains about the scope and effects of disappointment.

• • •

Homo singularis is a flexible being, since his cognitive abilities change with the judgment devices. Frégoli populates the marketplace of singu-

---

[14] A. Appadurai, *Modernity at Large: Cultural Dimensions of Globalization* (Minneapolis: University of Minnesota Press, 1986), p. 7 and chapter 4.

larities. His judgment criteria are countless, his principles of calculativeness, many. Yet the upwelling of the practices of Homo singularis is regulated by judgment devices, which serve to aggregate, and objectivate values. When the joint action is coherent, when it draws strength from the cultural complex, it reinforces the primacy of qualities. It does not exclude the possibility of defining rational—or rather reasonable—behavior, without having to ratify the usual definition of rationality. Which represents a perplexing issue.

Moreover, Homo singularis is a complex entity. If we were to make a list of actions he or she is supposed to carry out, we would have to recognize that he or she is characterized not only by the faculties of judgment and of calculation, but also by the faculty of interpretation—not to forget the faculties of belief and trust. The two case studies that follow—one on the red Michelin Guide, and the other on the search for a "good" version of Beethoven's Ninth Symphony—should help clarify the issue of action in the singularities market.

### THE RED MICHELIN GUIDE: A PAPER ENGINE

How does one choose a "good" restaurant? When the qualifier "good" contains all of the characteristics applicable to restaurants as a function of the possible tastes of their clients, the question has no simple answer. Before the advent of guidebooks, this information was local and circulated in networks. Tourists had absolutely no means of gaining access. They had no way of dissipating the market's opacity. For a century, the Michelin Guide has been the most reputed guide to tourism and fine dining.[15] Its supremacy and longevity are attributed essentially to the integrity of its staff, to the absence of advertising, and even to the rigor of its judgments, but rarely to the object itself. And yet this veritable paper engine is worthy of consideration. It has the rare ability to create the conditions of large-scale comparisons of incommensurable entities while thoroughly respecting their particularisms: it thus eliminates unwelcome surprises for those exploring the unknown and it does so without (or almost without) restricting the user's autonomy. *It is a technology marvelously suited to the economics of singularities.*

In order to dispel ignorance or uncertainty about the qualities of its hotels and restaurants, the guide does three things: it selects, it compares, and it rates. First of all, *relegation* leads to associating belonging and minimum quality requirements: the Red Guide retains a mere one-tenth

---

[15] Concerning this twin historical development, see L. Karpik, "Le Guide rouge Michelin," *Sociologie du travail* 3 (2000): 369–389.

of all of the restaurants in France, and this harsh selection is fine tuned every year. User trust is fundamental here insofar as the guide's decision, although never explicitly justified, is definitive and leads to banishing nine-tenths of the restaurants in France to nonexistence—absent the intervention of other guides and/or local networks. This founding act establishes a minimal quality: without the guide, random choice can lead to dire disappointments; with the Red Guide, "catastrophe" is in principle excluded.

Even strongly restricted, this world is heterogeneous and still does not authorize a reasonable choice. It is therefore necessary, insofar as it is possible, to render the incomparable comparable. Since each restaurant is a singularity, it can be evaluated against all the others only by adopting a particular criterion of evaluation or, better, a configuration of particular criteria of evaluation. But who proposes this criterion or these criteria? The consumer, the producer, or the guidebook? To overcome arbitrariness in its most developed versions—which applies to Paris restaurants— for the past half century the Red Guide has engaged in an apparently commonplace practice: the use of a relatively long list of judgment criteria. Therefore the chances that the preferences of the various users will overlap are high.[16] This very real decentering conceals the novelty of the guide.[17] A bit of history here is useful.

In the past fifty years, three sets of criteria have been used in succession to rate Parisian restaurants:

- Between 1949–50 and 1959, *sixteen criteria* were used: "luxury," "Parisian elegance," "very comfortable," "classic," "selected and varied," "original atmosphere," "renowned elegant cafés" (1950), "renowned cafés and brasseries," "small typical restaurants," "wine merchants," "the cuisine trumps the decor," "specialties," "outdoor dining," "open late," "snacks" (1950), "following the prices" (1957).

- Between 1960 and 1970, *twelve criteria* remained after simply deleting from the previous list "Parisian elegance," "very comfortable," "selected and varied," and "small typical restaurant."

- Since 1971, and after deletions and additions, nine criteria have remained: "outdoor dining," "dinner after the theater," "starred establishments," "traditional dishes," "cuisine by type," "typical bistros and brasseries," "menus for . . . ," "private dining rooms," and "open at weekend."

[16] The list of these dimensions is the fruit of a long history; it includes location, quality of the cooking, setting, decor, view, service in the garden or on the patio, dishes, price, and so on.

[17] The study is based on data collected from (1) the Red Guides published every five years from 1900 to 1990, together with those in between that featured an innovation in the presentation; and (2) all of the Red Guides published between 1990 and 1998.

The changes of category indicate the methods used by the Red Guide in an effort to foster the best match between restaurant and client. Initially, a deliberate policy aimed at expanding the clientele can be seen in the widened diversity of evaluation criteria. The guide thus increased the probability of an elective encounter between customer and restaurant. Ten years later, the itemized list had been simplified without its overall logic having been altered. Perhaps the change resulted from the difficulties encountered in dealing with too many criteria whose specific meanings were hard to determine and whose exact boundaries were difficult to define. Another ten years, and the list was pared down again. It would seem that the guide eliminated the least-used criteria and offered the user the benefit of an already long collective experience.

Must we therefore conclude that, over time—and with the growing popularity of gastronomy, in which the Red Guide played an essential role—tastes have become less and less diversified? This would be a strange interpretation, even if it seems to fit the facts. In reality, without saying so, the guide uses a new way of producing judgment criteria. Between 1949 and 1959, eleven out of sixteen criteria were mutually exclusive; this was also the case for eight criteria out of twelve between 1960 and 1970, while after 1970, the mutually exclusive criteria disappear. All of the terms can be combined: there is nothing to prevent associating one, two, three, and up to nine criteria, and thus circumscribing ever more closely the restaurant's qualifications. This method was the major invention of the Red Guide, after the use of a system of signs to characterize the restaurants.

The reader can now pick the judgment criteria that seem the most relevant and combine as many of the nine as he wants. He can therefore make his choice as a function of the most general qualification, which results from using a single criterion, a restaurant that is part of a large class of restaurants, or as a function of the most specific qualification, which results from combining all nine criteria, or any of the solutions in between. The free variation of the nature and number of the criteria enables the user to reasonably explore all possible choices; but as the number of intersecting dimensions grows, the number of restaurants decreases, of course, and at the same time, their qualification becomes more and more precise.

The individual consumer's taste is a configuration of logics of action whose richness dictates the specificity and therefore the suitability of the adjustment between object and actor. These variations depend on the user's decision, his ingenuity, his activism, and the time he has available. In sum, as a judgment device, the Red Guide defines the restaurants and, through the qualities demanded, defines the consumer as well. Since it also makes it possible to benefit from choices extended to personal tastes without demanding a heavy commitment in exchange, the guide goes even farther by proposing ready-made combinations: "starred establishments" (combination of culinary stars + setting + comfort), "dinner after the theater" (late-night dining + setting), "typical bistros and brasseries" (tradition + area), "menus for less than . . ." (price + setting + area).

The Red Guide allows every combination within the available criteria. More specifically, by combining a maximum number of criteria, it accommodates not only value commitment but also instrumental rationality, which imposes itself in the form of constraints on price or time and leads to either using ready-made formulas or setting limits on the search for the best choice. Choice is based on a polyphonic approach that allows the instruments of the orchestra to enter and exit, or, in another register, on a technique (known to the social sciences as multivariate analysis) remarkably well suited to dealing simultaneously with the diversity of user tastes and the varying degrees of user commitment.

●   ●   ●

The Red Guide's technology dispels opacity, reduces quality uncertainty, and establishes economic regulation for incommensurable products while at the same time making them all momentarily equivalent. Within the common framework of a list of evaluation criteria shared at least in part by the guide, producers, and consumers, the user is free to combine his tastes, his actions, his skills, and his available time. By its technology, the Michelin Guide is indeed an ideal figure of the judgment devices used in the economics of singularities.

### How Many Ninth Symphonies Did Beethoven Compose?

Choosing a singular product is a process whose outcome varies with the actor and the judgment device. The journey of Recordo, a young music lover, reconstructs this dynamic, combining logics of action, available time, competence, the qualification and requalification of the singularities and the consumers, and the unexpected bifurcations of the purchase path. The story of Recordo is a realistic fiction: it is fiction because the story is invented and realistic because everything is true.

Our character received the gift he had been hoping for: a hi-fi system. He wanted to inaugurate his CD collection with Beethoven's Ninth Symphony. This story of apprenticeship tells of the discovery of the paths taken in view of making the reasonable choice of a classical music recording.[18]

---

[18] The versions and prices cited are real, but the study was done on French documentation carried out a few years ago. Music journals can be consulted for more recent data.

## Qualities or Price?

Recordo has gone to a big record store, where his head spins at the sight of the number of CDs bearing the name "Ninth Symphony". He now unexpectedly finds himself forced to choose between the two terms of an alternative: is the work the only thing that matters or should he also take other criteria into consideration? In the first case, after having discovered the many versions, Recordo sees that the prices range from 5€ (Bela Drahos) to 23.50€ (Jane Eagler) or a ratio of one to four, for reasons that escape him. If all of the Ninth Symphonies were alike, the only pertinent criterion would be the price, and he should buy the Drahos version.

The definition of the product depends on the consumer's viewpoint. If he is unaware of the constituent features of singular products, he is faced with homogeneous goods, and the only differentiating criterion is price. The hypothesis is by no means arbitrary, for interest in various musical interpretations supposes that this means something to the buyer, which is by no means obvious. This explains the fact that low-cost CDs of unknown origin are sold at bargain prices in shopping centers. In the event that the comparison bears exclusively on price, choosing a "Ninth" is devoid of uncertainty. The Drahos version is the best because it is the cheapest.

## Differentiation or Diversification?

Nevertheless, Recordo hesitates because the case cover is dull and the CD is relegated to a "Misc." bin, whereas there are a half dozen slightly more expensive versions (7.5€), but with more attractive cases; in addition, certain versions are stacked on the "New" rack and, even better, Recordo recognizes a name from an ad; he therefore chooses the Barenboim version. And at any rate, he tells himself that these elements are not crucial because they're all the same Ninth Symphony.

When, alongside price, the consumer's choice relies on differences in appearance, the version can be compared at a general level.[19] Differentiation of the CDs comes from packaging and from the way they are displayed in the store or in advertising. However the jacket design and colors had more influence in the case of 33 rpm records than in that of CDs. Since the differences are associated with different prices, price competition is

[19] F. Cochoy, *L'âne de Buridan: Les emballages et le choix du consommateur* (Paris: Presses Universitaires de France, 2002).

maintained, and Recordo chooses the version (Barenboim) that seems to offer the best quality-price ratio.

> In reality, Recordo has often heard that interpretations are not all alike, so he knows he has to find a "good" interpretation. It is then that he discovers, to his discouragement, that the store has some sixty versions. Because he lacks the competence, he is unable to make a reasonable choice. The listening stations are not enough. This place where all of the classical CDs are on offer and where the prices are known—an example of perfect information—is thus for him a perfectly opaque market where he can make only random choices.

Without judgment devices, the singularities market is opaque. The difficulties begin with the refusal to regard the Ninth Symphony as a homogeneous/differentiated good. How can Recordo select the "right" version from among the sixty-odd candidates? How can he pick one singularity from among the many. This is the question that time and again distinguishes the market of singularities from other markets. And the first general observation Recordo makes is that, without help, he is condemned to inaction. Whereas the logics of competitive pricing and of packaging do not require help, as soon as the choice implies a judgment as to the relative aesthetic value of a musical interpretation, Recordo has to find devices capable of helping him—in spite of his total incompetence—to make the "right" choice.

### Devices or Luck?

> To extricate himself, Recordo realizes that three forms of aid are available to him. He can phone certain members of his family or certain friends who have probably already been faced with such a situation and ask them what solution they chose. He can, as some clients are doing, ask the salesperson for advice. Finally, he can rely on the best-seller list that is posted in the store and which proposes, in order of sales: Erich Leinsdorf (7.50€), Georges Szell (8.10€) and Leonard Bernstein (12.90€). In all three cases, the solution is simple and quick: the Leinsdorf, which is among the cheapest, is the public favorite.

A novice, but curious all the same, Recordo decides to look at the aids available to him. The best-seller list, when one is interested only in the top-selling version, and the advice asked of the salesperson are among the devices that offer a "single preference," which greatly facilitates the consumer's task, whose action now comes down to an alternative between refusing and consenting. Ratifying the Leinsdorf recommendation is a

TABLE 1
Awards Displayed on the Ninth Symphony CD Jackets

| Versions | Awards | Prices |
|---|---|---|
| Harnoncourt | "Diapason d'or"<br>"10 de *Répertoire*"<br>"*ffff*" "Choc du *Monde de la musique*" | 14.00 € |
| Fricsay | "Diapason d'or"<br>"10 de *Répertoire*"<br>"Choc du *Monde de la musique*"<br>Recommandé par *Classica*"<br>"Indispensable"<br>"******" | 12.90 € |
| Furtwängler (1951) | "Diapason d'or"<br>"10 de *Répertoire*"<br>"Choc du *Monde de la musique*"<br>"Indispensable"<br>"******" | 12.80 € |
| Herrenweghe | "*ffff*" | 22.10 € |
| Toscanini | "Choc du *Monde de la musique*" | 12.90 € |
| Karajan (1962) | "******" | 11.90 € |

quick and simple solution, and what is more, one that is guaranteed by the judgment of common opinion.

### Awards

And yet Recordo refuses to inaugurate his CD collection by giving into suggestions based on judgment criteria in which he has little faith. Ignorance is back, but, as he walks through the store, he notices that judgments of excellence awarded by record journals feature directly on the CDs in the form of colored stickers carrying texts that had until now mystified him: "Diapason d'or," "Diapason historique," "10 de *Répertoire*," *Télérama*'s "*ffff*," "Choc *Le Monde de la musique*," or "Recommandé par *Classica*." He also notes the distinctions "Indispensable" and "******" in the *Guide Hoffelé-Kaminski* and the *Guide du CD*, respectively. (See Table 1.) Recordo is now on the alert as he moves more confidently among the displays, shelves, and bins of CDs, on the lookout for these signs. With a little patience, he draws up a list that should help him make a confident choice.

These awards are public devices based on musical expertise. Eliminating those that seemed dubious, Recordo is left with six different versions that have received a total of eighteen awards for artistic excellence. Recordo observes that there is no systematic relation between artistic value and price and that the record journals converge only partially in their judgment. The criterion of artistic excellence helps him reduce the choices, but it leaves him undecided about the six possibilities. If it were a matter of number of awards, which is one way of rating them, he should choose the Fricsay version.

### Apprenticeship and Competence

With the awards, Recordo finally has assessments that concern the musical value of the records. And at the same time, the pluralism of the judgments further aggravates the difficulty of choosing. What explains these differences? He does not have a clue. He therefore needs at least partially to dispel his ignorance. At the reception desk, he noticed a set of specialized journals and guides available for consultation.

He looks up the reviews of the Fricsay version and thereby begins to connect the highest awards with what the critics say about the musical interpretation. But to justify choosing among the six versions, he must broaden his reading. And so Recordo reads. For the interpretations of Beethoven's Ninth, he seems to detect a split between what the critics call the Baroque interpretation and the "classical" tradition, with, on the one side, Harnoncourt and Herrenweghe and, on the other, Fricsay, Furtwängler, Karajan, and Toscanini. But there can also be major differences within each of these two broad categories, though they concern different criteria, as he has discovered by reading the journals' criticisms: "Fricsay is the absolute antithesis of Furtwängler."

Finally Recordo realizes he is unable to decide on the basis of comparison because not all critics apply the same criteria to the same musical interpretation, so that the singularity of the critics doubles the singularity of the interpretations, something that was until then concealed by the "objectivity" of the awards. Things are getting more complicated. But Recordo has discovered a public space of discussion, and one critic's arguments were persuasive: he is going to choose the Harnoncourt version.

The interpretations and evaluations advanced by the critics only increase the incommensurability of the singularities. The arguments can be compared from an individual standpoint, but the difficulty of making a choice becomes greater and the detour longer. Quality indicators such as awards, which had created a restricted world devoted to merit and apparent objectivity, are suddenly replaced by the pluralism of the judgments of the critics, many of whom had been involved in attributing the awards. The texts offer several largely justified possible choices, and Recordo once again changes his mind: the Harnoncourt version replaces the Fricsay.

### The Logic of Personal Choice

Yet Recordo is still not sure. It seems all the harder to rely on someone else as everyone seems to believes that he, as the client, has personal preferences. What he has read has taught him that judgments vary with points of view and that the propositions do not take into account his own taste. His indecision now concerns what he personally wants.

Fortunately he realizes that the buying process, as he goes about it, is also a learning process. He has also understood that he can identify his own taste only progressively, by trial and error. He decides on the Harnoncourt version: it is a record that should help him get his bearings, or at least partially, among the various interpretative styles. He has an inkling that this is one of the ways whereby he is going to discover his own tastes and acquire a specific competence.

To make life easier for himself, he thinks he should discern the logics used by the journals and the specialist critics in making their choice so as to rely on those closest to his own logic of action—when he finally has one. . . . When that day comes, he will perhaps be able to trust his own judgment.

To avoid unpleasant surprises when choosing a singularity, it is preferable to know the logic of one's own choice. After having identified the tastes of others—friends, salespeople, critics, conductors—Recordo discovers that his choice should revolve around his own taste. The realization comes late, which is not abnormal given that commitment in this market entails a demanding "apprenticeship." He knows it will take time and experience to shape this taste, to recognize his criterion or criteria of evaluation. But when he finally does, not only will the recommendations and arguments of the judgment devices take on another meaning, but he will also be able to mobilize his own competence in making his choices.

Recordo has come to the end of his journey. He could just as well have stopped at each stage as added still others. One way of summing up would be to list the various versions and their corresponding logics of action: Bela Drahos for the lowest price, Barenboim for price and jacket, Leinsdorf for musical conformity, Fricsay for the music world's judgment, Harnoncourt after comparing the specialists' arguments, and later, another version founded on his own judgment. For Recordo, there is no doubt that Beethoven wrote several Ninth symphonies.

This journey contains several lessons: (1) Without credible judgment devices provided by market professionals and music critics—advertising, specialized salespeople, best-seller lists, award stickers, record critics— there is no way to make a reasonable choice. (2) The intervention of these devices transforms the qualifications of both the singularity and the consumer. (3) The consumer's action is defined by the relative influence of logics of action and of economizing principles. (4) The adjustment between singularity and consumer varies with the degree of concordance between product logic of action and consumer logic of action. (5) Recordo's journey illustrates some of the configurations of judgment criteria and economizing principles that can be involved in the process of making a purchase.

## Chapter Eight

# THE METAMORPHOSIS OF SINGULARITIES

TWENTY YEARS after his "Theory of monopolistic competition," E. H. Chamberlin penned a spirited critique of the conception of the product in mainstream economics.[1] As the title of his paper clearly indicates, the product should not be considered as given and stable over time but rather as an "economic variable." Although the argument was forceful—"Products are actually the most volatile things in the economic system, much more so than prices"—and although he insisted that what was true for given products was not for variable ones, he ended on a radical rhetorical criticism: "It seems difficult to understand how the economists can pretend to explain (or to prescribe for) the economic system and leave products out of the picture,"[2] but his call for a theory of product variations met with only scant success.

Two big changes were needed: one in the economy and the other in the social sciences. In the economy, it was the proliferation of commodities, which began in the 1970s. The increased mobilization of diversified and costly resources (marketing, packaging, advertising, R&D) bolstered a dynamic of deliberate production of differences with an increasing pace of *product renewal*.[3] In the social sciences, it was the notion and the problem of *product qualification* constructed by heterodox economists and (orthodox) sociologists. The second change was reinforced by an analogous evolution that occurred at the same time in anthropology, where, after having posited that, like persons, commodities also have "social lives," a research program was developed to study the multiple changes "from commodity production to the final consumption."[4]

*Qualification* may be defined as "any change in the product meant to stimulate the desire of the buyer and increase the economic gains of the seller."[5] Unlike the generic product, the *qualified product* has undergone

---

[1] "Products are not in fact 'given'; they are continuously changed—improved, deteriorated, or just made different—as an essential part of the market process." E. H. Chamberlin, "The product as an economic variable," *Quarterly Journal of Economics* 67 (1953): 3.

[2] Ibid., pp. 8, 27.

[3] See Chapter 18.

[4] A. Appadurai, *The Social Life of Things: Commodities in Cultural Perspective* (Cambridge: Cambridge University Press, 1986). esp. "Introduction: Commodities and the politics of value," pp. 3–63.

[5] A. Barcet and J. Bonamy, "Qualité et qualification des services," in Jd. de Bandt and J. Gadrey (eds.), *Relations de service, marchés de services* (Paris: Editions du CNRS, 1994), p. 161.

changes that make it a commercial product. Recent economic sociology has made great strides in the description and interpretation of the practices and transformations that intervene in both devices and products: product conception, packaging, advertising, choice of tastes and scents, marketing, communication, logistics, informal or public promotion, spatial organization of selling sites, codification of seller practices, use of stars, construction of beliefs, sponsorship, brands, multiplication of logos, and so forth. These interventions mobilize huge budgets and a growing number of market professionals.

Product qualification and requalification may be the result of direct intervention on the product, the result of the interpretation of judgment devices through oriented knowledge, as well as the result of the consumers' interpretations. Since the same generic product can undergo several different forms of qualification at the same time, *the unit of analysis is no longer the generic product but the qualified product.*

In the market of singularities, the action of qualification raises several questions. Can it change differentiated goods into singular goods? Or, vice versa, can it desingularize singularities? Can it modify the states of the singularity? The range of possible transformations is usually underrated; it will be explored and sociological studies will be presented when we come to the concrete market of singularities. Here we merely wish to show, first, how judgment devices can singularize (overqualify) or desingularize (dequalify) the products, and second, how, using linguistic practices, judgment devices can create incommensurability from sameness.


## THE WEIGHT OF WORDS

Linguistic and interpretative practices can be associated with overqualification and dequalification alike, as is clearly shown by two examples devoted to fine wines and workers' jobs. In the last twenty or thirty years, there has been a surge in the cultural complex surrounding fine wines. It has multiplied its interventions through specialized publications—guides, magazines, and books—and through the mass media. It has produced and transmitted a variety of sensorial, historical, and cultural knowledge; it has elicited and ratified new practices and new products; and in the case of a few great wines, it has, year after year, developed and repeated a celebratory discourse that explains the transformation of these wines into "works of art" and/or "luxury goods," independent of their material transformation. These metamorphoses have produced their effect in the form of changes in symbolic value, price, taste, and clientele.

While a good deal is known about the upward social mobility of fine wines, much less is known about the downward social mobility of workers' occupations in industrial firms. For a given job that is about to open up, it makes a big difference if its description is provided by colleagues at the plant or by a recruiting agency. In the first case, the account will mention the specific skills required and the sometimes subtle qualities that are indispensable, thereby describing a particular configuration of competencies and commitments. In the second case, the agency will use classified ads, and in view of obtaining a maximum response, the wording will combine general characteristics—age, diplomas, experience—and a formalized job description. Such an all-purpose presentation—a common practice—is by no means insignificant, since it cannot help omitting the specific job characteristics. The essential is therefore lost. As a logical consequence, the practice leads to recruiting an employee with qualifications that are lower than they could or should have been, which in turn leads to the likely dequalification of the position, thus confirming and justifying a posteriori the initial practice of dequalification. [6] The linguistic practice of transforming a singular job into a trivialized one produces a real dequalification of the work.

In the same perspective, in the early days of the Internet, the CVs sent out by job seekers devoted a good deal of space to freestyle descriptions of work experience, skills, and personal aspirations. Once the information attained a certain volume, firms began using search engines to make a preliminary selection on the basis of predefined grids.[7] Then the distinctive characteristics—which might represent relatively scarce and therefore valuable resources—disappeared, and the suppression of information once again resulted in a dequalification of many candidates.

In both cases, specific linguistic and interpretative practices were enough to overqualify or dequalify goods and services as well as people. However, we should not let the similarity of the operations mask the difference of scale between the two phenomena. The overqualification of certain fine wines, which can sometimes attract the public's attention, concerns only a limited number of actors. Alternatively, job dequalification, by its magnitude and continuity, has altogether real though invisible effects on the market and society.

## CAN SAMENESS ENGENDER INCOMMENSURABILITY?

Can sameness engender incommensurability? There should be no hesitation in answering this question. The achievements of logic are too certain to even think of questioning them. Nevertheless, let us look at the results

[6] F. Eymard-Duvernay and E. Marchal, *Façons de recruter* (Paris: Métailié, 1997).

[7] J.-P. Neuville, "Les bons 'tuyaux' du marché de l'emploi: Internet peut-il faire de 'l'économie de la qualité' un marché?" *Sociologie du travail* 3 (2001): 349–368.

of two comparisons of the same hi-fi components in two journals: one made and circulated by a specialized cultural superstore, here called Superstore; the other, *Diapason,* a specialized classical music journal that publishes a special issue each year devoted to evaluating hi-fi material. Table 2 shows the evaluations and comments for the *same* hi-fi components at the *same prices* in 2002.

The Superstore uses two kinds of rating—technical stars reflecting the tests run in its own laboratory (from one to four) and quality-for-price stars (from one to four)—while the magazine *Diapason* relies on a "subjective," "impartial and detailed" listening test to provide a commentary and to award between one and six stars, which also take price into account: one or two stars for "not recommended," five or six stars for "very good," and the "Diapason d'or" for "exceptional." The table further lists ratings and commentaries for the same components.

Summing up the results contained in Table 2, here are the judgments concerning the *same components* proposed at the *same prices*: (1) For the CD players, the Superstore does not make a recommendation, although the remarks vary considerably from one to another; whereas *Diapason* recommends a player that is "very good" and the cheapest as well. (2) For the amplifiers, one that receives a low rating from one is recommended by the other. (3) For the speakers, one set rated low by the Superstore receives the highest recommendation given by *Diapason*.

These disagreements are only of limited interest as long as they have not been put into perspective. For the CD players and the amplifiers, the Superstore relies on technical measurements as well as on design (refined, handsome), quality of the front panel (superb, spare), sturdiness of the mechanism, presence of technical components (Alpha processor, double converter, HDAM modules, double transformers, copper shielding, case, five docks, etc.), filtering, signal attack (optimized, unusual power), dynamic (stunning), price (low), and musicality (splendid, dynamic). With the exception of one reference to design, *Diapason* uses the language of the music listener: timbres (ordinary, full-bodied, less shimmering), high-high range (short), low range (lack of), sound images (depth of planes, limpid, readable), definition (lacking in clarity, sharp), and overall reproduction (lacking in body, should be more "open," natural, lacking in weight, limpidity, subtlety, fairly sharp, clearer). For the speakers—whose physical quality and performance depend largely on craftsmanship—the convergence is greater.

One remark made with small variations from time to time by *Diapason* gives the general tenor of this comparison: "Experience shows that there is practically no correlation between technical measurements and musicality." The Superstore relies on the objectivity of technical tests to construct ratings that seem indisputable—unless we question the validity

TABLE 2
Two Ways of Evaluating the Same Hi-Fi Elements

| Equipment | Price | Superstore 1–4 stars | FNAC Comments | Diapason 1–6 stars + Gold | Diapason Comments |
|---|---|---|---|---|---|
| Player | | | | | |
| Denon DCD-1450 | 575 € | Q: ****<br>Q/P: *** | Superb faceplate, superbly refined design . . . sturdy mechanism eliminates all vibration and the Alpha digital processor, produces a linear transparent signal . . . quality filtering . . . and natural, splendid musicality. | **** | Clean reproduction, no major defects. Ordinary vocal quality. Full image but lacking details. Subjective dynamic "a bit washed out." The musicians seem to have lost their taste for playing. More cons than pros. |
| Marantz CD 6000 | 380 € | Q: ****<br>Q/P: **** | . . . a few interesting improvements . . . double differential transformer and especially the HDAM modules, which optimize the signal attack and ensure an impressive dynamic, close to 130 db as well as significantly less surface noise. | **** | Clearer and sharper definition than the CD 67 but less color and body to the sound. Vocal quality less shimmering. Short high high range. Overall reproduction more "electronic," less expressive. We would like a fuller sound and a more open image. |
| Phillips CD 723 | 150 € | Q: ****<br>Q/P: **** | For a rock-bottom price, here is an excellent player! It is equipped with the necessary minimum (remote, 26 buttons, coaxial digital cable and can satisfy any set-up. Reliable, having largely proven itself. | *******<br>1999 Gold. | Still unrivaled at the price. Natural and subtle nuances. Total absence of tension or shrillness in the high range. A certain lack of weight in the low range . . . compensated by a great limpidity . . . |

*(continued)*

TABLE 2 (cont.)

| Equipment | Price | Superstore 1–4 stars | FNAC Comments | Diapason 1–6 starts + Gold | Diapason Comments |
|---|---|---|---|---|---|
| **Amps** | | | | | |
| Denon PMA 1500 | 760 € | Q: \*\*\*\* Q/P: \*\*\*\* | . . . the best technology has to offer: double transformer power cable, specific UHC-MOS transistors, all on an ultra-rigid copper coated chassis. As for the musicality, it is the living reflection of the care lavished on the craftsmanship, quite simply superb! | \*\*\*\* | A handsome integrated amplifier, with a fairly well-defined and balanced result. The subjective passband seems broad with fairly tense lows. The mid-highs are precise and detailed . . . the sound image tends to lack depth at high volume with a flattening of the planes. |
| Marantz PM 7000 | 460 € | Q: \*\*\* Q/P: \*\*\*\* | . . . a few mandatory practical features: 5 ports of which one phono, 2 series of HP terminals, complete remote control with possibility of correcting vocal quality. | \*\*\* | Balance less warm than the PM6010OSE. Clearer but much less subtle in both timbre and dynamic. Lows lack definition. Fairly limpid and legible image with sharp focus. |
| Yamaha AX-496 | 380 € | Q: \*\*\* Q/P: \*\*\*\* | A dynamic that requires the addition of excellent columns Yet it's punch does not prevent rendering every subtlety of a lyrical piece with finesse. | \*\*\*\*\*\* | The lowest priced integrated amp. Clear, well-defined balance. Timbres not harsh but lack natural. Energetic restitution. |

## Speakers

| | Price | | Description | |
|---|---|---|---|---|
| Boston CR 75 | 500 € | Q: ***<br>Q/P: **** | Finely crafted and reveals the quality of the care taken in their manufacture. For their size the shape of the sound is stunning, the timbers are clear, the lows hard hitting and the highs finely chiseled. | Gold — Clear, very detailed and agreeably lively. Astonishing amplitude and relief for a speaker this size. Quality of conception and craftsmanship comparable to products in a higher category. |
| Elac ELT 7 | 380 € | Q: ***<br>Q/P: **** | These speakers "ring" remarkably well with ample, airy lows and an excellent dynamic. | ***** — Sound both airy and dynamic with good fusion between the two speakers. The energy in the low range gives the reproduction body. If the upper register is somewhat lacking in neutrality, it is nonetheless rapid and well defined. |
| Triangle Polaris | 600 € | Q: ***<br>Q/P: *** | . . . reasonable size, original presentation . . . and of course agreeable, well tempered musicality. | ***** — Small column. Very spontaneous, rapid, light. Honorable transparency. Clear, deep image but the planes are not clear enough. A hint of color to the timbers due to a flattering sheen in the upper highs. |

*Note:* Q = Quality; P = Price; Q/P = quality/price ratio.
Stars: 1 to 5 from Superstore; 1 to 6 from Diapason.

of technical measurement as an indicator of musical quality, whereas *Diapason* posits that the ear of the music critic is the only good judge. Each system of comparison is associated with a specific conception of musical reproduction so that the evaluation is based on a choice between measuring instruments or highly trained human senses. And since their modes of production cannot be observed, the trust they enjoy, and without which they would have no influence, comes from their link with institutions considered as trustworthy.

Dissociation of technique from music is not restricted to comparison of hi-fi components. It characterizes products, firms, judgment devices, and clients. Two mutually autonomous and indirectly competitive markets coexist: one is organized around specialized superstores and the other around dedicated hi-fi stores. The differences between them center on the hi-fi producers' nationality (big Japanese firms, on the one hand, and small English and French companies, on the other), on the size of the market, on the extent of economic concentration, on the importance given to packaging, on the competencies of the sellers and the buyers, on clients' average age, on the showrooms, and on listening practices. And, if the prices are in theory the same for the same material, for other types of material they can be much higher in the dedicated stores than in the specialized superstores. The separation of the two markets is almost complete.

Two global logics organize the adjustment relations within each of these markets. In the specialized superstore, the product sold is a polymorphous machine that is all the more excellent because the price is low and the technical assessment high: the client is considered to be an interchangeable individual who fits into a limited number of general categories. In the dedicated hi-fi store, what is sold is not so much the quality of the sound reproduction as the fit between the sound and the ear, the hi-fi system and the person. The listening experience can only be personalized and, given that many clients do not have a truly strong option, it often leads to unexpected choices. The merchant is the principal judgment device, and the outcome of his intervention varies with the clients' competencies and reactions. *Under these conditions, the same is no longer the same.*

Identical hi-fi materials have become incomparable: social logic has its own rules. However, a number of conditions must be present for the metamorphosis to occur. The goods must be multidimensional, and the clients must have different grasps for making their judgments. Moreover, the products should be part of processes of collective interaction articulated around peculiar judgment criteria that integrate the strategy of the producers, the viewpoints of the devices, and the interpretations of the buyers.

How is it that, in the specialized musical circuit, new systems are always cropping up without ever claiming to target the mass market; that innovators and entrepreneurs are still as numerous; that public supports like the specialized press continue to exist; that clients buy—sometimes costly—hi-fi materials; and that stores stay in business even if they do not show the same growth and profit as other sectors? The phenomenon is no more intelligible when linked, for instance, to economic rent. Indeed, such terminology misses everything that had to be put together for the specialized market to exist: a passion for music, a shared belief in the greatness of music, a particular conception of sound reproduction—everything that goes into the devices, that underpins the market, and that places individual identity within a collective identity. If the two conceptions of the hi-fi system persist over time despite the inequality of the forces, it is because they belong to two worlds that are not only different but also largely alien to each other.

• • •

From the general presentation of the qualification operation and from the exploration of the metamorphosis of products, several consequences can be derived: (1) The consumer has a power of interpretation whereby he transforms the representation of a singular product as proposed by the judgment device; this is the expression of a greater or lesser autonomy. (2) Judgment devices are the central mechanism in the qualification of singular products because consumers are obliged to use them. (3) Judgment devices qualify consumers by qualifying the products, because they indicate more or less clearly and stringently the dispositions and behaviors that are the most appropriate to the particular product qualification. (4) Multigrasp products lend themselves best to totalizing reinterpretations.

Through the interpretive representations they propose as well as through their concrete interventions, judgment devices aim to make the products more desirable: this is achieved by qualification. Unlike the generic product, the *qualified product* has undergone changes that make it into a commercial product. Reasoning directly from the "official" characteristics of singular products therefore involves the risk of erroneous interpretations of the way the market works. The hi-fi comparison is an extreme case. To believe that all of the qualification possibilities are systematically explored and utilized leads to a symmetrical error. In reality, the power to qualify and to requalify is a capacity for action that is stimulated by certain forces, such as competition, and hindered by others, such as collective representations. These transformations cannot be taken for granted.

## Chapter Nine

# THE REGIMES OF ECONOMIC COORDINATION

JUDGMENT, JUDGMENT devices, trust devices, judgment criteria, quality competition, price competition, junction, and adjustment are the main tools designed for analyzing of the markets of singularities. However, the conditions under which they are brought into play are still to be determined. Can they be applied directly to all singularities marketplaces, as though the latter were merely a surface effect of a general form of economic coordination, or shall we look at these marketplaces as being structured by a plurality of invisible collective logics, which are articulated and are more or less present and active, according to their location within the global space? In fact, the multiplicity of the singularities, the diversity of the judgment devices, and the multitude of tastes make the choice easy: such a world is far too complex to lend itself to direct study.

A new tool has to be developed: it should meaningfully simplify the concrete reality. This very general formulation means that we need a typology of markets such that (1) each specific type of market is built with the minimum components necessary to make it work; (2) each specific type of market functions differently; (3) all specific types of market taken together should account for all relevant concrete differences; and (4) all specific types of markets come under the same theoretical viewpoint.

We call this intermediate tool *a regime of economic coordination*. It is not a Weberian ideal-type: it is a pure form, a model. Each of these models is defined by a particular adjustment between the products, the judgment devices, and the consumers. More precisely, because singularities on the market are distinguished not by their generic characteristics but by their types of qualification and because these types of qualification are mainly the effects of specific types of judgment devices, each model is a *system of relations between particular qualified products, particular judgment devices, and particular forms of consumer commitment*. Consequently, each regime of coordination is distinguishable from all others by *a particular working logic*. For reasons that will be given later, forms of consumer commitment *are not part* of this typology.

As a result of these choices, each model is distinguished from the others and yet is defined by the same types of devices and the same types of products. It should become easier to study the variations in the forms of competition and in the market equilibrium. Thus, each regime of coordination is an abstract model exclusively composed of the same judgment devices. Alone or in combination with other regimes, it should explain the diversity in the functioning of the concrete markets of singularities.

These regimes of coordination are the products of a *general classification* whose scope encompasses all market places and whose *analytical construction is based on the judgment devices*. Such a perspective is the logical consequence of the strategic position of the judgment devices in the markets of singularities, since they are simultaneously consumers' representatives, cognitive aids, active competitive forces, trust supports, axiological operators, and the main qualifiers of the singular products. With this classification, products whose qualification is similar are placed in the same model, and each generic product can be represented by several qualified products allocated to two or more specific models. This will be the case, for example, of a book evaluated by a critic, recommended by friends, and distinguished by the best-seller list; and because the arguments and judgments envelop the "same" novel in different interpretations, several qualified products will coexist. Qualified products are thus more numerous and more varied than generic products, and through this process those that share the same generic product may be distributed among several different specific models. This is the path followed in constructing the regimes of coordination.

The rules governing this classification are: (1) Each coordination regime is built around a particular qualification of the singular products. (2) This qualification is brought about by judgment devices, and, therefore, the general classification of the coordination regimes is the result of a typology of the judgment devices designed to reveal the pertinent forms of product qualification. (3) The categories of the classification should not only be relevant, they should also be as few in number as possible. (4) In addition, a typology of *consumer commitments* has been elaborated. Although it should correspond to the classification of the particular logics governing the regimes of coordination, *it has no part in constructing this classification*.

For the presentation and discussion of the classification of the regimes of coordination, we will deal successively with the construction of the classification and with the forms of consumer commitment. Before beginning Part 3, which is devoted to the use of the regimes of coordination for explaining concrete markets, we will discuss several general topics that arise when one wants to situate economics of singularities within economic sociology.

## A Classification of the Economic Coordination Regimes

There are seven regimes of coordination. This classification is the central tool for analyzing the markets of singularities, and it is built on a series of divisions and subdivisions that take in all of the judgment devices. It is the product of three steps: (1) the division of all judgment devices into impersonal and personal devices; (2) the subdivision of the impersonal devices according to the nature of the knowledge provided to the consumers and according to the market size, which also measures the strength of the market's profit orientation; and (3) the subdivision of the personal devices according to the relative strength of the rules that are linked to the shared network-market. The presentation will follow the visual representation provided by Figure 1, which organizes all the relevant information.

### Impersonal Judgment Devices versus Personal Judgment Devices

To start with, the universe of judgment devices is split into the two general categories of impersonal and personal devices. The first comprises appellations, cicerones, rankings, and confluences; that is to say, all those devices that provide buyers with an impersonal knowledge of the products. The second encompasses all networks, those invisible realities that ensure the circulation of knowledge through interpersonal relations.

Each of these categories of devices has different general characteristics and a particular logic of subdivision. Essentially, *impersonal devices* combine impersonal knowledge and an aesthetic universe (this is the originality model), but nothing prevents other criteria of judgment from becoming pertinent. *Personal devices*—networks—can provide knowledge of content as well as of rankings, but the first predominates by far; their spheres of action are more restricted than those of impersonal devices, but they are also more precise and more credible. Networks are linked to the "personalization model," and as a result, they are associated with personalized knowledge, interpersonal trust, and professional excellence.

The distinction between the two categories of judgment devices is often assimilated to that between general and local, or between far and near. But that can lead to confusion. In effect, personal relations by telephone or by Internet are not local; furthermore, world brands can cleverly multiply their local presences. For judgment devices, it is still their common designations that best pin down their respective meanings: impersonal devices ensure the circulation of the same discourse, the same knowledge for everyone, with the caveat that such knowledge lends itself to individual interpretations and reinterpretations; whereas the network is the product of relations between singular persons, a discourse modeled on mutual idiosyncrasies. Using this separation, we will construct, first, the coordination regimes founded on impersonal devices and, then, the ones founded on personal devices.

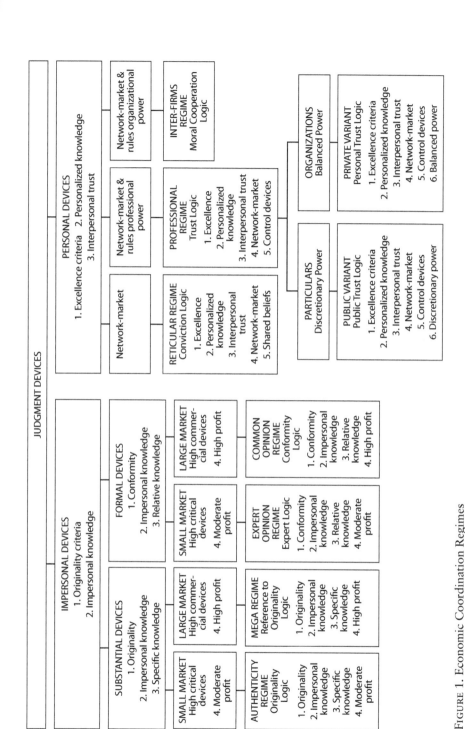

FIGURE 1. Economic Coordination Regimes

## Impersonal Devices and Coordination Regimes

Impersonal devices are subdivided according to two dimensions: on the one hand, the nature of the knowledge provided to the consumers, with a distinction between *substantial* and *formal* devices, and, on the other hand, the strength of the market's profit orientation, with a more formal distinction between the primacy of *critical devices* (small market) and that of *commercial* devices (large markets).

### SUBSTANTIAL DEVICES VERSUS FORMAL DEVICES

When devices are substantial, the knowledge that circulates concerns the *specific contents* of the singularities. A substantial device would be criticism of a book or a movie, and is thus an absolute qualification of the product, since the latter is evaluated for itself according to its particular characteristics, whatever the judgment may be. Substantial devices would thus be critical reviews, guides, brands, promotions, and so on: they are usually oriented by criteria of an aesthetic nature and are distinguished by the value given to originality. The knowledge they bear can be detailed and reasoned or can be as little as a sign or an image; but in all events, it is *specific knowledge*.

When the devices are *formal*, the knowledge concerns the *relative positions* of the singularities. A formal device would give the rank attributed to the product, and is thus a relative qualification. Some formal devices give awards in accordance with specific contents; others—the most numerous and influential, those which are found in a great variety of domains—take their rankings from the charts. This distinction highlights two ways of relating to products, which have crucial differential effects on the market and on the consumer.

### COMMERCIAL DEVICES VERSUS CRITICAL DEVICES

Size separates the *small market* from the *large market*: the first is made up of small and medium-size businesses with low barriers to entry; the second is composed of large firms often geared to short- and middle-term profits. Depending on the products and the clientele, the small market—which is usually local—can also be national or international; while the large market, with its mass production and volume sales, is characterized by an oligopolistic structure, rationalization of production processes, multiplication of brands, and importance of promotion. The distinction between the two market models according to size is necessarily blurred, since the border shifts with activities and historical periods.

One pertinent indicator of size is the ratio of *commercial devices* to *critical devices*, in which the first term covers all those devices devoted to selling products and increasing corporate profits, while the second term encompasses the devices devoted to product evaluation—such as critics and guidebooks—and to consumer protection in the form of laws, certification, and so forth. The assumption is that the larger the market, the higher the ratio of commercial devices to critical devices and the stronger the orientation toward short- and middle-term profits. This distinction makes it possible to explore the degree of tension between profit seeking and maintaining singularities.

The combined dimensions of the nature of the knowledge and the market's profit orientation define four regimes of coordination: (1) the *authenticity regime* (specific products; small market, which means moderate profit; and logic of originality); (2) the *mega regime* (specific products; large market, meaning high profit; and logic of the reference to originality); (3) the *expert-opinion regime* (ranking of specific products; small market, meaning moderate profit; and expert logic); (4) the *common-opinion regime* (rankings; large market, meaning high profit; and logic of conformity).

The *authenticity* regime concentrates the multiplicity of the tastes proposed and sought; it valorizes loyalty to personal logics of action. It is embodied by, among others, the markets of art, fashion, books, or fine wines. Organized around the twofold requirement of "cultivated" and "distinguished" taste, these markets differ by the value ascribed to the cultural references of both the past and the present and by the influence of cultural complexes. The *mega* regime—megafilms and megabrands, for example—is defined by tension between aesthetics and profitability in large markets. The *expert-opinion* regime rests on choices made by experts entrusted with selecting the best singular products—for example, literary-awards juries—but the judgment on the representatives' choices is conditional and that means the consumer maintains the capacity to defect. The *common-opinion* regime is characterized by ranking based on purchases—as is the case with the hit parades' Top 10/20/30/40/50, box offices, best-seller lists—by the tension between profitability and aesthetics and by a relation of delegation that implies consumer conformity justified by convenience.

## Personal Judgment Devices and Coordination Regimes

The network does not lend itself to the classification used for impersonal devices. First, a distinction between the two kinds of knowledge is, in this case, pointless, for word of mouth freely mixes specific contents and rankings. Second, the market embedded in the network can grow, but only up to a point, beyond which impersonal devices intervene to compete with or to complete the network; the distinction between small and large markets is therefore useless as well. Lastly, personalized products and above all personalized services have in principle to adapt to all consumers. Consequently, at least at an initial stage, forms of consumer commitment are not pertinent either. Thus neither the nature of the knowledge nor market size nor forms of consumer commitment can be used to construct network-based regimes of coordination.

Our approach is based on two sociological findings: first, under conditions of uncertainty, the seller-buyer network spontaneously produces the trust necessary to exchange; and second, the personal network occupies a key position in the market of singularities for the distribution of credible product knowledge. These two propositions will be discussed later, but we can already assert at this time that, first, under certain conditions, conflicts of interest and the ensuing opportunistic practices can be moderated by the trust produced by the network; and second, when the use of impersonal judgment devices is forbidden or when the effectiveness of these devices is limited, the personal network enables the client to marshal the knowledge needed to choose the "right" personalized service and thus ensures market continuity. It is therefore not unrealistic to consider that certain markets of singularities can operate on the basis of networks alone.

The relationship between the composition of the network and the way it helps the market operate leads to a distinction already presented, that among personal networks, trade networks, and practitioner networks. The first is composed of family members, friends, and colleagues; the second is made up of sellers and buyers; the third consists of practitioners. Together, these three networks provide the knowledge and trust necessary for the market of singularities to function. Intertwined in a *network-market*, they delineate the foundations shared by the three coordination regimes, which are subdivided according to the ways their networks are implemented: the *reticular* regime, or network-market alone; the *professional* regime, or network-market plus rules stemming from a professional authority; and the *interfirm* regime, or network-market plus rules stemming from organizational power.

The reticular regime rests, exclusively or primarily, on the network-market. It is as though, under certain conditions, this foundation could single-handedly and durably underpin many markets of singularities and as though shared convictions could, on their own, spark the shared quest for excellence. The professional regime—which takes in many trades and professions—is defined by the combination of the network-market with *control devices* aimed at channeling professional practices around a logic of excellence and trust. The interfirm regime is more exploratory and concerns the autonomy of a market or a quasi market in the context of moral cooperation between firms; it encompasses subcontracting and partnerships.

## Consumer Commitments and Coordination Regimes

Although the coordination regimes are exclusively the result of the combination of judgment devices, it may be useful to propose a typology of consumer commitments that will help to understand how these regimes of coordination function. Today there are almost as many consumer types as there are producers, marketers, and analysts. It is not the scarcity that is the problem, but the proliferation. How can we simplify reality in a way that is relevant? Comparison of two historical states of the literature on consumption may help.

There is an impressive difference between the representation of the consumer in the 1960s–1970s and that in 2000. In the first period, the consumer was "controlled," "conditioned," "manipulated," and "alienated." A few decades later, the book titles speak for themselves: *The Active Consumer, The Unmanageable Consumer, The Authority of the Consumer, Consumption as the Vanguard of History.* Apparently today's consumer is "active," "personalized," "experienced," "demanding," and "selective."—as well as "autonomous," "unpredictable," "versatile," and "secretive." Furthermore, it seems that he is also a "producer," "coproducer," "businessman" and "professional," as though the dignity of the consumer could only be truly expressed in the vocabulary of production.

What do these two portraits represent? Not meticulous depictions of a reality that we know has always been diversified and hard to pin down, but collective interpretations that are a source of intelligibility and action. The figure of today's consumer is thus inseparable from the action of the media, consumer associations, marketers, economists, and sociologists, all of which, for different reasons, are involved in constructing a collective representation that began its rise just as the figure of the worker was fading.[1] This "new" consumer serves as a reference for comparing the present with the past, and developed societies with the rest of the world. His sudden rise justifies the work of the "market professionals" and partakes of a history that is purportedly characterized by the disappearance of class struggle. Moreover, these simplifications and generalizations are not entirely arbitrary; they contain a grain of truth.

[1] F. Ohl, "La construction sociale des figures du consommateur et du client," *Sciences de la société* 56 (May 2002): 8; R. Rochefort, *Le consommateur entrepreneur* (Paris: Odile Jacob, 1997).

The "passive," "dependent" customer of the 1960s and '70s is to be seen in the context of the mass consumption that developed in the shadow of Fordism. Product diversity was still limited, as were the tastes of the consumers, who were assimilated at the time to interchangeable entities. In John Galbraith's then highly popular theory of the "revised sequence," large industrial firms planned their development and "conditioned" demand.[2] Critical minds were discovering that behind the apparent freedom of choice lay the creation of "false needs" purported to be necessary for the development of capitalism and the reproduction of the social class structure. In the ten years following the turn of the millennium, the post-Fordism era expressed itself in the rapid renewal of new goods and in the development of the "customization" of products. The consumer became "active" and "autonomous." This change cannot be explained by market demands alone; other forces such as individualism intervened as well. It became harder and harder to link the consumer—now omnipresent, now elusive—with the manifold processes that were transforming society.

Both periods questioned the scope of these representations: Illusion or reality? Yesterday, the dawn of the "affluent society," largely experienced by the first generation as a form of emancipation, was interpreted as a collective alienation. Today, when the rationalization of supply is meant to channel behaviors, the consumer is said to be active and autonomous. In spite of these contradictions, however, this historical comparison is useful, providing we look not at what changes but at what remains constant. In both periods we find the same two dimensions: activity-passivity and autonomy-heteronomy. For yesterday as for today, it is not either-or, it is both.

Thus in the market of singularities, where one is confronted with the multiplicity of possible choices, the search for the "right" product can be conducted through an *active commitment* to satisfy the conditions of a reasonable choice or by means of the *passive consent* that goes with the purchase made through a representative. *Autonomy* is asserted through the capacity to define and maintain one's personal tastes, while *heteronomy* indicates an actor's propensity to accept the tastes embodied by the devices and/or the products. Combining these dimensions produces four forms of consumer commitment: (1) activity and autonomy; (2) activity and heteronomy; (3) passivity and autonomy; (4) passivity and heteronomy. The assumption is that, if the coherence of the regime of coordination is to be maintained, the first type should be associated with the authenticity regime, the second with the mega regime, the third with the expert-opinion regime, and the fourth with the common-opinion regime. No relationship between regimes of coordination based on personal de-

---

[2] J. K. Galbraith, *The New Industrial State* (Boston: Houghton Mifflin Company, 1967).

vices and forms of consumer commitment, especially for the professional regime, can be identified, as they are supposed to accommodate very diverse types of clients.

Thus in the authenticity regime, ordinary consumers tend to adhere to a consumption ethos that includes veneration of artworks, choice as an adventure, and autonomy as a form of dignity. But their cognitive deficit obliges them to compromise with demands they are usually unable to satisfy without external help. In the mega regime, consumer autonomy represents far too great an economic risk not to marshal, on a large scale, (1) the devices that foster at least partial conversion to the aesthetic judgments awarded to financial success and (2) the primacy of a heteronomy imposed by, among others, the constant arrival of new products on the market. In the expert- and common-opinion regimes, success is based on conformity to the judgment devices, which also means convenience. But in the expert-opinion regime, consumers can take critical positions, while, in the common-opinion regime, the pressure of convenience works much more strongly in favor of conformity.

The main justification for this consumer typology is underscored by the following questions: What would be the consequences of an imbalance between the particular logic of a coordination regime and a de facto prevailing adequate or inadequate form(s) of consumer commitment? Could the distribution of the forms of consumer commitment help to understand the changes in the market equilibrium or in the dynamic of singularization and desingularization? And what about the eventual transformation of consumption into a central political issue?

• • •

The general classification contains seven regimes of coordination: four rely on impersonal devices, and three on personal devices. If the degree of homogeneity is not high enough, nothing forbids—as we will show in the case of the lawyers market—further subdivision so long as the rules of the approach are respected. Alone or combined, regimes of coordination should explain the ways all markets of singularities work. Using this tool, we will present several analyses of concrete markets.

The concept of regimes of coordination justifies rethinking the way we define the market. Neoclassical theory assumes that whatever falls outside of supply and demand *stricto sensu* can be bracketed without changing the observed relations; thus the market can be exclusively assimilated to the interplay of supply, demand, and price. But for markets of singularities, judgment devices have powerful, systematic, and *diversified* effects; and therefore the judgment devices of the market are inseparable from the concrete exchange. *The singularities market is equipped or it is not.*

An "interlude" is defined as "a brief period when a situation or activity is different from what comes before and after it";[3] it is also "a brief distraction."[4] It is the first meaning that I want to convey; the second is too ambitious.

Usually it is in the introduction to a book that an author situates his work among others. It is a place at which the presentation cannot mean too much since the reader does not yet have a precise idea of the book's content. I have chosen to locate this text at the half-way point of the book, where the reader knows something, but not everything, about the work. Doing so does not entirely resolve the issue, though. To place one's work in context requires establishing some distance, but, even though it is made of paper, a world was nevertheless reconstructed as the work was being written. This is what gives particularism to the text located in between the "before" and the "after."

I intend to present a not-too-organized tour of some issues and works that, for diverse reasons, I consider to be relevant for understanding the position of the economics of singularities within economic sociology: Polanyi and his legacy, the debates around the notions of embeddness and the self-regulating market, the theory of pluralistic forms of exchange, the relationship between judgment and calculation, and finally, the relations with some contemporary approaches.

• • •

Several configurations of sociology and economics attest to a break with classical tradition that must be attributed most particularly to Karl Polanyi. It was in effect his work that created the conditions and the notions for defining a new research program on the market. It would be difficult to understand the present situation without looking at the originality and strength of his approach; at the lucidity of his *Great Transformation*, whose validity extends to our times; and at the relevance of some issues and notions that are still alive and well, although his intellectual undertaking ended in semifailure. To take the measure of this attempt and of his achievement, we need first to take a trip back in time.

For a long while, the field of political economy was a mixture of economics, sociology, and political science. Adam Smith's founding work, *The Wealth of Nations* (1776), contains analyses of the market as an auton-

---

[3] *Cambridge Advanced Learner's Dictionary*, dictionary.cambridge.org/define.asp?key=41480&dict=CALD.

[4] *Chambers 21st Century Dictionary*, http://www.chambersharrap.co.uk/chambers/features/chref/chref.py/main?title=21st&query=interlude.

omous reality (theories of value, of wages, and of the "invisible hand") and interpretations concerning division of labor, the State, and social-class relations. Adam Smith went even farther in another work, which was devoted to action guided by *sympathy* as the capacity for forming judgments about others.[5] He was interested in the problem to which he would ultimately fail to provide a satisfactory solution, a problem which other analysts would tackle, in particular Durkheim, and which is more relevant today than ever: How can the quest for profit maximization be reconciled with respect for moral obligations? How can an individualistic profit orientation, supposedly inherent to human nature, be combined with reciprocity, which presumes sharing a system of common values? In sum, how can the market and society be held together? In this initial stage, economics did not separate the market from social institutions and social forces: the market structured society but it was also structured by society. Karl Marx would continue along the same path, for he would not separate the study of capitalism from Ricardo's economic theory.

Although the tension between economics and sociology began earlier, it was the creation and development in the 1870s of the marginalist theory that widened the gap. For a long time thereafter, market theory was purely and simply assimilated to price theory and was defined by three axioms: the economic agent is rational and self-interested; the balance between supply and demand is achieved by price variations; the market optimum requires conditions of pure and perfect competition.

Paradoxically, at more or less the same time—between 1880 and 1920—a brilliant generation of sociologists sprang up: each in his own way attempted to rebuild a unitary knowledge under the label of sociology. Some, like Weber, Pareto, and Schumpeter, set out to complete the theory of "pure economics," while others, like Simmel and Veblen, wanted to replace it. Weber stands out as having the most elaborate, diverse, and original work: it contains a systematic sociological conceptualization of economic reality; many writings on the formation and development of capitalism (which led him to maintain links with Marxism); and a monumental conception of the relationship between religion and economics.[6] All these authors did brilliant work, and yet the same sad fate awaited them. Unnoticed by the economists of the time, their message did not strike a chord, and they remained without disciples or schools to expand their work. The separation between sociology and an increasingly mathematical economics grew wider and wider. It would be hardly an exaggeration

[5] Adam Smith, *The Theory of Moral Sentiments* (London: A. Millar, 1790; repr., Mineola, NY: Dover Publications, 2009).

[6] P. Steiner and J.-J. Gislain, *La sociologie économique 1890–1920* (Paris: Presses Universitaires de France, 1995).

to say that those who took an interest in the market ignored society,[7] and with the exception of Marxism, those who devoted themselves to society no longer studied the market. The disjunction between the two disciplines became complete.

It was in this intellectual context that Karl Polanyi published *The Great Transformation* (1944) and *Trade and Market in the Early Empire* (1957). Whereas the sociology and history of the time focused on the study of culture, the state, or capitalism, from the outset Polanyi underscored his originality by placing the market at the heart of his study of both European and traditional societies. His essential contributions are concentrated around the distinction between the *embedded market* and the *self-regulating market* and around a *general theory of the forms of economic exchange*.

*The Great Transformation* explains the succession of economic, political, and military catastrophes that regularly punctuated European history between 1914 and 1945, after a century of peace. Unlike the usual interpretations, the book advances a single cause: the formation and development of a *self-regulating* market, of a market without interferences, a market governed exclusively by price. This unprecedented historical reality appeared in the eighteenth century and attained its perfect form in England's Poor Law of 1834, which imposed the commoditization of human labor.

Unlike the forms of exchange that, beyond their differences, had until then shared the common feature of being "embedded" in different social and cultural regulations of society, the self-regulating market was no longer governed by external rules or constraints: on the contrary, it was the market that controlled society.[8] For nearly a century, this mechanism, through the alternating development of prosperity and poverty, drove European history toward the social dislocations and self-defense movements that were to become unmanageable at the start of the twentieth century and would inevitably lead to revolts, uprisings, and two world wars.

The notion of a self-regulating market has given rise to a number of different interpretations. The ambiguity of the term has to do in part with Polanyi himself, who scattered various meanings of his concept through-

---

[7] And they did so despite an institutionalist school of thought which had a limited influence.

[8] "Instead of economy being embedded in social relations, social relations are embedded in the economic system. . . . This is the meaning of the familiar assertion that a market economy can function only in a market society." K. Polanyi, *The Great Transformation: The Political and Economic Origins of Our Time* (Boston: Beacon Press Books, 1944, 1957), p. 57.

out his work. For some analysts, the self-regulating market is the opposite of the embedded market; the first is a market governed uniquely by the logic of price, cut free from society, and in this sense, it purely and simply coincides with the standard market. And it is true that some of Polanyi's statements point in this direction. Other interpretations of this notion have been proposed, though, and their discussion will be pursued below.

The theory of the plurality of forms of exchange is directly opposed to the unity and universalism of neoclassical theory. Using historical and ethnographic material, Polanyi distinguished three institutionalized forms of integration—production, exchange, and consumption—governed, respectively, by the three principles of reciprocity, redistribution, and exchange. These three forms of integration also differ by their forms of embeddedness, which means by their configurations of kinship, religion, and culture. Economic systems are "embedded and enmeshed institutions, economic and non-economic," and a general theory of economic organization should take into account the changing place of the economy in society.[9] Thus, any economic system expresses a different way of combining reciprocity, redistribution, and exchange, and varies with the country and the historical period.

During the period between 1960 and 1980, anthropology became the main arena of confrontation. Everything revolved around the issue of the relevance of neoclassical economics for studying primitive societies, an approach to which most anthropologists of the time were hostile since primitive societies did not seem to have any price system. For these anthropologists, the difference between primitive and modern economies was therefore not one of degree but of nature, and on that basis, some of them rallied around the argumentation developed by Dalton, one of Polanyi's disciples: the so-called substantivist theory, which defines the economic system as the institutionalized process of the relationship between production and distribution.[10] Those who belonged to the "formalist" school, that is to say, the neoclassical school, found themselves on the shakiest of grounds: how can one justify a theory of price where there is no such thing as prices? The solution was found in the principle of economizing in order to increase satisfaction.[11] Like modern human beings,

[9] K. Polanyi, "The economy as an institutionalized process," in K. Polanyi, C. Arensberg, and H. W. Pearson (eds.), *Trade and Market in the Early Empires* (Glencoe, NY: Free Press, 1957, 1975), pp. 243–270; p. 250.

[10] G. Dalton, "Economic theory and primitive society," *The American Anthropologist* 63 (1961): 143–167.

[11] R. Burling, "Maximization theories and the study of economic anthropology," *The American Anthropologist* 64 (1962): 168–187.

primitive peoples seek to use the means at hand to best advantage: they are rational; and, therefore, the validity of neoclassical theory is universal. Notwithstanding a few resurgences, this long debate is over.[12] The formalist argument won out in the end. The chief contribution of this controversy, which mobilized a great deal of knowledge and passion, lies in the issues that provided food for thought in the years that followed.

Polanyi's final position was paradoxical: de facto, neoclassical analysis was relevant for developed societies, and the theory of the plurality of forms of exchange for the rest of the world. Both became regional sciences. This division was historical as well territorial. For feudal Europe and through the eighteenth century, a period that witnessed the development of international trade and national markets, economic systems were considered to be the product of variable combinations of reciprocity, redistribution, and exchange.

That composite reality gave way to the "total transformation" brought about by the advent of the market governed by price alone. This *unique* historical change led to the replacement of "regulated markets" by the self-regulated market *alone*. With hitherto unknown speed and radicalism, the "price"-market swept away the organizing principles of traditional economy: "The self-regulating market was unknown; indeed its emergence of the idea of self-regulation was a complete reversal of the trend of development."[13] This historical process led to the disappearance of the forms of integration, to the leveling that is the true meaning of a history with a fatally tragic ending. The absolute domination of the self-regulating market explains all the effects that accompanied its development over the long term.

Often quoted and having become the emblem of heterodox economic theory as well as of economic sociology, Polanyi appears as both a crucial and an ambiguous figure. Even though he regarded the pluralist theory of market as the only one that is universally applicable, he was led to a planetary Yalta that separates, on one side, developed countries, the self-regulating market and neoclassical economics from, on the other side, traditional societies, embedded markets and the pluralist theory of forms of integration. Such a dividing line consecrated a failure. By the same token—and no less important—his theory found itself deprived of the conceptual resources that it needed to study the eventual plurality of forms of exchange *within* the developed countries. Such an obstacle was insurmountable. Yet even so, Polanyi's legacy remains considerable.

[12] M. Granovetter, "The nature of economic relationships," in R. Swedberg (ed.), *Explorations in Economic Sociology* (New York: Russell Sage Foundation, 1993), pp. 3–41; M. Sahlins, *Stone-Age Economics* (Chicago: Aldine-Atherton, 1972), and *Culture and Practical Reason* (Chicago: University of Chicago Press, 1976).

[13] Polanyi, *The Great Transformation*, p. 68.

## Is the Self-Regulating Market Embedded?

WHERE "SELF-REGULATION" DOES NOT MEAN WHAT IT SEEMS

The search for the meaning of the self-regulating market has become the center of a flourishing debate that is important for the interpretation of Polanyi's work and for delimiting a common view of the phenomenon.[14] Such a quest must begin with a few questions: Is it theoretically possible that Polanyi could have used a "pure" conception of the self-regulated market to understand his times? Is it possible that he had transformed the abstract economic model into reality? Did he accept the idea that a real market could be completely disembedded?

These questions are of course merely rhetorical, since Polanyi answered them several times over. He stated explicitly that "no market economy separated from the political sphere is possible."[15] And he took great pains on several occasions to make it clear that the formation and development of the self-regulating market has not been spontaneous: it has been the product of a deliberate, systematic, and continuous state action: "There was nothing natural about laissez-faire . . . laissez-faire itself was enforced by the State"; "Laissez-faire economy was the product of deliberate State action"; "Laissez-faire was planned"; "The market has been the outcome of a conscious and often violent intervention on the part of the government which imposed the market organization."[16]

Furthermore, his study of nineteenth-century state policy is far from being merely allusive. Not only are the concrete indications precise and numerous, they are moreover put into the general perspective of the development of the "liberal State," characterized by a powerful administration that neutralized traditional restrictive regulations, built the management tools of the financial and trade markets, ensured social protection and established protectionism, and also diffused a system of knowledge and skills that combined information, statistics, economics, and ideology.[17]

[14] For a critical discussion of embeddedness, see G. T. Krippner, "The elusive market and the paradigm of economic sociology," *Theory and Society* 30, no. 4 (2001): 775–810; R. Le Velly, "La notion d'encastrement: Une sociologie des échanges marchands," *Sociologie du travail* 44 (2002): 37–53; J. Maucourant, *Avez-vous lu Polanyi?* (Paris: La Dispute, 2005); P. Steiner, "Encastrements et sociologie économique," in I. Huault (ed.), *La construction sociale de l'entreprise: Autour des travaux de Mark Granovetter* (Colombelles: EMS, 2002), pp. 29–50; P. Steiner, "Who is right about the modern economy: Polanyi, Zelizer, or both?" *Theory and Society* 38 (2009): 97–110.

[15] Polanyi, *The Great Transformation*, p. 196.

[16] Ibid., pp. 139, 141, 250.

[17] For factory legislation and social laws, land laws and agrarian tariffs, central banking and the management of the money system, bureaucratic control, police, municipal reforms as well as for "an enormous increase in the administrative functions of the state," the "sta-

The market emancipated from social and cultural constraints, the market obeying exclusively the free play of economic forces, the market which, for all these reasons, could only be explained by neoclassical theory, was in fact the state's creature. The state was necessary not only because it brought together the very conditions necessary for the market's development but also because it protected the market from its tendency to go too far, to lapse into a utopia by imposing, for example, constraints such as social-protection laws in order to prevent the dislocation of society. Nevertheless, *this market was considered as autonomous*. To understand such a paradox, one needs to take into account two remarks made by Polanyi: first, "a belief in spontaneous progress must make us blind to the role of government in economic life," and second, "the liberal creed assumed its evangelical fervor only in response to the needs of a fully deployed market economy."[18] Autonomy as a collective representation cannot be separated from the strength of shared beliefs.

Nevertheless, the logical task of reconciling the two contradictory questions—Is the market emancipated from society or does it rely on state intervention?—remains. The solution offered by Polanyi is that *the modern market is disembedded (self-regulated through price) because it is embedded in the political reality that creates the conditions for an apparently autonomous functioning*. The statement looks paradoxical but it is not. We have been experiencing exactly the same strange reality for the last decades without being overly disturbed. It is only when a crisis threatens that the "modest state" suddenly reappears, sometimes as an instrumental actor, sometimes in all its glory; but the difference is one of degree, not of nature. Thus there is no contradiction between public intervention and laissez-faire, as the second is the product of the first. What is here called *disembeddedness is nothing but another form of embeddedness*. It appeared, as Polanyi demonstrated, that the state has succeeded the market embedded in social and cultural reality without completely replacing it. The main conclusion is clear: *no market can exist without being embedded*. Such a proposition justifies a new look at the standard market.

### IS THE STANDARD MARKET EMBEDDED?

It would be easier to describe and explain the functioning of concrete, heterogeneous markets if we could use not only the regimes of coordination but also the two notions of *price-market* and *judgment-market* as meaningful shorthand ways to refer to neoclassical economics and to the

---

tistics and information, to foster science and experiment," and "the innumerable instruments of final realization in the field of government," see ibid., pp. 132, 139, 140.

[18] Ibid., pp. 37, 135.

economics of singularities. As these two notions belong to two different theoretical perspectives, such a pragmatic practice may create some confusion. But not to use them would amount to accepting the idea of two theories whose validities correspond to different realities: this is the compromise Polanyi embraced, and it was hardly a success. But why should we accept the conception that the standard market is not embedded?

I will refer to a famous study often used for demonstration, which deals with the Marché au Cadran in Fontaines-en-Sologne.[19] This market still exists; it handles transactions in strawberries. It was built at the instigation of an economist who was at once ingenious, committed, and economically strictly orthodox. He brought the theory of pure and perfect competition down from the ivory tower to dwell as faithfully as possible in the real world.

Three main features distinguish this market. First of all, there is a building with an interior layout deliberately organized to prevent all communication between sellers, between buyers, and between both groups: the only thing the economic actors share is the view of the electric signboard that posts the varieties of strawberries and the fluctuations in their prices. Moreover, the presentation of the strawberries for auction is standardized according to two rules: the physical separation between the varieties and the separation of the berries in the form of boxes of identical weight, which are therefore interchangeable. In this case, price is the only differentiating feature. Lastly, a disciplinary authority enforces the rules inside the market as well as outside the market perimeter, watching for forms of sociability that might favor price-fixing.

The Marché au Cadran is an extreme reality because it has been purposely and faithfully built to incarnate an abstract theory. To use it as a reference amounts to walking around with a textbook in hand. Concretely, it is an arrangement mediated by a whole set of devices—technical, architectural, organizational, ethical, and cultural—which turns the neoclassical price theory into reality.

The equipment of the Marché au Cadran is twofold: one is simple and deals with the products, the other is complicated and deals with human beings. The first includes (1) a technical device for showing the prices, (2) a technical device for showing the product varieties, (3) a technical device for the auctioneer, and (4) a corresponding logistic. Under these conditions the actors have all the (objective) information they need to make the best choice. The second includes a whole set of disciplinary devices necessary to obtain the conditions of pure and perfect competition.

[19] M.-F. Garcia, "The social construction of a perfect market: The strawberry auction at Fontaines-En-Sologne," in S. MacKenzie, F. Muniesa, and L. Siu (eds.), *Do Economists Make Markets? On the Performativity of Economics* (Princeton: Princeton University Press, 2008), pp. 20–53.

Without this global equipment, the market would not exist. *The price-market as well as the judgment-market is embedded.*

The main differences between the market of singularities and the standard market lie elsewhere: first, in *the nature and the format of the information/knowledge, and that justifies the distinction between decision devices and judgment devices*; and second, in the differential use of *bracketing*. For neoclassical theory, it looks legitimate to place the market equipment in brackets and, as a result, to deal only with the demand/supply/price system because it is assumed that it produces the same effects on the whole market. But the same assumption cannot be made for the economics of singularities, since the different types of devices exert different effects on the different products and actors.

Thus, *all markets are embedded, but the forms of embeddedness are different for making decisions or judgment, and they also differ according to the differential conditions of bracketing the market equipment.* Such a difference does not forbid the alternative or combined use of the judgment-market and price-market to explain a heterogeneous reality. In fact, this distinction fits nicely with the findings of a study by Paul DiMaggio and Hugh Louch on the relationship between types of product and types of consumer market preferences.[20] The authors distinguish the network-market from the impersonal market and show that, when it comes to purchasing a used car, a house, legal services, or maintenance services, more consumers are satisfied with "personal-networks"; but when buying a new car, more are satisfied with "general market sellers." In other words, the judgment-market is preferred for singular products because uncertainty can be removed or at least reduced by trust, and the price-market is preferred for differentiated products, because uncertainty is low and in any event the risks can always be calculated.

### MORE ABOUT EMBEDDEDNESS

The term *embeddedness* was revived by Granovetter in 1985.[21] Its subsequent success stems both from the maintenance of its critical function and from a change in what it designated: the network replaced religion, culture, and the state. The *new economic sociology*—the term at least, as the reality already existed—arose from this mutation. Both before and after 1985, developments in the sociology of networks—of which Granovetter was one of the main protagonists—concentrated on the relations between the differential effects exerted on the standard market by the variable

---

[20] P. DiMaggio and P.L.H. Louch, "Socially embedded consumer transactions: For what kinds of purchases do people most often use networks?" *American Sociological Review* 63 (1998): 619–637.

[21] M. Granovetter, "Economic action and social structure: The problem of embeddedness," *American Journal of Sociology* 3 (1985): 481–510.

density of the networks, the variable trust within the networks, the variable strength of the ties between the networks' actors, and the relative positions these actors occupy in the structure of the networks. It was during the same period that the network served as a basis for elaborating a structuralist market theory.[22]

*Embeddedness* is a widely shared reference and a notion whose meanings are multiplied by the domains of reality[23]—cognition, culture, religion, politics[24]—and by the scale of action—networks, institutions, the state, etc.—in which it is used. Furthermore, since this evolution intersects with the new developments in institutional analysis,[25] the position of the notion within economic sociology is shifting.

The historical significance of the notion of embeddedness lies in a critical function with respect to neoclassical theory—the refusal to separate economic relations from social forms—and in a research program respecting this requirement. These principles and this overall conception are now largely accepted; numerous and various studies rely on the notion of embeddedness without necessarily using the term as more than a generic reference.

These considerations explain the approach taken in the economics of singularities, which makes reference to embeddedness as a generic category. The economics of singularities sticks closely to exchange (an initial and provisional choice, which is only partially respected, as the reader will discover in the conclusion); it proposes to study markets of singularities using coordination regimes, which stem from the different types of judgment devices, all of which should lead to fleshing out the relations between judgment devices, culture, and the state.

## The Plurality of Forms of Exchange

Can we identify a pluralist conception of forms of exchange? Can we bring together studies and approaches whose authors would define themselves by this conception and who, therefore, would be aware of sharing a common set of problems and solutions? If we cite names and approaches

---

[22] H. C. White, "Where do markets come from?" *American Journal of Sociology* 87, no. 3 (1981): 517–547, and *Markets from Networks* (Princeton: Princeton University Press, 2001); M. Grossetti and M.-P. Bes, "Encastrements et decouplages dans les relations Science–Industrie," *Revue française de sociologie* 42, no. 2 (April –June 2001): 327–355; E. Lazéga, *The Collegial Phenomenon* (Oxford University Press, 2001).

[23] S. Zukin and P. DiMaggio, *Structure of Capital* (Cambridge: Cambridge University press, 1990), pp. 1–36.

[24] B. G. Carruthers, *City of Capital* (Princeton: Princeton University Press), 1996.

[25] B. Chavance, *L'économie institutionnelle* (Paris: La Découverte, 2007); G. M. Hodgson, "The return of institutional economics," in N. J. Smelser and R. Swedberg (eds.), *Handbook of Economic Sociology* (Princeton University Press, 1994), pp. 58–76.

like Polanyi, Williamson, Viviana Zelizer, Harrison White, DiMaggio, and Louch, as well as the economics of conventions and the economics of singularities—the list is by no means exhaustive—we are struck by the disparity of the collection. Rarely or never have these names been assembled around a unitary principle. And yet one does exist.

The similitude is grounded first of all in the same refusal: no description or explanation can be satisfying that uses a single form of exchange as a tool for observing and explaining because reality is considered to be too complicated, too diverse, and too changing. The positive counterpart of this refusal is the use of at least two forms of exchange, which, independently or together, become the components of the explanation.

Although the theory of forms of integration is the very epitome of this orientation, Polanyi's theory must nevertheless be removed from the analysis as, unlike the other approaches, it does not apply easily to modern societies. On the contrary, this is the case for Williamson, who, after connecting organization and the market via the changes in transaction costs, multiplied hybrid forms of governance[26]; for Zelizer, who refuses the generalized neutrality of money and highlights instead, alongside the general form of circulation, specific monetary circuits[27]; and for White and convention economics, which distinguish three models of coordination[28]; while DiMaggio and Louch, like the economics of singularities, stick to two. The list is short, but there is no need for it to be longer to see both the plurality and the diversity of forms of exchange.

The meaning that can be ascribed to this grouping depends on the specific causes that are used each time to justify such pluralism. For Williamson, the diversity of forms of coordination results from variations in transaction costs. But this monetary reality hides a particular materiality: products are essentially qualified by smaller or greater numbers of legal texts drawn up to limit the effects of opportunism. For Zelizer, culture and social structure explain that "special monies" must be added to the general monetary function; these are sums of money that are withdrawn

[26] O. E. Williamson, "The economics of organization: the transaction cost approach," *American Journal of Sociology* 87 (1981): 548–577.

[27] V. Zelizer, "Making multiple monies," in R. Swedberg (ed.), *Explorations in Economic Sociology* (New York: Russell Sage Foundation, 1993), pp. 193–212. For Zelizer, "monies" are like products.

[28] O. Favereau, O. Biencourt, and F. Eymard-Duvernay, "Where do markets come from? From (quality) convention," in O. Favereau and P. Lazega (eds.), *Conventions and Structure in Economic Organizations: Markets, Networks and Hierarchies* (Cheltenham, UK: Edward Elgar, 2002), pp. 213–252; A. Orléan (ed.), *Analyse économique des conventions* (Paris: Presses Universitaires de France, 1994). The economics of convention is theoretically linked to L. Boltanski and L. Thévenot, *De la justification: Les économies de la grandeur* (Paris: Gallimard, 1991) (*On Justification: Economies of Worth* [Princeton: Princeton University Press, 2006]).

from general circulation and assigned specific purposes: "domestic money," "charitable money," "ritual gifts." For White, as for convention economics, for DiMaggio and Louch, as well as for the economics of singularities, it is the diversity of product qualifications and of evaluation criteria that leads to constructing two or three forms of coordination. In the final analysis, the heterogeneous character of the viewpoints hides a unitary principle: the construction of the forms of coordination is adjusted to the interpretation of the differential features of the exchange products. *Pluralist theories of forms of exchange are based on the object missing in economic theory: namely, the product, insofar as it cannot be reduced to the sole characteristic of homogeneity/differentiation.*

Despite their diversity, then, these approaches share a common representation of reality, which produces similar effects on sociological knowledge. Causality, far from working in its usual form as a determinism that goes directly from one point to another, encounters the coordination logics, which can only divert it from its original path before it goes on to produce its effects down the line.

Embeddedness and the plurality of forms of exchange, which are rooted in Polanyi's legacy, are thus today two unifying principles and therefore ways of marking one's position in the arena of economic sociology. But whereas the first term casts a wide net, the second delimits a much smaller cluster.

## Judgment and Calculation

Judgment holds a key position in the economics of singularities. It is defined by the tension between axiological rationality and instrumental rationality; it designates the configuration of logics of action that make it possible, on the one hand, to compare, evaluate, and choose the "good" or "right" singularities and, on the other hand, to apply all forms of calculation to the singular products qualified by the same configuration of logics of action.

Yet for economists, judgment and calculation have long been the most general, as well as the most useful, antinomy for invalidating economic sociology. Indeed, without superfluous explanations, demonstrations, and interpretations, the two terms would make for a radical separation between economics—a science of calculation; in other words, a "true" science—and sociology, which would be "relegated" to qualitative studies. Of course, some have done their best to show that the question was badly put, that the difference was not as great as it seemed, and even that certain domains of sociology were largely mathematical—all to no avail. Rituals are not sensitive to history and it is not their job to tell the truth.

Though the habit is longstanding, the comparison between judgment and calculation is fallacious. It would not enter anyone's mind to compare a horse and a carriage, the first being the driving force, and the second the more or less useful means of transportation. The relationship between judgment and calculation is the same. One is a modality of choice and the other an instrument of action. The connection between them is as external and arbitrary as that between the horse and the carriage. The comparison can be repeated over and over, and it will still be just as absurd because judgment is a modality of choice and as such can be compared only to other modalities of choice. So we must come back to *decision* to extend the comparative exercise. And the question of calculation must be attached to the two modalities of choice.

By definition, decision belongs to a world grounded in generalized equivalence whose actors are guided by a single criterion of action, while judgment belongs to a world in which the products, devices, and actors are characterized by a plurality of evaluation criteria. This fact has major consequences for calculative practices. But they have to be identified with precision.

The difference between judgment and decision must not be confused with the opposition between calculation and noncalculation: *calculation (in the usual meaning of the notion) is (almost) everywhere.* But the conditions under which calculation is used vary widely. Decisions are linked to generalized equivalence and a single criterion of action, both of which represent the conditions for applying any type of calculation to an indefinite calculability; the limits of the lists of actors and products caught up in the same calculation are purely pragmatic and contingent. On the contrary, with judgments, the calculation comes up against two limits. One is set by the sharing of the same evaluation criteria: any type of calculation may be applied to more or less broad spaces of calculation. The other comes from the restricted calculative possibilities between judgment criteria. To sum up: to set judgment and calculation in opposition is a linguistic absurdity; calculation is involved in judgment as well as in decision, but the conditions for using calculation are not the same in each case. We are already far from the initial caricature.

Can we go from a market organized around judgment to one organized around decision? (This comes down to asking about the conditions that make it possible to construct a space of unitary calculation.) The answer is "yes," providing we add that this transmutation entails procedures and consequences that are problematic. To simplify, let us distinguish three conversion procedures. First of all, when the judgments produce only small differences, that is, when the actors attribute only a secondary value to these differences, suspension of the evaluation criteria can be the result of persuasion, negotiation, compromise, and sometimes payments. Second, more vigorous means can be used—from marketing to advertizing—that bring into play both conversion and imposition:

proselytizers are not lacking in resources and continually ply the world. Third, the bearers of judgments can be excluded or destroyed.

When addressing the process of market transformation, sociologists and economists alike often use a particularly euphemistic language, of which *negotiations* and *compromise* are the key words. What could be more democratic than peaceful bargaining? However, this style is deceptive. To be sure, transformations in the market can be the result of negotiations, but they are also associated with a violence that is not necessarily physical. It is often a matter of imposing on the unwilling a world that will be called rational, modern, cosmopolitan, postmodern, etc., in which profit-oriented action will glide over the at-last smooth surface of the market. This is the sense that can be given to the passage from the judgment-market to the decision-market.

We need to add that presenting and discussing this question exclusively at the technical-commercial level all too often makes us forget that more is at stake than simply the functioning of the market and the exchange of goods and services. Also and above all there is an ongoing struggle over values, what Weber called the struggle between gods, and there is no guarantee that it can be resolved by compromise. In the market as in society, the question is as much political and cultural as it is technical and commercial.

I would not have undertaken this review and formulated this argumentation if I had not seen the issue of the antinomy between judgment and calculation raised once more, this time at the instigation of two sociologists.[29] According to Michel Callon and Fabian Muniesa, all economists, sociologists, and anthropologists have shown that they are unable to study the market as a collective calculating device. Instead of arguing for a change in the methods of observation, the authors propose a radically new approach that should lead to restoring the actual, heretofore largely concealed, reality of the market. For them, the functioning of concrete markets, especially the stock market or supermarkets, comes down to an indefinite process of calculation, which implies calculable products, calculating machines, and calculative actors. In order to achieve that aim, four conditions are needed: the calculative reality must be extended,

[29] M. Callon and F. Muniesa, "Economic markets as calculative collective devices," *Organization Studies* 26, no. 8 (2005): 1229–1250. This paper is a shortened version of the French one. The article was the object of three critiques that were written from different perspectives: P. François, *Sociologie des marchés* (Paris: A. Colin), pp. 236–267; D. Miller, "Turning Callon the right way up," *Economy and Society* 31, no. 2 (2002): 218–233; and P. Mirowski and E. Nik-Kha, "Markets made flesh: And a problem in Science Studies, Augmented with Consideration of the FCC auctions," in D. MacKenzie, F. Muniesa, and L. Siu (eds.), *Do Economists Make Markets? On the Performativity of Economics* (Princeton: Princeton University Press, 2005), pp. 190–225.

judgments must be eliminated from reality, the theoretical foundations of that change should be formulated, and only generalized equivalence should exist.

How can calculative reality be extended? The easiest way, the one that is adopted here, is to call *calculation* all the practices that until now have not been regarded as such. This is done for all practices of classification, separation, and grouping of products and persons that precede the numerical operations. This transmutation is termed by the authors "wide but usual," although it seems very wide and completely unusual.[30]

To get rid of judgment is a little more complicated. It is explained by the authors that judgment and calculation are part of a third notion: *qualculation* (a neologism proposed by F. Cochoy), which finds its concrete expressions on the continuum between pure judgment and pure calculation. In this case, both judgment and calculation should logically be reported missing.

But the story is not straightforward. Elsewhere, judgment is the subject of strange qualification operations that lead it to be associated for example with *agapè*, meaning spiritual and unconditional love: undoubtedly after that, judgment will be hard to find![31] And, meanwhile, calculation makes a triumphal comeback. This is easy to verify: once the definitions are laid out,[32] all one has to do is to count up the occurrences of the three terms in the rest of the article.[33] The results show that the notion of judgment, like that of qualculation, is *never* used, whereas that of calculate/calculation and related terms occurs over one hundred times. It is therefore no exaggeration to consider that "qualculation" is nothing but a decoy, and that judgment has indeed disappeared from the language and from the world. From now on, the market reality can be purely and simply assimilated to calculation. Nobody should be astonished: it is the result of a careful construction.

What is the aim of Callon and Muniesa's analysis? As far as we can tell, it is to replace a pluralist, fragmented, divided, conflictual market with a market characterized by generalized equivalence, which amounts to producing the much desired calculative market. How can this be done?

[30] *Calculation*: "when you use numbers in order to find out an amount, price or value" (Longman Dictionary of Contemporary English, *http://www.ldoceonline.com/dictionary/calculation*); or "to determine by mathematical processes" (Merriam-Webster Online, http://www.merriam-webster.com/dictionary/calculate); and in French, *calcul*: "Opération ou ensemble d'opérations portant sur des nombres ou des symboles numériques" [Operation or set of operations involving numbers or numerical symbols], (*Trésor de la Langue Française*, http://atilf.atilf.fr/tlf.htm ).

[31] M. Callon and J. Law, "On qualculation, agency and otherness," *Environment and Planning D: Society and Space* 23, no. 5 ( 2005): 717–733.

[32] Callon and Muniesa, "Economic markets," pp. 1129–1132.

[33] Ibid., pp. 1132–1150.

The practical means have already been shown but their use has to be theoretically grounded. Here the replacement of judgments by calculation rests on two general arguments: that there is a common etymological origin for the two words; and the "trick" by which the authors "try to avoid the distinction (also conventional, but too sharp) between judgment and calculation."[34]

There is nothing useful to be said about the second reason since it is difficult to discuss feelings. However, if every social scientist chose to modify the terminology at will, common understanding would become difficult. The first reason is more interesting. For the authors, the blurring of judgment and calculation is based on the observation that, etymologically, *calculation* derives from *judgment*. But I do not see how this observation could justify such a practice. Moreover, in all dictionaries, *calculation* is derived not from *judgment* but from the Latin *calculus*. That is a problem in itself. In fact, the authors' reference is a paper published by Emile Benveniste.[35] Although I am not a linguist, it seems useful to take a look at this study. In this short paper, Benveniste does not present a general analysis of the etymology of *calculation*; he is interested in two comparisons: one between two words whose historical evolution is different, and the other, which concerns the converse: two different words that have finally converged. First, he shows that, although the meaning of the two terms *duco* (L.) and *hegéomai* (Gr.) have moved from *commander* (command) to *juger* (judgment), one may observe with *duco* a drift toward calculation that is not found with the Greek term. Second, he shows that two Latin terms—*duco* and *puto* (meaning *tailler la vigne*, "to prune a vineyard")—moved toward *judgment*, and that both show *calculation* as a derived term.

Thus the etymological origins of *calculation* are diverse: they are not always linked to *judgment*. Benveniste's paper does not substantiate the general link between the two words inasmuch as it does not invalidate the general link between *calculation* and *calculus*, an issue Benveniste does not address at all. It is therefore hard to see how *calculation* can validly replace *judgment* and therefore to accept the general reasoning that organizes the authors' paper.

Moreover, the practice of excluding such-and-such word from language and from reality is worrying. A few years ago, Williamson asked the readers of a paper of his own to forget about the word *trust* because, for him, it should be replaced by *calculation*.[36] This time, it is the "disappearance"—of

---

[34]Ibid., p.1231.

[35]E. Benveniste, "Le compte et l'estimation," *Le vocabulaire des institutions indo-européennes* (Paris: Ed. de Minuit, 1969), vol. 1, pp. 151–154.

[36]O. E. Williamson, "Calculativeness, trust and economic organization," *Journal of Law & Economics* 36 (1993): 453–486.

judgments and, as a consequence, of singularities—that is proposed. Logically, "pruning a vineyard" should also be replaced by *calculation*. After losing trust and judgment and singularities, shall we lose wine as well? Some may regret it.

Even if they were right, Callon and Muniesa had a last step before them: to transform the goods, because actors and machines can calculate only if the products are calculable. This is not a given. It is the process that is nowadays known as *qualification*. But in fact, the solution has existed for a long time in Chamberlin's major work. And still, according to the authors, once again all economists, sociologists, and anthropologists, after having demonstrated their incapacity to restore the calculative practices of the market, have shown the same inability to understand the book in which Chamberlin formulated the general proposition that "in all cases, there can be no transaction without the individualization of the product," a process the authors from time to time called *singularization of goods*. For them, the product becomes calculable only following a process of qualification that takes the form of a transformation in which the product becomes attached to the consumer, the strength of the attachment being evaluated by the price. This would be Chamberlin's thesis, which was "unknown" until its revelation by our authors.

We therefore need to turn directly to Chamberlin's work.[37] This will be laborious, since the authors do not cite specific pages. Essentially, the work is devoted to the analysis of the, necessarily, varied relations between the "product as a variable," and price and sales volume. Chamberlin uses the term *individualization of the product*, but its meaning is adjusted to its theoretical aims, and these were concentrated on the study of the relations between differentiation and the price theory. *Individualization, uniqueness, product "variation,"* and *differentiation* have the same meaning and refer to any differences in products, "real or fancied," that result in profit on the market. Because these differences are countless and because the greatest number of them are "produced" by the producers, these notions designate the same general reality and are linked to the same theoretical perspective and the same research program. If the differentiation theory has been integrated in the neoclassical theory, the same is not true of the "individualization process": orthodox economists were not interested in the "product as an economic variable" research program. However, as I show below, that was not the case for some sociologists and heterodox economists around the 1990s, although at that time the impetus would come from other sources.

At the most general level, the notion of individualization (along with its synonyms) only provides Chamberlin with the ways to distinguish his

---

[37]E. H. Chamberlin, *The Theory of Monopolistic Competition: A Re-orientation of the Theory of Value* (Cambridge, MA: Harvard University Press, 1933, 1969).

theory from the one he is combating. All these terms are centered on the products and their qualifications. That is well known. But in this book, Chamberlin is not very interested in generalities: he wants to elaborate a theory of value that will take into account the diverse "varieties" and "classes" of the products.[38] So let us follow him.

For his analysis, Chamberlin proposes two main divisions of products. First, he distinguishes two broad categories of differentiation and, their corollaries, two categories of mutual adjustments between product and consumer. One rests on *"certain characteristics of the product itself"* such as "trade-marks; trade names; peculiarities of the package or container; or singularity in quality, design, color or style"; and the other on *"the conditions surrounding its sale,"* which includes, for the "retail trade," the seller's location as well as his "way of doing business," "reputation," and "all the personal links which attach his customers either to himself or to those employed by him."[39] Second, he proposes a more sophisticated division when he opposes to ordinary goods the idiosyncratic personal relations and the personalized relations that cannot be "duplicated," that are "not interchangeable," that are incomparable, such as "reputation, skills and special ability in the professions"—the physician, for example.[40]

For Callon and Muniesa, qualification is unidimensional: "The product wavers between a high level of singularization (weak substitutability) and a high level of standardization (strong substitutability). The good has been placed in a frame with other goods."[41] But for Chamberlin, the two categories of qualified goods belong to two different markets, to two different frames: "The skillful physician does not sell his services in the identical markets with the ordinary for their services are not interchangeable and do not sell for the same price."[42] The seeds of the personalized, singular service are present! But Chamberlin stops there.

Yet, this analysis allows us to draw some conclusions. First, individualization, like differentiation, is a generic type that points globally to what we will call qualification, because it implies a very great diversity of relations with the consumers. Second, the category of products related to consumers by personalized relationships represents, in Chamberlin's view, a subdivision of individualization or differentiation, since it does not belong to the same market, to the same universe, as that of interchangeable products. If one wants to name them, they are closest to the

---

[38] Ibid., p. 113.

[39] Ibid., p. 56.

[40] "Peculiarities of any individual establishment which cannot be duplicated (such as the personality of the proprietor for instance) lead to profit . . . likewise reputation, skill, and special ability, in the profession." Ibid., p. 112.

[41] Callon and Muniesa, "Economic markets," p. 1235.

[42] Chamberlin, *Theory of Monopolistic Competition*, p. 113.

products of the process of the "singularization of goods," as it is used in this book. Third, since the world is heterogeneous, generalized calculation can only be done when personalized, singularized goods and services are dequalified. So, in fact, Chamberlin's position is the opposite of what Callon and Muniesa claim it to be.

• • •

The paper prompts some astonishment on a number of grounds. The first has to do with the altogether classic—and fallacious—opposition between judgment and calculation. One might have thought that, after Weber, sociologists would have avoided using this distinction. In all events, the antinomy between judgment and calculation makes no more sense when it is used by sociologists than when it is used by economists. The second follows from the observation that sociologists caught up in the fantasy of generalized calculability could so easily jettison the values and conflicts that punctuate the market's workings and maintains its heterogeneousness, with *perhaps* a very few exceptional cases, like the stock market. The third, is to discover sociologists elaborating a theory that so perfectly performs the conditions that are necessary for the neoclassical theory to be valid.

### Situating the Economics of Singularities

Where does the economics of singularities stand among the various viewpoints within economic sociology? We have already presented three answers with the specific and situated references that will be continued with Polanyi's legacy connections and with the examination of a line of analysis that effaces singularities as an object of study. For a more systematic comparison, we need to rely on general interpretations of present-day economic sociology and take stock of the main features of the economics of singularities, namely, (1) it does not apply to the standard market but to the market of singularities; (2) quality competition prevails over price competition; (3) it uses a conception of action oriented by the tension between logics of action and the principle of economizing; (4) it integrates personal and impersonal judgment devices as supports for action; and (5) the combinations of judgment devices determine the coordination regimes that make up the markets of singularities.[43]

[43] The general interpretations include B. Carruthers and B. Uzzi, "Economic sociology in the new millenium," *Contemporary Sociology* 29, no. 3 (2000): 486–494; F. Cusin and D. Benamouzig, *Economie et sociologie* (Paris: Presses Universitaires de France, 2004); F. Dobbin, *The New Economic Sociology: A Reader* (Princeton: Princeton University Press, 2004); M. Fourcade, "Theories of markets and theories of society," *American Behavioral*

The first two features are found nowhere else. In order to draw this comparison, we would need to confront not only dimensions or problems but whole approaches, which is beyond the scope of the present book. I have therefore retained a different strategy, which may also be more useful for the English-speaking reader. I have chosen to include the elaboration of the economics of singularities in the overall development of a large part of French economic sociology, which is not sufficiently known owing to the language barrier, and has, it seems to me, something original to offer. This necessarily sketchy examination should lead to a wider comparative framework.

In the early 1990s, France's economic sociology landscape contained mainly, alongside the new economic sociology, field theory (P. Bourdieu), the theory of regulation (J.-D. Reynaud), the economics of quality (L. Karpik), sociotechnical analysis (M. Callon, B. Latour), later, network structural analysis (E. Lazéga), and, within heterodox economics, the economics of conventions (F. Eymard-Duvernay, O. Favereau, A. Orléan, R. Salais, L. Thevenot, and others) and, finally, the theory of regulation (R. Boyer).[44] At the time, these were more or less elaborated, and soon they would produce empirical studies. From this period, I will merely retain a feature whose importance has been generally underestimated: the relative ease of the exchanges between heterodox economists and sociologists. This mutual openness, riskier for the economists than for the sociologists, was to have two consequences: a mutual, broader, as well as more solid, knowledge of economics and sociology, and a shared set of problems that would appear over time.

---

*Scientist* 50, no. 8 (2007): 1015–1034; P. François, *Sociologie des marchés* (Paris: Armand Colin, 2008); M. Guillen, R. Collins, P. England, and M. Meyer (eds.), *The New Economic Sociology: Developments in an Emerging Field* (New York: Russell Sage Foundation, 2002); J. Lie, "Sociology of markets," *Annual Review of Sociology* 23 (1997): 341–360; J. Rauch and A. Casella, *Networks and Market: Concepts for Bridging Disciplines* (New York: Russell Sage Foundation, 2001), pp. 1–29; N. J. Smelser and R. Swedberg (eds.), *Handbook of Economic Sociology* (Princeton: Princeton University Press, 1994, 2005); P. Steiner, *La sociologie économique* (Paris: La Découverte, 2007); P. Steiner and F. Vatin (eds.), *Traité de sociologie économique* (Paris: Presses Universitaires de France, 2009); R. Swedberg, *Principles of Economic Sociology* (Princeton: Princeton University Press, 2003); V. Zelizer, "Pasts and futures of economic sociology," *American Behavioral Scientist* 50, no. 8 (2007): 1056–1069.

[44] Respectively: P. Bourdieu, *The Social Structure of Economy* (London: Polity Press, 2005); J.-D. Reynaud, *Les règles du jeu* (Paris: A. Colin, 1989); L. Karpik, "L'économie de la qualité," *Revue française de sociologie* 30, no. 2 (1989): 187–210; M. Akrich, M. Callon, and B. Latour (eds.), *Sociologie de la traduction: Textes fondateurs* (Paris: Presses de l'Ecole des Mines, 2006); E. Lazéga, *The Collegial Phenomenon: The Social Mechanisms of Cooperation among Peers in a Corporate Law Partnership* (Oxford: Oxford University Press, 2001); "L'économie des conventions," *Revue économique* 40, no. 2 (1989); R. Boyer, *Théorie de la régulation* (Paris: La Découverte, 1986).

This inventory seems to describe the most classical model of science, but this order was to be gradually muddled by another dynamic whose unity and extension could be identified only retrospectively.[45] The starting point was the intervention of an economist and a sociologist— F. Eymard-Duvernay and Catherine Paradeise—who each independently of the other transmuted the topic of *job qualification*, on which they had worked in economics and sociology of labor, into *product qualification*.[46] Rejection of the thesis of natural aptitudes found its corresponding expression in the rejection of the product as a given; the same happened with the transformations by which labor is put into work and the transformations by which products are put into the market. What was being proposed, discreetly, was nothing less than a new object of study.

There followed a necessary period of elaboration, as a number of publications testify, before concrete studies were undertaken, and then the dynamics was extended, especially with the arrival of committed young researchers. After a decade or so of dispersed involvements, a common research domain had been built. The list of the questions studied is long: product qualification in the narrow sense, coordination devices, market strategies, forms of consumer action, networks, prices, and later, calculation, consumption, politics, etc. I will limit myself to a summary presentation of the first three, which occupy a strategic position.[47]

[45] See the English translation of the debate , which was organized by C. Musselin and C. Paradeise, "Quality: A debate," *Sociologie du travail* 47 (Supplement 1) (2005): 89–123, with contributions by M. Callon, F. Eymard-Duvernay, L. Gadrey, L. Karpik, C. Musselin, and C. Paradeise. See also A. Stanziani, *Histoire de la qualité alimentaire XIXe–XXe siècle* (Paris: Seuil, 2005), pp. 23–36.

[46] F. Eymard-Duvernay, "La qualification des produits," in R. Salais and L. Thevenot (eds.), *Le travail* (Paris: Economica, 1986), pp. 239–247; C. Paradeise, "Acteurs et institutions: La dynamique des marchés du travail," *Sociologie du travail* 1 (1988): 79–105.

[47] The global number of references has been severely limited, first of all, because the number of references for each topic discussed itself has been severely limited and, second, because a number of topics have not been discussed. The reference list should therefore not be taken as a reflection of the global sociological movement, which largely exceeds the number of entries found here. On *product qualification*, see S. Barrey, F. Cochoy, and S. Dubuisson-Quellier, "Designer, packager et merchandiser: Trois professionnels pour une même scène marchande," *Sociologie du travail* 3 (2000): 457–482; C. Bessy and F. Chateaureynaud, *Experts et faussaires* (Paris: Métailié, 1995); S. Dubuisson-Quellier and J.-P. Neuville ( eds.), *Juger pour échanger: La construction sociale de l'accord sur la qualité dans une économie des jugements individuels* (Paris: Editions de la Maison des Sciences de l'Homme & INRA, 2003); L. Karpik, "Le Guide rouge Michelin," *Sociologie du travail* 3 (2000): 369–389; M. Storper and R. Salais (eds.), *World of Production: The Action Framework of Economy* (Cambridge, MA: Harvard University Press, 1997); A. Stanziani (ed.), *La qualité des produits en France, XVIII–XX siècle* (Paris: Belin, 2004). On *devices*, see F. Cochoy, *L'Ane de Buridan: Les emballages et le choix du consommateur* (Paris: Presses Universitaires de France, 2002); F. Eymard-Duvernay and E. Marchal, *Façons de recruter* (Paris: Métailié, 1997), O. Favereau, "Marchés internes, marchés externes," *Revue économique* 2

First, *product qualification*, taken in its narrow sense, includes the operations and the professionals that are mobilized to make products desirable. It explains the rise of studies on the representation of the consumer in the products' conception, studies on the many product transformations that intervene between production and sale, on the arrangements that ensure the encounter between product and consumer, not to mention the interest devoted to the skills of the numerous professionals of the market: designers, merchandisers, packagers, marketers, publicists, and so on.

Second, the *devices*, a term widely used and borrowed from Michel Foucault, indicates the break with the institutional view and identifies the symbolic-material arrangements that ensure the products encounter their consumers. Broadly speaking, this meant the discovery, exploration, and analysis of a great number of concrete mechanisms and the building of numerous classifications and interpretations. This disorderly collection can be subsumed under the generic term of *coordination devices*, which was proposed by O. Favereau.

Third, the *consumer*, whose representation wavered between sovereignty and alienation, finds himself reconstructed through the possibilities offered and the constraints imposed by the product qualifications and coordination devices. The consumer became multiple, and his action was linked to the orientations and margins of freedom that were the results of the products and devices uses as well as of the actors' forms of commitment.

This brief overview calls for four general remarks. First, with the products, devices, and professional actors as well as producers and consumers, the previously almost empty market was replaced by a populated one with numerous new problems to study. Second, this development, which, once again, *does not hold for all French sociologists working on economic reality*, unfolded according to two apparently contradictory and yet persistent modalities: competition between different approaches and the sharing of a knowledge grounded in the same concrete domain. Each of these two perspectives has favored different orientations, interactions,

---

March (1989): 273–328; A. Hatchuel, "Les marchés à prescripteurs. Crise de l'échange et genèse sociale," in A. Jacob and H. Verin (eds.), *L'inscription sociale du marché* (Paris: L'Harmattan, 1995); A. Hennion, *La passion musicale* (Paris: Métailié, 1993); L. Karpik, "Dispositifs de confiance et engagements crédibles," *Sociologie du travail* 4 (1996): 527–550; A. Mallard, "La presse de consommation et le marché: Enquête sur le tiers-consumériste," *Sociologie du travail* 3 (2000): 391–410; P. Trompette, "Customer channeling in the funeral business in France," *Revue française de sociologie* 48, Supplement: An Annual English Selection (2007): 3–34. On *consumers*, see S. Dubuisson-Quellier, "Le prestataire, le client et le consommateur: Sociologie d'une relation marchande," *Revue française de sociologie* 40, no. 4 (1999): 671–688; J. Gadrey, "Les relations de service dans le secteur marchand," in J. de Bandt and J. Gadrey (eds.), *Relations de service, marchés de services* (Paris: Editions du CNRS, 1994), pp. 23–41.

and solidarities without leading to mutual destruction. One may wonder if the collective research dynamics may not have been the result of this interweaving.

Third, beyond the diversity of theoretical views, methods, and studies, something like a common framework can be distinguished, which is grounded in the product as the grasp, to understand the markets' functioning. As such, that framework expresses an original collective accentuation compared to the development of research in other countries.

And finally, coming back to the initial question on the economics of singularities: the product as a principle of market intelligibility was at the root of this approach, even before this multiform development arose. The separation between homogeneous/differentiated products and singular products (at the time called *quality products*) was in place from the outset: of necessity it led to the development of a new schema of analysis, used for the first time to account for the functioning of the lawyers market. [48] Throughout this entire period, therefore, the economics of singularities could not help finding itself both inside and outside this collective movement. This position was the condition for pursuing and enlarging the systematic construction of the theory.

[48] For the main steps in the development of the theory, see L. Karpik, "L'économie de la qualité," *Revue française de sociologie* 30, no. 2 (1989): 187–210; *French Lawyers: A Study in Collective Action, 1274–1994*, trans. Nora Scott (Oxford: Oxford University Press, 1999) (chapter 8, "The market," is a limited extension of the 1989 paper "L'Economie de la qualité"); "Dispositifs de confiance et engagements crédibles," *Sociologie du travail* 4 (1996): 527–550; "Le Guide rouge Michelin," *Sociologie du travail* 3 (2000): 369–389; "Pour une conception substantive de la confiance," in L. Quere (ed.), *La structure cognitive de la confiance* (Paris: Economica, 2003); and *L'économie des singularités* (Paris: Gallimard, 2007).

PART THREE

# Economic Coordination Regimes

Part 3 puts on trial, within the limits of the available data, the capacity of economic coordination regimes to explain the functioning and evolution of markets of singularities. Each of the regimes differs from the others by a specific configuration, which combines a particular qualification of the singularities, a particular form of the intervention of judgment devices, a particular form of consumer commitment and a particular form of global logic governing the matching between these elements.

Each chapter in Part 3 analyzes a different coordination regime on the basis of one or several concrete studies, though none is intended to be systematic or exhaustive. The elaboration of each study deals with a particular theoretical issue—which varies from one study to the next, from one coordination regime to another—thus making it possible to address several different problems within a limited number of pages. The final chapter is devoted exclusively to price.

The coordination regimes under consideration are divided into two categories, according to their reliance on impersonal or on personal devices. The distinction is unevenly strict, however; when impersonal devices predominate—even strongly—the network is never completely absent, whereas in the case of personal devices the reverse is possible.[1]

One last explanation before we begin: the book contains very few references to the Internet, but not because I underrated the phenomenon; on the contrary. After an initially tentative period and the premature announcements of major innovations, the rapid proliferation of new products and new actors now tells another story. The Internet can be used as a judgment device alongside the other devices; but it would be more realistic to consider it as a new, global, and largely autonomous reality. That means that the relentless expansion of its exchange system supposes as a corollary the development of its market equipment. And this requirement is all the more necessary for singularities. The Internet thus allows us to observe the invention and implementation of new judgment devices called for by the generalization of the exchange of singularities. With the same approach, this huge construction site—this *market in progress*—needs a separate analysis.

[1] To avoid having to turn back to Figure 1, which presents the classification of the economic coordination regimes, a sidebar on the first page of each chapter refers to the portion of the table containing the analytical dimensions that constitute the regime to be analyzed.

## Impersonal Devices Regimes

THE REGIMES OF coordination built on impersonal devices include the *authenticity regime*, the *mega regime*, the *expert-opinion regime*, and the *common-opinion regime*. In the chapters that follow, one or several concrete markets are associated with each of these coordination regimes: fine wines, megafilms, megabrands, luxury goods, literary prizes, "concept stores," and popular music.

## Chapter Ten

# THE AUTHENTICITY REGIME

THE AUTHENTICITY REGIME is composed of *names.* Fine wines, popular- or classical-music CDs or Internet downloads, and book titles number in the thousands and tens of thousands. And thousands of new names are added every year. Reliable identification of each entity requires the combination of two, three or, exceptionally, four such names: for example; J. S. Bach + *The Well-Tempered Clavier* + Sviatoslav Richter; Graves + *Haut Brion* + 1995; Charles Parker + *Ornithology* + Dial Records; Shakespeare + *Theater* + New translation. Such

| Impersonal devices Substantial devices Small market |
| :---: |
| *Active and autonomous consumers* |
| Originality/ Aesthetic logic |

names are inalienable, and their bearers are the producers of a singular work, although in some cases they may have merely participated in a coproduction that combines human skills and natural resources.

These names designate apparently heterogeneous entities: some are unique (paintings), others are rare (wine vintage years), others are reproducible (CDs and DVDs, books). Although the forms of production vary, each singular product, because it is a symbolic product, is open to an indefinite number of interpretations. Not all products lend themselves equally to interpretation, however; for the public, the symbolic richness of a singularity varies with its age, the criticism it has received, and the debates it has sparked. Due to the indefinite number of possible interpretations, the reproducible symbolic product is also a singularity. It carries with it all of its past interpretations and is formally prepared to receive new ones.

By and large, the singularities of the authenticity regime are linked to the originality model and, most often, more specifically to the artistic model, whose main characteristics appear clearly in the painting market, the embodiment of its purest form. Thus, pictorial works are subject to the requirements of creation, uniqueness or at least scarcity, incommensurability and artistic value.[1]

Since paintings are displayed before their sale, the commercial exchange should (in principle) not encounter the obstacles that follow from

---

[1] For Nathalie Heinich, the world of modern art is distinguished from the pre-Renaissance art world by the predominance of an ideal-typical artist who comes under the "singularity regime" (see "Façons d'être écrivain: L'identité professionnelle en régime de singularité," *Revue française de sociologie* 36 [1995]: 499–524).

ignorance or radical quality uncertainty. But a painting is a work that deals in meanings. Thus prior knowledge does not suffice to eliminate uncertainties about a work's interpretation, its authenticity, its aesthetic value, or about the action of those involved in the exchange. Uncertainty about the interpretation: what are we to make of the interpretations of Rembrandt's *Night Watch*, when it became "Day Watch" after restoration. Uncertainty about authenticity, which has become more acute than in the past with the advent of new techniques and a more and more exacting demand for rigor; uncertainty about aesthetic value, which increases with proximity to the contemporary period. And finally, uncertainty about the intensity of the sellers' and/or buyers' passion, which is proportionate to the social value ascribed to this symbolic activity and to the more or less absolute belief in the greatness of art, artists, and art history.

All of these uncertainties mean that ignorance places a constraint on the buyer that is all the more restrictive because the aesthetic judgment that recommends the choice must include a vast array of knowledge, and because the price of error or of being misled is not limited to the money lost but also threatens self-esteem. Aesthetic value, social value, and economic value all intertwine to make it difficult to arrive at a reasonable choice.

The art market exists only because there also exists a diversified cultural complex composed of critics, art historians, museum directors, professors, collectors, dealers, auctioneers, and experts. It encompasses embodied knowledge, writings, judgments, arguments, and proofs. Credible expert knowledge is indispensable for qualifying paintings and reducing the sphere of ignorance and uncertainty.[2]

On this condition, although it is transfigured by the artists, the intermediaries, and buyer commitment and by the knowledge, passions, and ideals it arouses, competition between works can be linked to the clients' logic of action so as to construct the comparable without destroying the incomparable. Today purchase paths are more disconcerting than they were when the art market was restricted to a few important dealers and a small clientele. Nevertheless, the adjustment between sellers, judgment devices (experts, instruments, catalogues, writings, etc.), works, and buyers comes about—although not without the occasional hitch.

Aside from masterpieces, what other singular products belong to the authenticity regime? For Charles Taylor, "authenticity" encompasses moral

---

[2] On painting, see, R. Moulin, *Le marché de la peinture en France* (Paris: Minuit, 1967) (*The French Art Market* [New Brunswick, NJ: Rutgers University Press, 1987]); R. Moulin, *De la valeur de l'art* (Paris: Flammarion: 1995); R. Moulin and A. Quemin, "L'expertise artistique," in F. Aubert and J.-P. Sylvestre (eds.), *Confiance et rationalité* (Paris: Editions INRA, 2001), pp. 185–199; O. Velthuis, "Visual arts," in R. Towse and A. Khakee (eds.), *Handbook of Cultural Economics* (Berlin: Springer Verlag, 1992), pp. 470–475. On music, see A. Hennion, *La passion musicale* (Paris: Métailié, 1993).

ideals, self-determined freedom, self-realization, dialogue, and stakes among the "inescapable horizons."[3] For Christian Bessy and Francis Chateaureynaud, authenticity is developed through forms of apprenticeship associated with the objects, and the interpretation of sensations through forms of bodily engagement completely excludes the possibility of a closed universe of meanings.[4] These two conceptions readily apply to singularities but under the control of the aesthetic judgment criterion, which expresses itself in singular products, in judgment devices, and in particular forms of self-fulfillment. Concrete markets in the authenticity regime are thus defined by the exacting encounter of the products' and the clients' tastes, mediated by the tastes conveyed by the judgment devices.

The authenticity regime encompasses the greatest number and the strongest diversity of singularities, as is shown by the multiplicity of names; furthermore, new products are appearing every day. The authenticity regime also brings together the greatest number and the strongest diversity of consumer logics of action. Thus choice of the "good" or the "right" singularity meets with numerous obstacles. One difficulty stands out: how can one reduce or eliminate the *cognitive deficit*, which measures the gap between what the consumer knows and what he should know in order to make reasonable choices. It is this issue that clearly dominates the market of fine wines.

## THE MARKET OF FINE WINES

Preference for a "good" or fine wine cannot be separated from the value ascribed to taste and the pleasures of fine "cuisine."[5] But France produces and sells tens of thousands of wines, each of which differs from the next by its "specificity and its particular character." Quality uncertainty is therefore widespread. Unaided, the consumer is rarely able to distinguish an "outstanding" wine from a "good" wine, a "good" wine from a "not-so-good" wine, and so on. Ignorance prevails.

[3] C. Taylor, *The Malaise of Modernity* (Toronto: House of Anansi Press, 2003), pp. 31–41.

[4] C. Bessy and F. Chateaureynaud, *Experts et faussaires* (Paris: Métailié, 1995), pp. 320–327.

[5] For France, the surveys agree on three general findings: (1) "eating right," "quality foods," and "the most important food quality criteria" are associated with pleasure; (2) taste tops the list of purchasing criteria; (3) the food product has a high cultural value (*Enquêtes CREDOC–CAF*, June 2000; *CREDOC–INC*, 2000; *CREDOC*, January 2001; *CREDOC–INC*, February 2001). Of the six criteria of food quality, 79 percent of French respondents chose taste as the most important (*Enquête, CREDOC–INC*, February 2001). A decade later, "pleasure" and "taste" still occupy the first ranks, although taste has acquired a strong competitor with "health." See P. Hebel, "Synthèse des baromètres sur l'alimentation," no. S3424, CREDOC, December 2008, http://www.credoc.fr/.

The consumer may rely on the 1855 ranking of the best Bordeaux wines or on the AOC, *appellation d'origine contrôlée*, or *Registered Denomination of Origin*, the official certification guaranteeing the "superior quality" of certain French products (called Protected Appellation of Origin by the European Commission, and also known in EU parlance as Protected Geographical Indication) which is attributed to approximately five hundred wines. Created in 1935, the AOC label is based on geographical origin (the *terroir*) and imposes specific production techniques and yield standards that wine producers are supposed to respect. All AOC wines have a name protected by law (e.g., *château*, *domaine*), all are obliged to list certain information on the bottle label, and all are subject to inspection by the National Institute of Appellations of Origin (INAO). All identify "unique," "typical" wines associated with a taste, a place, and a memory. While appellations of origin distinguish singularities and allow the consumer to avoid the most serious disappointments, they are nevertheless of limited help for two different reasons: on the one hand, the number of possibilities is too great to be really helpful for individualized and reasonable choices and, on the other hand, general faith in the "superior quality" of AOC wines has become less general or absolute than it once was. If fine wine belongs to the AOC universe, all AOC wines should not be automatically equated with fine wine. And according to some critics, a few fine wines do not even belong to the AOC universe at all.[6]

The fine-wines market has a long history. *Grands crus*, haute cuisine, and social elites have long been linked. Technical guides appeared, but only for the use of professionals, in the second half of the nineteenth century. It was only between the two world wars that taste and taste criteria became a matter of knowledge, especially in gastronomic circles. And the real boom did not occur before the 1970s–1980s, with the development of wine criticism (which emerged earlier in England and in the United States) and more generally with the building of a wine world.[7] With its journalists, cellarmen, supermarket and restaurant sommeliers, and merchants, with its allies—producers and consumers—and its means of public expression, it undertook to develop the mediation between supply and demand in the name of a central justification: "*we are here to inform and guide you when you go to buy.*" By using and proposing diversified judgment devices, wine criticism grew, constructing as it went the

[6]AOC is still a valid label for the present and the past, but a law passed in 2006 stipulated that it would be replaced by a new classification in 2009. At the top, AOP (*Appellation d'Origine Protégée*), with more stringent requirements, will replace AOC, and at the same time more freedom will be given to other wine producers. For a more developed discussion of the French appellation system, see T. Coleman, *Wine Politics* (Berkeley: University of California Press, 2008), pp. 37–66.

[7]The history of wine-book publishing is a good expression of this transformation; see J.-L. Fernandez, *La critique vinicole en France: Pouvoir de prescription et construction de la confiance* (Paris: L'Harmattan, 2004), pp. 189–238.

aesthetic, economic, and social world of fine wines. Embodied in the roles of technician, judge, teacher, guide, journalist, and high priest, wine critics managed to be present on all fronts.

As technicians, wine critics codified a vocabulary increasingly accepted by the public, they invented a language, they worked out protocols of judgment for comparative tasting, they supported the development of sensorial techniques, and some acted as consultants to producers. As judges, they applied themselves to knowing and making known a wide palette of wines, to organizing comparisons, and to formulating judgments, all of which relied on the systematic practice of tasting. They ensured that the outcomes were known by using a broad range of reputedly independent means of public expression, in particular the Betanne and Desseauve, Gault Millau, and Hachette guides, as well as some translated foreign guides like those of Hugh Johnson and, later, Robert Parker.[8] As journalists, they invented the specialized journals—in particular the *Revue du vin de France, Cuisine et vins de France,* and the "special wine" issue of *GaultMillau* magazine; they published there as well as in other less-known journals and in newspaper columns, and they held forth on radio and appeared on television.[9] They also invented a form of writing that would transmit sensations, and they succeeded in sharing their passion for wine, in particular with the new, well-heeled social classes eager to learn an art of the table that they assimilated to an art of living. As guides, wine critics were present through their daily advice in restaurants, in wine shops, and sometimes in supermarkets. As teachers, they developed training tools and instituted the moral rules of the art of drinking. As high priests, they devoted themselves to celebrating the belief in great wines as works of art.

All experts assert that critical evaluations are not expressions of pleasure or displeasure but rather of true knowledge, and for some of them, of science, although tasting—regarded as a professional tool of the competent expert—based on the twin criteria of convergence and repeatability of results, demonstrates more than anything the limits of oenological knowledge.[10] And yet the disappointments do not seem to perceptibly

---

[8] There is no shortage of wine guides in the New World or in the Old, especially as translations are numerous. French guides like Bettane and Desseauve, Hachette, Gault Millau are being or have been translated into English, and Robert Parker and Hugh Johnson lead the foreign guides in France.

[9] M.-F. Garcia-Parpet, "Styles de vie et manière de boire: Un marché de l'offre des biens de prescription oenologique," *Cahiers lillois d'économie et de sociologie* 41–42 (2003): 177–197; G. Teil, "La production du jugement esthétique sur les vins par la critique vinicole," *Sociologie du travail* 1 (2001): 67–89.

[10] Tasting a wine is . . . not a trivial task. We expected to find as much. . . . On the other hand we did not expect to find that training visibly did not make much difference." G. Morrot and F. Brochet, "La force des représentations dans la dégustation des vins," *Revue des oenologues* 97 (November 2000): 27–30.

lessen their authority. The respect extended to the vast array of knowledge deployed by critics may be one explanation, but another equally valid reason could be the collective belief—ceaselessly bolstered by public reference to art—that the choice of a fine wine introduces devotees into a (more) civilized world.

Critical devices—newspapers, radio, guides—predominated at the beginning of this evolution. They owed their diversity to wine critics, who combined a heterogeneous milieu with strong networks of personal contacts. This period was characterized by a plurality of aesthetic judgments, a more or less public discussion process, a generalized struggle over the definition of "fine" wine, and a belief in the validity of aesthetic judgment criteria and thereby a common reference to *art*.[11]

For a long time, the French market of fine wines relied on a conception deemed too obvious to be open to discussion. Based on the fragmented organization of wine production (reinforced by the creation of the AOC designation) and on a transformation that recognized the validity of tradition, the market's development was underpinned by three aporia: fine wines are incomparable; fine wines are defined by a plurality of taste judgments; fine wines are to be kept. Since choices were and still are guided by more than one logic, many producers are allowed their chance, for the universe of wine is one of mystery, discovery, judgment, and possible consecration. There is no clear limit to the number of fine wines, and the market is constantly pushing back the boundaries.

Since the 1970s–1980s, the market equipment has changed. Wine judgment devices have multiplied, diversified, and reached an ever broader public, while critics have come to occupy an increasingly central position and to assert themselves by the multiplication of judgment devices and qualification operations.

## The Hachette and the Parker Guides to Wine

Fine wines exacerbate the features that make it so hard to choose between singular products. All these wines have different tastes, which vary with the *terroir* and the year: this combination produces a very large number of singularities. Moreover, the judgment criteria used by producers, experts, and connoisseurs do not necessarily coincide, and the logics of action—when one exists—behind laymen's choices are diverse and usu-

---

[11] "The basis of this culture, that which constitutes, as it were, its basic belief, is that wine is regarded as an object of passion, of estheticization, of collection, of expert commentary." J.-L. Fernandez, *La critique vinicole*, p. 28; "a taste reference founded on esthetic appreciation," G. Teil, "Savoir si un vin est bon: le jugement de gout," *Revue des oenologues 96* (July 2000): 17–23.

ally vague. In these conditions, the reasonable adjustment between products and consumers can only be highly complicated—even unfeasible. It is to deal with such an opaque situation that guides were created. They occupy a strategic position, and as far as oriented credible knowledge is concerned, each of them offers its own solution.

Wine guides share one paradoxical characteristic: works devoted to the celebration of incommensurable individualities and to the demarcation of incomparable universes of taste turn into one-dimensional arrangements.[12] Of course they are substantial devices, and that means, theoretically, that the commentaries accompanying each selected wine cannot be separated from the ratings. In principle, the commentaries should make it impossible to confuse wines receiving the same rating or the same number of stars, but the social use of the guides often leads to a complete separation between the two forms of evaluation, for example, when advertising or sales catalogues use the rating in isolation as added information or for ease of consultation by hurried users.

Each guide also aims to express a particular aesthetic viewpoint. For instance, *Parker's Wine Buyer's Guide* has long asserted its preference for powerful, fruity wines and woody scents,[13] while the *Hachette Wine Guide* celebrates variety. Although these orientations may be the source of lively controversies and, according to some, may explain relative success and influence, other differences exist that may be more relevant and influential, like linguistic differences[14] or, of more interest to us here, the ways wine knowledge is constructed, organized, and presented, which amounts to studying the particular relationship that guides build with their readers. This can be seen from a comparison between the two guides.[15]

*Parker's Wine Buyer's Guide* and the *Hachette Wine Guide* are both big books, but comparing their indexes one discovers that the number of producers selected is around 2,000 for the first guide and 5,000 for the

[12]Robert Parker thus relentlessly maintains, in various ways, that "what makes a wine interesting is its individuality, . . . its unique taste," even though he gives the most detailed ratings of all of the critics.

[13]If a guide like Parker's is well enough known to influence producers' choices, it may have widespread effects. That explains the movie *Mondovino*, the sometime heated debates in France, and critical reactions even in the United States; see A. Feiring, *The Battle for Wine and Love: Or How I Saved the World from Parkerization* (Boston: Harcourt, 2008).

[14]Linguistic analysis of the commentaries of Jacques Dupont (*La Lettre de Gault & Millau*), Robert Parker (*The Wine Advocate*), the *Hachette Wine Guide*, and of a French winegrower shows the existence of different lexical universes, the only common feature being the existence of two different universes of terms for red and white wines. G. Morrot and F. Brochet, "La Force des représentations dans la dégustation des vins," *Revue des oenologues* 97 (2000): 27–30.

[15]*Hachette Wine Guide: The French Wine Bible* (Paris: Hachette, 2001), in English, and 2008, in French; *Parker's Wine Buyer's Guide* (New York: Simon & Schuster, 2002), in English, and 2008, in French.

second, and that the number of wine names is a little over 2,000 in one case and almost 10,000 in the other.

These large differences engender two main consequences. First, the Parker guide gives half-points on a scale of 50 to 100, but scores below 70 are rare (even though they do exist), so that the real scale runs from 70 to 100; while the Hachette guide distinguishes five categories of wines (one, two, or three stars, no star, and "our favorite"). It is therefore not hard to see from the indexes that each Parker rating is associated with an average of 330 wines, whereas the corresponding Hachette guide rating is linked to around 2,000 wines. As a result, when the wines are subdivided by color and by region, it is quite clear that the *Hachette Wine Guide*, with its broad categories, is a more "extensive" device than the Parker: it gives (or imposes on) its consumer a broader autonomy of choice.

Second, from one guide to the other, the world of wine is very different because the units of analysis are different. The Parker offers a selection of elite producers and several ratings for each wine according to year; while the Hachette guide selects only wines of the year, without taking into account whether or not the producer is well known. The first guide is oriented more toward historical diversity and the second toward territorial diversity. As a result, the world of the first guide is on the whole simpler and more elitist with fewer discoveries than the second. Each guide has created a different world. The same is true for the other guides as well.

This comparison helps in formulating a loose definition of a fine wine. The notion is delimited neither by rules—general, administrative, or other—nor by common norms: it is a convention. Therefore the composition and extension of the world of fine wines vary with the different viewpoints. Fortunately, the "great guides" share a large core of names with, of course, some confusion and conflict along the boundaries.[16] Perhaps should we accept at least that a wine should be considered as "fine" if the ratings given by the most influential guides serve as a true asset in the competitive struggle—and of course if they follow the particular logic of the singularities markets.

By circumscribing the market and structuring the supply, guides offer direct help in coming to a decision. Their relative effectiveness depends on how well the presentation of knowledge fits the user's skills and competences. The more "restrictive" the guide, the more useful it is to laymen; the more "extensive" it is, the better suited it is to connoisseurs. This relationship is one of the causes of the strategic position occupied by *Parker's Wine Buyer's Guide*, since it is more useful to laymen, who are by far the most numerous buyers.

[16] In an essay on the same topics, after having listed several relevant dimensions, each followed by a few examples, Parker, without making a general list, reaches the same conclusion; see introduction to *Parker's Wine Buyer's Guide*, 2002.

## The Intelligentsia, Connoisseurs, and the Layman

The development of the fine-wines market has seen a continuous rise in the number of judgment devices; commercial devices have joined the "critical" devices, and both have multiplied with time and have added to the personal networks that always existed. Purchasing practices reveal their degrees of effectiveness.

For many, reasoned access to the market is complicated, and yet in various forms, large numbers of clients display an active and autonomous commitment. Connoisseurs and those laymen who use a guide or some other system of evaluation that suits their level of competence have the means to make a relatively sure choice, but they are only a small minority. Connoisseurs belong to networks, clubs, and associations, and they read and criticize the guides and journals. They are the militant base of the wine world, and they often distinguish themselves by the sales circuit they use: direct purchase at the winemakers and shopping at specialty wine shops, which sell some unknown wines and dispense learned advice. Neither of those options prevent informed buying at the supermarket.

Laymen and semi-laymen are by far the most numerous. They drink occasionally. They are not unaware of the specialty stores but usually shop at the supermarket, which accounts in France for 70 percent of all wine sales.[17] Some are drawn to wine fairs, where they seek out advisers—when they can find one—and some rely on personal networks. These consumers are following rather useful cues. The rest are faced with aisles of shelves displaying several hundreds of bottles of fine wines at various prices.

In this situation, the consumer's action expresses the tension between the desire to choose for him- or herself and the distress engendered by comparisons that are all the harder to make as the shelves are so ill-suited to that purpose. Everything can therefore come into play for those who follow the autonomous individualized path: advertising, labels, bottle aesthetic, color, brand name, information, region, and so on.[18] Furthermore, while supermarket prices can vary by a factor ranging from 1 to 100, the lowest price is not "highly determining."[19] Even when they are on their own, this is not a criterion consumers use. Or to put it other way,

---

[17] ONIVINS-INFO 106 (2003): 39 (the review of the Office National Interprofessionnel des vins [Interprofessional National Wine Association]).

[18] The marketing-studies reviews list a large number of causes affecting individual choices. But this result has to be taken with caution as it comes from surveys and not from studies of purchasing behavior; see "Comprendre la démarche d'achat des consommateurs en grande distribution," ONIVINS-INFOS 100 (January 2003).

[19] "Certain characteristics of wine are not particularly determining, for example price." Survey by ONIVINS INRA on wine consumption in France in 2000 with a representative sample of 4,000 persons, ONIVINS-INFO 91 (March 2002): 11.

they use it quite often, but in reverse: the higher price is taken for a sign of quality. However, they are by no means sure of winning their wager.

If those unfamiliar with wine criticism still do not feel free to choose on the basis of the lowest price or of random indicators, it is because the wine world has succeeded in building a social norm and having it recognized: the choice of a fine wine should be based on a judgment, one's own or another's. In not following this rule, one would be committing an *ethical* sin. A reasonable choice of wine is a civilized practice. Such an obligation, expressed and conveyed in many ways, has become general; it suffices to observe the care with which wine labels are read and the assiduity with which advice is sought to understand that this is a serious matter.[20]

The same rule also explains that the guides do not take price into account when rating wines. Prices feature (though not always), but with the exception of specific guides devoted to good, low-cost wines, they play no part in the judgment. The same is true for tastings, except when one wants to highlight ratings in which a much less expensive wine has outperformed the others. And the same rule explains that, in supermarkets, buyers would hesitate less if they were basing their purchase on price alone. No better demonstration can be found that quality competition prevails over price competition.

These observations enable us to draw the portrait of the lay consumer. For him or her, gathering information is a matter of hit and miss, itineraries are diverse, deliberations can take some time, and purchases can hold surprises: sometimes pleasant, sometimes unwelcome. This consumer is not irrational; he simply relies on the wrong signals for comparing his possible choices. One might think that tasting would be "the" solution. This is not the case, however, since the layman is usually not looking for the wine he likes but for the wine experts say he is supposed to like. With time, practice, and experience, some manage to acquire a sufficient repertory of "good" wines and, from then on, are no longer game for an adventure they know to be costly and whose outcome is unpredictable. That outcome accounts for the often observed but largely unexplained fact that, for fine wines, purchases are often guided by habit.

How is it that, in spite of the changes that have occurred in the market over the past twenty or thirty years, when it comes to buying fine wine, more than half of the clientele find themselves on the spot? Why have the

[20] "More than any other product, the gustatory qualities (of wine) are the most determining attributes of quality. . . . Even rank novices do not think twice about using a specific vocabulary to express their impressions of a wine's taste and voice a judgment about its quality." L. Sirieix, "L'apprentissage de la qualité par le consommateur: L'avis des experts est-il pertinent?" *Actes de la 5ème journée de Recherche en Marketing de Bourgogne* (Dijon, 2000).

increasingly numerous judgment devices and the many forms of wine criticism not been able to do a better job of expanding the domain of knowledge so as to allow reasonable choices? For instance, in supermarkets, seven out of ten consumers—the percentage is virtually the same regardless of sex or age—agree that it is "hard to choose a wine."[21] More than one in two customers has neither the competence nor the help without which it is impossible to make an enlightened choice. Why do they persist?

What are the French drinking when they drink wine? A long history, which combines *grands crus* with social elites—first churchmen, then princes and kings, and finally the grand bourgeoisie—with an extreme diversity of tastes, soils, and skills, with literary celebration and with brotherhoods. To the question, what does it mean to be French today? we find in fourth place the answer, to be French is first of all to like fine wine.[22] Wine bears a collective identity rooted in the past and in the soil. It gives rise to knowledge and belief—and to loyalty, passions, and commitment. This legacy has enabled wine criticism to engage actively in a triple qualification of wines, of consumers, and of its own function.

The periodical requalification of wines is the inevitable outcome of the struggles between critics as they become more and more knowledgeable and as they incessantly redefine the fine wines at the same time as they alter their systems of justification. The growing singularization of fine wines results from a strategic alliance between critics, producers, and *grande cuisine*; it also stems from the expansion of a literature devoted to the aesthetic celebration of "outstanding vintages," which escorts them on their rise to the status of luxury and art.[23] Lastly, it is inseparable from a new well-to-do bourgeoisie and a new international clientele, who have become the actors of the formation and development of the new beaux-arts which bear the names gastronomy and oenology.

Judging wine has become more exacting as wine criticism, with the new knowledge it has produced and mobilized and with its increasingly assertive cultural reference, has been transformed into a new intelligentsia. The overqualification of fine wines, accompanied by the rising technical competences and upward social mobility of critics, had as its inevitable by-product the loss of the cognitive and social position of part

---

[21] For regular and occasional consumers, the percentages are 67 and 79 percent, respectively. Survey by INRA-ONIVINS 2000 on a sample of 4,010 persons over fourteen years of age, *ONIVINS-INFOS* 84 (June 2001): 11.

[22] See G. Durand, "La vigne et le vin," in P. Nora (ed.), *Les lieux de mémoire*, vol. 3 (Paris: Gallimard, 1997), pp. 3711–3741.

[23] "Numerous French products are the embodiment of luxury, whether haute couture or fine cuisine. I do not think the image of France is hurt by the most prestigious "grand crus" being rated like works of art." R. Parker, *Le Monde*, 16–17 September 2001.

of the consumers. Unwilling to retrain periodically or unaware of the necessity—even though wine schools are on the increase—semi-connoisseurs or semi-laymen of good will are experiencing a partial loss of their competence and joining the ranks of layman. In other words, rapid production of new knowledge, when not balanced by equivalent training, engenders a *cognitive pauperization* of those buyers whose competence is the most fragile.

Together the equipment of the fine-wines market and the dynamics of the wine-culture complex define the terms of a problem encountered sooner or later by every market of singularities: how much ignorance is compatible with continuity, not to say development, of the market?

## Vulnerability of the French Fine-Wines Market?

The fine-wines market in France is based largely on small producers and on barriers to entry that do not bar newcomers: small winemakers can be very successful. But alongside the small and medium-size wineries, one finds the most famous châteaux, whose development is the result of heavy technical investments and energetic marketing: these are on their way to the mega regime.

Upon this material basis, the fine-wines market concentrates the main characteristics of the authenticity regime: large numbers of products carrying a rich symbolism, numerous judgment devices, primacy of quality competition over price competition, relatively balanced competitive forces, critical pluralism, promotion of customer competence, activity and autonomy, and fairly strong consumer commitment. The close link between this market and the authenticity regime presupposes relative independence between the symbolic and economic logics.

The fine-wines market relies on two antithetical types of consumer: the expert and the connoisseur driven by a sufficiently strong aesthetic passion to invest thought, time, and money to arrive at the desired choices; and the layman, often thrown back on trial-and-error. And there is a large variation in between. But the fact that one in two consumers considers it hard to choose a wine gives a realistic idea of the *ineffectiveness of the existing judgment devices*. The persisting cognitive deficit explains that disappointing purchases are far from the exception. The extent of the cognitive deficit distinguishes the market of fine wines from most of the other markets.

Logically, a lack of competence should be compensated by judgment devices. When these are not sufficiently effective, the market can only fall back on the strength of trust. The collective belief in the symbolic value of wine, particularly in France, is deep-rooted. Wine is considered to be part of an identity linked to culture, art and, even, civilization; it may also be conceived as an *adherence* relation to a quasi world of pleasure or distinction. Whatever the case may be, belief must be robust and enduring, continually reinforced by the action of a cultural complex in order to explain why—for so long—so many buyers have engaged in practices whose repetition does not really reduce their difficulties and their wanderings.

The market's strengths can become its weaknesses. France, which has for so long a time held the top position in the foreign markets, is now threatened by increasing exports from America, Australia, and Chile, to Great Britain in particular, but in reality, to the whole world—including France. Given the growth of the wine industry in new countries, some of this redistribution of international trade is inevitable. But as it happens, the evolution is all the more dangerous for France because the economic struggle also challenges the French model of wine qualification and thus the entire French system of production.

As the story is often told, the competitive struggle amounts to a conflict between small and medium-size producers and a few big firms, between the Old World and the New, between the *appellation wines* and the *brand wines*. Such a picture is only partially true, since appellation wines are also produced in the New World, and brand wines are already produced and will be increasingly produced in the Old World.[24] Even if big American and Australian firms are the present leaders of the brand-wine industry, the great divide will probably run through both the Old and the New Worlds.

What is at stake in this opposition? It is not quality versus no quality, but two different conceptions of quality. Brand wine is characterized by large-scale production of good, pleasant-tasting, stable, and homogeneous wines, while appellation wines feature particularism, variability, and surprises—some pleasant, some unpleasant. Or, to put it differently, on the one hand, there are a limited number of wines with an easy choice and a predictable outcome and, on the other, numerous wines with a complicated choice and uncertain results. Even so, the picture is too simple if one takes seriously Parker's observation that technology brings "standardization to such a point that it becomes difficult to distinguish between an Italian, a French, a Californian or an Australian chardonnay."[25] And he would certainly not disagree with the reminder that "the

[24] M.-F. Garcia-Parpet, "Markets, prices and symbolic value: Grands crus and the challenges of global markets," *International Review of Sociology* 18, no. 2 (July 2008): 237–252; E. Giraud-Heraud and Y. Surry, "Les réponses de la recherche aux nouveaux enjeux de l'économie viti-vinicole," *Vignes et vins* 60–61: 1–24. See also Coleman, *Wine Politics*, pp. 103–106.

[25] Introduction to *Parker's Wine Buyer's Guide*, 2002.

infinity of possible combinations makes the individuality of each appellation, of each vintage year, of each producer and almost of each bottle."[26]
The conflict between the different universes is both real and global. It
involves different tastes, different relations to nature and technology, and
different conceptions of the consumer.

In the debate prompted by the crisis in the French wine industry in
2002–2005,[27] which only marginally affected the *grands crus* but more
seriously the AOC wines, the brand-wine threat was largely raised and
discussed. Two kinds of solutions were evoked: those linked to the traditional crisis of overproduction and proposals to develop brand wines.
Nothing specific to the appellation wines was really considered: no pro-
posal to transform the judgment devices, no appeal to technical ingenuity
to reduce—in France and elsewhere—the ignorance and uncertainty concerning the appellation logic that so severely hampers the possibility of
making reasoned choices and is weakening the wine industry. It is odd
that producers and sellers have not been and are still not concerned to
invent new or to improve existing judgment devices, whereas this is the
only way—in France or elsewhere—to enlarge informed choice.

Thus the choice, in terms of the tastes of wines and consumers' tastes—
no small issue in France and elsewhere—rests mainly on the solidity of belief and on its corollary, the mixture of goodwill and hesitation long displayed by those who attempt to make reasoned choices. To be sure, brand
wines and appellation wines are incommensurable realities: they thrust together two worlds. But such incommensurabilities have already been compared, and the barrier of the belief in the superiority of appellations has
already been partially breached abroad. Is it going to hold more successfully in France? And elsewhere? No one knows. But we do know that the
competitors are megafirms with enough technical and financial resources
to eventually succeed in dismantling their opponents' symbolic systems,
even those with a long history. And we also know that trust/belief does not
always follow the model of slow erosion over time. In all events, there is a
theoretical consequence to the comparison: one world is based on differentiation and the other on singularization. One should be addressed by mainstream economics and the other by the economics of singularities.

•   •   •

Because it is an extreme example, the fine-wines market clearly shows the
combination of characteristics that define the authenticity regime: (1) a

---

[26] M. Bettane and T. Desseauve, introduction to *The World's Greatest Wines* (New York: HNA Books, 2006).

[27] J. Berthomeau, *Comment mieux positionner les vins français sur les marchés d'expor-tation?* Report for the French Minister of Agriculture, 2001.

large diversity of product names and tastes as well as of consumers' tastes or logics of action, along with the threats rising from an opaque market; (2) the central position occupied by substantial impersonal judgment devices acting through competitive struggles and whose credible knowledge will orient consumers' action all the more because they possess a high degree of symbolic authority; (3) the active presence of trust/belief, which is all the more necessary for consumer choice and market continuity because knowledge should be credible; (4) varied forms of adjustment, which express the various forms of encounter between the tastes proposed by the devices, the tastes of the products, and the forms of consumer commitment; (5) a pervasive model of originality that reveals its presence, within financial constraints, mainly by the primacy of quality competition over price competition and by the relative adequacy of the regime components; and finally (6) the diversity of the efficiency of the coordination regime according to the effectiveness of the judgment devices, consumer competence, and forms of commitment. Even if one crucial cog is missing—price and pricing—the authenticity regime can be studied and characterized through the fine-wines market. In this sense, it is relevant to other concrete markets like art goods, some elite luxury goods, gastronomy, classical music, or books.

## Chapter Eleven

# THE MEGA REGIME

ORIGINALLY PART of the authenticity regime and then
its competitor, the mega regime differs by the scale
of its action. Megafilms, luxury-products megafirms,
and megabrands necessarily mean international, and
sometimes world, scales. While the aesthetic criterion tends more or less to prevail over the profitability
criterion, nevertheless the tension between them is
much more acute in the large market than in the
small market, and that explains the difficulty of formulating a general rule for the formation of the different balance states.

| |
|---|
| Impersonal devices<br>Substantial devices<br>Large market |
| *Active and<br>heteronomous<br>consumers* |
| Reference to<br>originality/<br>aesthetic logic |

The continuity of singularities therefore cannot be taken for granted.
In effect, it is not unconceivable that increasing production, expanding
exchange, and especially short-term high-profit seeking would lead to a
transformation of the product. And can we not assume that the transformations of these products necessarily entail parallel transformations in
the consumer such that their autonomy will not impede the logic of action required by the new products? The evolution of the mega regime is
quite problematic.

The internal diversity of the mega regime is too great to be embodied
in a single market. Megafilms, luxury-goods megafirms, and megabrands
have been selected as examples because, *in that order*, they show the increasing tension created by the large market. And in following that order,
the analysis will deal with effects of the changes in the balance between
aesthetics and profit criteria.

## MEGAFILMS

Year in, year out in all big French cities, the moviegoer can chose from
hundreds of new films in addition to many rescreenings. This market is
sufficiently familiar to allow us merely to list its characteristics: films are
singularities, quality uncertainty exists, advertising deploys its full arse-
nal to prevent the consumer from purely and simply reproducing his
tastes, and finding a "good" movie is the customer's first aim and implies

an active commitment. The adjustment between movies and moviegoers, all guided by diverse logics of choice, may look like a matter of hit and miss, but every week choices are made which must not all be disappointing, since customers come back more or less regularly.

The last thirty years have been marked by the production of blockbusters and their spectacular promotion. Invented in the United States as a means of preventing the disappearance of a movie industry threatened by television, the blockbuster employs means not used by television to seduce and captivate viewers from all cultures, countries, and social classes. This "world cinema" targets primarily young people, who make up the bulk of audiences everywhere: it aims for universal meaning.[1]

For most analysts in France, this evolution should explain the decline of "classical" movies. This category of films belongs more to the authenticity than to the mega regime, and it encompasses *films d'auteur*, arthouse cinema, and underground movies. It is characterized by reference to the film as a work of art,[2] as well as by stars, medium-size budgets, medium- or long-term profit, vigorous criticism, and a varied audience. Alternatively, while it retains the star and the search for originality, the blockbuster breaks with the classical movie by its megabudget,[3] and by the special effects and the sophisticated marketing strategies. Blockbusters are certainly not a new genre: crowds flocked to see *Ben Hur*, *Gone with the Wind*, and *The Ten Commandments* in their time, but these were exceptions; today the spectacular big-budget film is a regular production of the movie industry.

As the latest metamorphosis of the popular movie, the megafilm is supposed to correspond to the new moviegoers' tastes; and Americans, who are reputedly the only ones with the financial means, talent, and industry to produce them, are therefore held responsible for the disappearance of the classical cinema. The evolution of the film industry seems to confirm this prediction, since in France the number of moviegoers who usually prefer classical French films has grown, whereas ticket sales for theaters showing these films has not ceased to decline. Although statistics support this evolution, it does not mean that their usual interpretation is correct, as the examination of the relationship between movies, judgment devices,

---

[1] For example, George Lucas's *Star Wars* (1977), Steven Spielberg's *E.T.* (1982), or James Cameron's *Titanic* (1998).

[2] The claim that film is an art form is old. It found its most intransigent expression after the Second World War in André Bazin's criticism and in the *Cahiers du cinéma*. Serge Daney has maintained that rigor. The counterpart of the artistic conception of movies is the primacy of the *auteur*, that is, the director. As J. P. Esquenazi shows in "Le film, un fait social" (*Réseaux* (2000): 11–47), the conception of the cinema as an art leads to neglecting the "question of the audience."

[3] The average budget of the films produced by the American "majors" is ten times the average budget of a French movie. But every year a few French movies have similar budgets.

and customers' choices will show. Beyond this issue, the blockbuster has redefined economic success and is an expression of a specific form of rationality that can be identified in other markets of singularities. To resolve this small historical anomaly is to open the way to the global study of a market that has redefined economic success

## Movie-Market Judgment Devices

The rule is "nobody knows." Radical uncertainty about the success of movies persists however much talent is recruited, capital invested, and marketing launched. Nearly two-thirds of big-budget movies are financial failures, while medium-budget films can be big commercial successes.[4] Nevertheless, the inflation of blockbuster budgets continues since, when success comes, it comes with a bang.[5] In all events, the income from merchandising, and television and DVD sales limits the financial risks.

The continuity of this Hollywood policy is rooted in the belief that, whatever the theme, style, and worth of the films, sales techniques are sufficiently sophisticated to control the final market. Of course this does not guarantee success, but it should increase its probability. Such faith in market tools is fundamental:[6] it explains the massive role of marketing and the imbalance between critical opinion and promotion, between critical and commercial judgment devices. Stars, advertising, posters, trailers, TV launches, control of the screens, and merchandising are used to achieve commercial and financial success. In the mega regime, promotion seems to leave little room for viewer autonomy. Faced with huge and diversified audiences, judgment devices must make the film visible and desirable, as well as neutralize the influence of autonomous judgment processes embodied in word of mouth, criticism, and the cultural complex.

The megafilm cannot do without what we continue to call *stars* but which have become more like *celebrities*. The star of the 1950s was the personification of seduction and glory; he or she was above other humans and relied on fascination and adulation to captivate spectators: "Over an

[4]In France, in millions of ticket sales: *Trois hommes et un couffin* (English remake: *Three Men and a Baby*) (10.2 in 1985), *Les visiteurs* (13.8 in 1993), *Le dîner de cons* (9.2 in 1998), *Le fabuleux destin d'Amélie Poulain* (8.2 in 2001), *Les choristes* (*The Choristers*) (8.4 in 2004), *Les bronzés 3* (10.3 in 2006), *Bienvenu chez les Ch'tis* (11.4 in 2007).

[5]*Titanic* is in a class of its own. It was released in 1999, with worldwide box-office sales of $1 billion for a production cost of around $200 million.

[6]The proportion of marketing expenses out of the total film cost in the USA has risen on average from 10 percent in 1989 to 25 percent in 1999 to 37 percent in 2007 (*World Film Market Trends*, Focus 2007, Observatoire européen de l'audiovisuel [European Audiovisual Observatory], http://www.obs.coe.int).

immense part of the globe, in an immense sector of film production, movies revolved around a solar figure fittingly called the star." Composed of "the most valuable and therefore the most costly substance, the star was one of the mythic beings that people the collective imaginary."[7] It is not certain that today's movie stars are of the same order: fame matters more.

A symbolic gap separates the star from the celebrity. The star belonged to the world of demigods and merely inhabited his or her body,[8] whereas the celebrity stands at the summit of a trajectory that others can follow. They and we are of the same nature. Desacralization has made great strides. Film celebrities thus take their place among the other elites of a stratified and pluralist society, a position accessible to all who have won the competitive struggle. There was no economics of stardom, but there is an economics of celebrity. For celebrity—in film, popular music, fashion, and sport—attracts an audience.

Blockbuster launches include a range of operations programmed to mesh with the release: trailers, posters, publicity launch, press interviews, TV promotion. The programming is by now well oiled. Competition depends less on the price of the ticket than on the conception of the venue (traditional theater, art houses, and multiplexes) and on the number of film copies, a mechanism used to control the screens. Whereas in France the maximum number of copies for a release used to be around fifty, in the space of a few years it grew to seven hundred (for *Titanic*), and today approaches a thousand for exceptional launches. It is no longer enough to make movies, they have to get screened. Controlling the screens has become one of the strategic choices for, even if the film flops, there is the hope of bringing in the biggest audience possible before critical opinion gets around, and at the same time, perhaps a chance to block the release of rival films. The blockbuster launch provides all-in-one protection from other movies, film critics, and word of mouth. Megafilms therefore do not "travel" without their market equipment.

Some analysts consider the crisis of quality movies to stem from the evolution of the film and promotion.[9] Banality, according to this logic, is merely the consequence of a competitive dynamic that mobilizes increasing volumes of capital, favors economic concentration, intensifies the economic struggle by the inflation of megabudgets and short-term maximum-profit seeking, encourages the multiplication of film copies, and finally, imposes trenchant verdicts that increase the turnover rate and at the same time

[7] E. Morin, *The Stars* (New York: Grove Press, 1960).

[8] "The person called Elizabeth Taylor is a fabrication." Remark attributed to Elizabeth Taylor.

[9] L. Creton, "Le cinema et l'argent: L'emprise du paradigme budgétaire," in L. Creton (ed.), *Le cinéma et l'argent* (Paris: Nathan, 1999), pp. 31–44.

doom classical cinema, which is profitable only over the middle term. The reasoning looks irrefutable, but it is far from realistic. In effect, by this logic, judgment devices and the moviegoers' margin of action are excluded from the picture.

## The Effectiveness of Devices

Whereas in France the share of "frequent" and "regular" moviegoers, who are in principle the most drawn to French classical films, grew between 1986 and 1999, the share of the audience of American films screened in France also appears to have increased at the same time. Thus one more fraction of the movie audience seems to have succumbed to the attraction of American films in general and blockbusters in particular. But comparison of the distribution practices for French and American films suggests an entirely different reading of the figures.

Table 3 shows the promotion practices for French and American films, broken down into megafilms and small films. It shows that, for movies with small or medium-size diffusion budgets, American films are released to three times as many screens as French films, are promoted in more original ways, and spend twice as much on promotion.

Global comparisons of the budgets devoted to American and French movies are part of the usual explanation for the decline of the French film industry. But Table 3 fails to sustain the received wisdom. The gap between promotion budgets does not exist for blockbusters: it concerns only the medium-size and especially the small movies (fewer than twenty copies; and fewer than twenty-five thousand, and sometimes even fewer than ten thousand, tickets sold). Unlike the French, American producers use judgment devices to make *all* of their movies visible and attractive.

When distributors simply post copies of good reviews at the door, those who have already made their choice are happy, but those who have not gone down to the theater are left in the dark. If theaters showing classical French films clearly draw fewer viewers than those screening equivalent American films, it is not because moviegoers have suddenly gone over to American culture, it is more prosaically because the French movies are invisible and therefore do not exist on the market. Their fate depends on an exceptional event such as a review in a large newspaper or the commitment of a network. Without judgment devices, movies and movie houses play no part in the struggle to capture an audience.

The data clearly shows the increase in the number of viewers of American films and the decline in the numbers that go to classical films; but the explanation is not the draw of the American cinema, it has to do with the

TABLE 3
American Movie-Judgment Devices Compared to French
Movie-Judgment Devices (1996–1999)

| | |
|---|---|
| Number of screens for new releases | Twice as many for American as for French movies |
| Release date | In Summer too/Not in summer |
| Monopoly of release screens | Sometimes/Never |
| Marketing budget | Twice as much |
| Number of movie/TV trailers | Twice as many |
| Overall promotion budget | Twice as much |
| Promotion quality | Originality/Standardization |
| Megafilms | |
| Promotion budget | The same |
| Small Films | |
| Number of screens | Three times as many |
| Promotion budget | Two to three times as much |

Source: D. Goudineaud, *La distribution des films en salles en France*, Paris: Ministère de la Culture, 2000. (The table is based on years for which the complete series of data was available.)

modesty of the judgment devices accompanying classical French movies, which is tantamount to excluding them from the competition. The French market knows how to use traditional devices like criticism, the network, and film culture; however, for whatever reasons, in the case of the small and medium films, it seems unaware that judgment devices are now part of the necessary conditions for putting these movies on the market.

## The Hit: Part 1

The economic model of blockbuster success is the "hit": the inescapable world mobilization of spectators to attend a movie whose foregone success says that nobody should miss it. But a majority of blockbusters are not hits, though they are very costly. Therefore we have to understand the strategies developed to limit risk before we go on to propose an interpretation of the distinctive hit market

Moviegoers should be separated neither from criticism nor from the cultural status of movies nor from their networks. Critics write and publish;

they are the only ones whose job it is not only to judge but also to justify their judgment. They occupy a key position in the authenticity regime and yet are not marginalized in the mega regime, despite the strength of promotion and the intensive use of a television culture that entertains a confusion between criticism and admiration-to-order. Newspapers seem no longer to be commensurate with promotion, but their influence should not be underrated insofar as they are read by those moviegoers who are themselves opinion leaders.

Movies are also a prime topic of conversation and sociability, and the movie-goer is infinitely more active, more autonomous, and better capable of interpretation than the whole mechanism of commercial persuasion suggests. Reactions, opinions, and rejections travel along the networks and can, on their own, sometimes make or break a work. Such surprises are not rare: they attest to viewers' autonomous and informed capacities for action.

Nowadays, the launch of a megafilm is organized to protect the blockbuster from criticism. It is based on the distinction between the *release of the film*, which rests on stars and promotion, and the *exploitation of the film*, which varies with critical opinion and word of mouth. The release is confined to the short interval of time before the film critics make their appearance. With respect to former practices, it is characterized by the replacement of time by space: a blockbuster is now released in the greatest number of countries and theaters possible, accompanied by stars and commercial promotion. It is during this short period that communication and advertising budgets can make all the difference. Between 25 and 50 percent of the box-office take is made the first weekend. In another one or two weekends, with the exception of very big hits, it's all over. If this is not a blitzkrieg, it is at least a blitz-capture of the audience at a moment when critical opinion is not yet known.

Implicit homage to the efficiency of the market of singularities: the transformation of the film release into an event designed to arouse desire for the singularity is fully effective only if it can fend off the intervention of independent judgment devices. When this strategy is successful, the blockbuster thrives in the market enchanted by stars and promotion. This is risk reduction.[10] Afterwards comes exploitation. This is the time of word of mouth and critical opinion; it is the period when the viewing audience vanishes or, on the contrary, seems destined to swell and swell and so to create *the hit*. This extension is also a mutation based on viewer action.

[10]L. Menand, "Is the blockbuster the end of cinema?" *The New Yorker*, 7 February 2005.

## The Hit: Part 2

How does one choose a film? The theory of social classes and the theory of *rational addiction* agree on the same proposition: culture is drawn to culture. [11] But this proposition is of little help in understanding the relationship between the diversity of influences and the diversity of viewer paths. We will use an impressionistic classification that helps to collect and put together data on works, devices, and customer choice logics: it is based on a typology that organizes the available statistics on frequent, regular, and occasional moviegoers.[12]

"Frequent" moviegoers go at least once a week and many rush to see all new releases: we can call them "first-week viewers." In France, they are relatively few—3.6 percent of the audience—but they represent nearly a quarter of all tickets sold. Insatiable and eclectic, all films interest them: new releases, innovations, *films d'auteur*. They get their information mainly from television, trade magazines, and networks. They display a great deal of cinematographic competence, nearly half are "erudite"; their logics of action are as much a matter of fashion as of love of the cinema. They tell on average some fifteen people what they thought of a movie, and three out of four follow their advice; they thus have a great deal of personal influence: these are the *opinion leaders*.[13]

"Regular" moviegoers—almost a third of the audience and nearly half of all tickets sold—see at least one movie a month; they are most often adults who choose films on the basis of available information and their own logics of action. Their capital of film knowledge, when it exists, is specialized and acts as a principle for choosing quality films. These viewers make up the bulk of the classical-movie clientele; it is among this group that one finds those who frequent the art houses. In general they use more than one source of information, they attribute great importance to the network, and it is they who are most interested in criticism. Actively

---

[11] On the theory of social classes, see P. Bourdieu, *La distinction: Critique sociale du jugement* (Paris: Editions de Minuit, 1979) (*Distinction: A social critique of the judgment of taste*, trans. Richard Nice ([Cambridge, MA: Harvard University Press, 1979, 1984]); O. Donnat, "La stratification sociale des pratiques culturelles et son évolution 1973–1997," *Revue française de sociologie* (January–March 1999): 111–119.

On rational addiction, see G. J. Stigler and G. S. Becker, "De gustibus non est disputandum," *American Economic Review* (March 1977): 76–90. See also R. Caves, *Creative Industries: Contracts between Art and Commerce* (Cambridge, MA: Harvard University Press, 2001), p. 177.

[12] On the respective sizes of the three categories in 2006: 3.6 percent of viewers and 24 percent of ticket sales; 31.2 percent of viewers and 47.3 of ticket sales; and 65.2 percent of viewers and 26.7 percent of ticket sales ("75 000 Cinéma," [*CNC-Médiamétrie*, 2006]).

[13] E. Katz and P. F. Lazarsfeld, *Personal Influence* (Glencoe: Free Press, 1955), pp. 296–308.

involved in interpersonal relations, they, together with their counterparts among the frequent moviegoers, form the group of proselytizers committed to the persuasion of their entourage.

"Occasional" moviegoers"—two-thirds of the audience but less than a quarter of ticket sales—prefer television to movies but make an exception at least once a year, usually prompted by a particularly sweeping promotional campaign on TV, to see the screen "event." They want to be entertained. Their presence explains the exceptional spikes in attendance, as in the case of *Titanic*. It is also in this group that one finds those who choose their film at random, particularly in the multiplexes.

The eclecticism of moviegoers with a great deal of cinematographic competence protects the market from a genre-based fragmentation and maintains the continuity of the singular products.

Although the data are not really adequate, they are at least compatible with a realistic view of the ways moviegoers participate in shaping a hit. *Hits are not based on imitation but on a large-scale multiplication of commitment, mobilization, and circulation of quality judgments*, together with the activation of a number of judgment devices, which, if given enough time, can balloon in unforeseen proportions. The interaction between the various judgment devices thus becomes inseparable from the interactions between viewers, analysis of which has shown that the great majority are active and ready to share what they like. They are the opinion leaders and proselytizers mentioned above. Insofar as each viewer is linked with another network, the mobilization can extend rapidly and on a potentially grand scale.

With increases in the strength and scope of the interaction between the star, movie criticism, promotion, and viewer networks comes a growing disparity in the success of different films, regularly resulting in a highly unequal distribution of income and profits: 20 percent of films account for 80 percent of the market's overall take, and between 5 and 20 percent of films concentrate 80 percent of the market's global profit.

•  •  •

The movie market is hybrid: it comes under both the authenticity regime and the mega regime. In the first, one finds the continuity of a culture and an aesthetic, which enables *each film to exist for itself*, as well as a capacity for judgment on the part of the critics, to be sure, but also on the part of the intelligentsia and a large share of the viewers. In the second, besides the usual industry, one finds big budgets, promotion, and commercial "coups." Between the two, the role of financial logic has changed considerably. Yet until now, profit seeking has not really jeopardized aesthetic demand, as attested to by the fact that a good portion of the audience has no difficulty in passing from one genre to the other, from classical films to blockbusters. Thus the continuity of the market of singularities is maintained.

The movie market is also heterogeneous. Two characteristics stand out as being more meaningful than others. On one hand, the market is equipped: no movie can do without judgment devices. On the other hand, from time to time, a movie scores an immense economic success. This cannot be explained by the impersonal or personal devices alone: it is the result of the rapid enlargement of their spheres of interactions under the impulse of movie-goers' commitments.

## THE LUXURY MEGAFIRM

While the magnificence of the objects with which the social elites surround themselves has a long history, the luxury industry itself did not appear until the nineteenth century, and then it only began to redefine itself in the 1970s by passing from the small to the large market, from familial capitalism to financial capitalism. At this point, the tension between singularities and profitability became a constituent component of the "luxury" firms.

The luxury-goods industry concentrates a number of contradictory features. It is rooted in the past and it plays the "high-tech" card. It was a traditional, largely national, artisanal activity; it is now largely composed of dynamic, big, world corporations with high rates of returns. Its creations used to be anonymous; today they are signed by famous names. And it practices the denial of luxury, which is supposed to have disappeared as the industry developed; the proof is said to be the make-up of the clientele, of which a large portion now comes from the middle classes. This line of reasoning will guide the elucidation of a collective logic that is not apparent at first sight; it will require clarification of the relationship between the opposing aims of "good taste" and the "disappearance of luxury goods"; it will demand determining what brands mean and what holds all these components of the megamarket together.

### Good Taste

In one of the supplements periodically published by newspapers and magazines, the advertising consists of superb pictures accompanied by lyrical prose. Such is the case, for example, of one brochure devoted to wristwatches. It claims to decipher the new trends, the old favorites, and the eternal classics;[14] it is dominated by luxury brands; and it presents a

---

[14] *Spécial montres*, Supplément publicitaire, *Libération*, 5 April 2002, 60 pp.

selection of watches that are original, partially incomparable, mostly produced in limited series—between twenty-eight and five hundred pieces—
and priced in the upper ranges. They are packaged in a discourse extol-
ling the creation of the "use value" of the high-tech object, time as an
"absolute luxury," "beauty," the "quest for singularity," "identity," "hedonistic pleasure," "nomadic intelligence." Here and there, a phrase suggests the resurgence of social standing by almost inadvertent euphemistic
expressions or by the casual juxtaposition of the unexpected with the
costly—"a few diamonds sprinkled on a steel mechanism gives it a new
worldly nobility," "Enriching the face of a platinum chronograph with a
circle of diamonds magnifies its function"— or by the celebration of watches
indicating the time zones, which become "multipliers of time" and give
rise to "temporal multichromatism," subtle references to the traveling
elites. The product is original and artistic, and its clientele is "select": a
definition of luxury goods.

Creation and handcrafted quality traditionally distinguish the luxury
industry. References to art are omnipresent: "our trades are bound up
with art and are part of the French *art de vivre*." The products aim to be
works of creation, tasteful, beautiful, and rare. The luxury product is
thus associated with noble materials, fine craftsmanship, and absolute
perfection, with everything that evokes supreme material excellence and,
increasingly, talents who are attested, recognized and whose names reinforce the company's appeal.

While the fine crafts are associated with art, luxury goods go with social superiority. Educated taste bows to *good taste*, the convention of the
elite. And, unlike the piece of art, far from being defined by a break with
the past, the luxury good asserts itself through the constant celebration
of tradition.[15] Recitation of the product's origins is a classic genre. Age
matters, but even more important is the antiquity of a privileged connection with the greats of this world: those who possess it cannot lose it, and
those who do not, cannot acquire it.

The relationship with the past involves more than social status, though;
the past is also a collective resource, a way of defining the products and
a conception of the company's policy. Luxury firms concentrate specific
intangible skills that are hard to acquire; this is one of their unbeatable
advantages. Changes introduced in the products do not follow the logic
of fast and radical renewal; they must fit into a continuity that is pro-
claimed in a style or an identity.

[15] Hence the older, the more valuable. For instance at an auction in 2002, previously
owned, special-order handbags went for between 5,600 and 10,200 euros: "The sale did
not escape the highly Parisian infatuation with 'vintage.'" Roxana Azimi, "Hermès à
l'encan," *Le Monde*, 16–17 June 2002. In November 2003, previously owned Philippe
Patek watches were selling for around a million euros (*Le Monde*, 3 November 2003).

The luxury product expresses its truth in the flesh: in the past it was designed for "high society"; and this continues to be true, even if the notion has acquired a broader meaning. The promise held out by the luxury product is not merely material or aesthetic, it is also a social promise. Its possession expresses belonging; it authorizes imitation and is supposed to favor the ascension of those who set out to convert (new) money into social status.

## Is the Luxury Product on the Way Out?

Traditionally the luxury product was associated with material, symbolic, and social excellence.[16] It was believed that these qualities could be found in the various manufacturing activities covered by the term *luxury*—perfumes, watches, jewelry, shoes, fashion, leather craft, gold work, lighting, crystal, or champagne. Similarly, it was believed that these features characterized both small businesses and big corporations. It was believed that the same characteristics applied to Vuitton, Hermès, Chanel, Gucci, Christian Dior, Prada, Bollinger, Cartier, Van Cleef and Arpels, Breguet, Rolex, Boucheron, Baccarat, Lalique, and other equally prestigious names.

Representatives of the luxury industry as well as certain analysts say that this conception ceased to correspond to reality in the 1970s.[17] According to these critics, elevated prices, scarcity, craftsmanship, high artistic standards, and social exclusivity are no longer found throughout the industry, while, on the contrary, they may be found in industries not dealing in luxuries. Above all, they claim that certain features disappeared with the "democratization" of the clientele: half of the turnover of the major luxury firms now comes from occasional purchases made by clients from the middle classes. This development, the reasoning goes, explains the greater variety of products and the replacement of handcrafted objects by industrial production, scarcity by small or medium series, familial logic by financial logic, and the national market by the international market. None of the traditional criteria defining luxury seems destined to stand the test of time.

The "democratization" thesis can also be used to criticize the "distinction theory,"[18] although it has the unfortunate property of bolstering the very argument it is supposed to weaken. How indeed could the middle classes come to resemble the dominant classes without imitating, to the best of their ability, their practices? And if luxury products appear so

---

[16] J. Baudrillard, *The Consumer Society: Myths and Structures* (Sage, 1970, 1998); Bourdieu, *Distinction*; T. Veblen, *The Theory of the Leisure Class* (New York: Modern Library, 2001).

[17] Declarations by those responsable for the association "Cercle Colbert," whose membership includes three-quarters of the French luxury industry.

[18] Bourdieu, *Distinction*.

desirable that clients from modest backgrounds succumb to temptation, it is clearly because they are associated with the signs of high status: for the occasional clientele, it is the certainty that the purchase cannot be a mistake, since its value is pegged to social standing. Imitation and legitimization are all it takes to make the theory of distinction work.

Denial of luxury is not a trivial attempt at dissimulation: it is a genuine issue. In 1973, Cartier was the first to double track its product line to different clienteles by creating its "Must" collection, which was a dazzling economic success. Thirty years on, Cartier discovered that, as a result of hedging its bets, it was on the point of losing all of its clientele. Banalization of the product led to the erosion of its image as a luxury brand and to the flight of its traditional clientele. It was a turning point.[19]

That result made an impression, but it did not convince the other major luxury firms engaged in the same practice to abandon their projects.[20] They still needed to figure out how to avoid the vicious circle: while an elite clientele attracts the middle classes, expansion of the middle-class clientele can lead to banality—commonness of the luxury product—and consequently drive away the elites. The dangers were not imaginary. The brand had been charged with signifying a primacy that could no longer be claimed.

### The Brand

The brand is a *name* that designates other names, a *sign* which points to a particular symbolic universe, a signpost that makes it possible to situate one brand with respect to others, and a *promise* whose credibility guarantees its reliability. It is the brand that creates the luxury product, not the reverse. It is the brand that underpins the unity of a set of goods; it is the brand—and its logo—that "carries" a universe of meanings, an "image," a "collective personality." All brands compete for the greatest differentiated visibility and the most social validity.[21] The symbolic concentration

---

[19] "This cycle, marked by unbridled exploitation, terminated with the end of the millennium. Already in 2001, we at Richemont asked ourselves about trivialization and the future of brand names. . . . We develop our markets on the basis of scarcity. . . . Our brands by far prefer to be demanded than to be proposed." Interview with F. Cologni, CEO of Cartier, *Le Monde*, 22 December 2001.

[20] "Every luxury brand must henceforth find and manage the right balance between diffusion and banality, expanding the brand name and respecting its identity and style, seeking out new, more occasional consumers while maintaining selectivity, which is the vehicle of desirability and strong brand value." G. Lipovetsky and E. Roux, *Le luxe éternel* (Paris: Gallimard, 2003), p. 106.

[21] J.-J. Lambin, "La marque et le comportement de choix de l'acheteur," in J. N. Kapferer and J.-C. Thoenig (eds.), *La marque* (Paris: McGraw-Hill, 1989), p. 140; E. Sommier, *Modes, le monde en mouvement* (Paris: Village Mondial, 2000), p. 51; A. Semprini, *La marque* (Paris: Presses Universitaires de France, 1995), pp. 5–30.

not only modifies the scale of the collective benchmarks or landmarks, it also changes their nature: *the brand is now more and more the reality, while the product has become more and more a sign.* The competition is waged between "Vuitton," "Gucci," "Dior," "Armani," "Hermes," "Versace," and a few others, not between their products,[22] and even less between their prices.

Singularities are qualified through collective representations associated with brands. This inverted relationship means that action and trust can be made to operate at a greater or lesser distance from producers/sellers. The brand is also embodied in selective publicity; in the sponsorship that associates it with the distinctive practices of the upper classes, whether it is a matter of high culture, high tech, or distinguished sports; in the repetition of public events; and in the social judgments conveyed during ceremonies, parties, receptions, and shows. The budgets devoted to social communication are so huge that they single-handedly account for the industry's strong economic concentration.

Over the long term, however, the reputation and appeal of a luxury brand cannot be the result of communication alone. The products must meet a set of aesthetic and physical standards; furthermore, in order to gain and keep clients' trust, the brand must act as a social "gatekeeper." It falls to the brand to establish and respect the social and aesthetic codes associated with the social positions occupied or coveted by its reference clientele. Whatever physical and aesthetic pleasure its products procure, the luxury brand would not exist if it did not reflect back to its clients, and therefore to society as a whole, the signs that designate a world of refinement and prestige. There can be no doubt: the luxury brand is defined by the summit of the social hierarchy.

The belief that goods can be converted into signs is what makes the luxury industry. It establishes the nature of the promise, as well as the nature of the quality uncertainty. And it measures its solidity by the volume of commentaries and evaluations emanating from the chorus that represents (high) society. A specialized press and mass media have become indispensable, as have active, committed critical circles at the international level, which, aided by their inevitable networks, create the resources of comparison and judgment, and counteract the pure exercise of power. These devices help decide among social and aesthetic codes, judge works, celebrate creators, fuel the *People* columns, accompany certain evolutions and refuse others, castigate denials or betrayals, spark genuine and false controversies, and play on images. The continued existence of the luxury product depends on a dense equipment of writings, discourses, images, representations, and social celebrations.

---

[22] "When creating a perfume, the choice of the *jus* is a secondary decision." G. Erner, *Victimes de la mode?* (Paris: La Découverte, 2004), pp. 174–178.

It is these critical social circles that choose between brands struggling to occupy the most prestigious spots in the collective imaginary and to earn the highest economic returns. They are also able to oppose a given policy or a given brand at any point. Not everything is possible, however, and certain brands have learned this at their own expense. Attached to famous names—those of movie and television stars, of top models, of sports heroes—brands have, over the last decades, shown exceptional capacities for capturing clientele without abandoning their economic rent.

### Integrating Opposites

How can the function of "gatekeeper" for the elites and the development of a socially heterogeneous clientele be held together? Can the clientele expand and diversify without posing a threat to the continuity of the singularities?

The solution has been to bring together under the same brand, on the one hand, singular products and a large range of geared-down products ever on the verge of becoming banal and, on the other, the social elites and the middle classes, and to smooth away the conflict or the threat of conflict by professional means and organizational solutions. It is in this context that both spectacular and more modest practices find their true significance.[23]

First, the construction of luxury palaces for brand stores in the up-market areas of the world's major cities, which, by their very appearance, produce the indisputable association of singularity, wealth, and social power. Not only do these palaces single out one brand from among the rest, but they also proclaim an independence, and thus a relationship with the clientele, that no intermediary can upset. Second, the increased scarcity of the products as a practice is tailored to the promise carried by the luxury good[24]—limited editions, special editions, or bespoke items. And third, preservation of familiarity throughout a far-flung territory:

[23] S. Dubuisson-Quellier, "The shop as market space: The commercial qualities of retail architecture," in D. David Vernet and L. de Wit (eds.), *Boutiques and Other Retail Spaces: The Architecture of Seduction* (London: Routledge, 2007), pp. 16–33. Sales personnel in Vuitton shops in France are trained in mock-up settings and the training is extremely "detailed." It is completed by a video and a house manual. Lipovetsky and Roux, *Le luxe éternel*, pp. 126–127. S. Dubuisson-Quellier, "Codification et ajustement: Deux moyens pour l'élaboration d'une mémoire de l'organisation. Le cas d'une activité de service," *Revue internationale de systémique* 12, no. 1 (1998): 83–98.

[24] "Question: 'But how does one reconcile the notion of volume with that of scarcity, which seems to me essential when talking about luxury?' D. Grumbach, CEO of Tierry Mugler: 'You are quite right. It is clear that a product that everyone can buy, whether in fashion or another domain, is no longer desirable. On this point, each brand and each product has its threshold of tolerance. It is therefore necessary to organize scarcity.'" "Le luxe, domaine du rêve," *Les Amis de l'École de Paris*, 1998.

the world over, one finds the same products, the same presentation, the same sales ritual. Everything points to the hidden but active presence of shared "codified memories," embodied in the forms of organization as well as in the practices of the market professionals. All of these add up to a repertory of specific rules for integrating two models for adjusting buyer and seller, two models that correspond to two types of clientele, who exist side by side without overlapping.

The middle-class clientele is so profitable and the probability of its expansion so great that luxury firms have probably never considered abandoning it. But it constitutes such a threat that the brand feels obliged to marshal rules, procedures, and arrangements, as well as its full symbolic weight to neutralize it. There where traditional industry played on separation and distance, the big luxury firms opted for integration and proximity: until now they have managed to combine two types of products, two types of production, and two types of clientele.

The passion for desingularization together with the financial interests that accompany mass production of differentiated goods is controlled, but it has not been eliminated. This integration is therefore not without risk. The continuity of singularities and the conquest of the world market can become contradictory, and choices for extending the market that have been made in the past and which are still reproduced may result in desingularization of the brand. To avoid this, the *reference to aesthetic logic* imposes itself by spectacular alliances with art in general and with contemporary art in particular.

Yet luxury goods continue to pose an enigma. We have an inkling of what luxury means in France, in Europe, or in the United States. However, the Japanese passion for collecting objects by Vuitton, Hermès, and a few others escapes us. Paradoxically, the idolization of objects is a threat for luxury firms, since it leads to sharing with others that which should not be shared.

## THE MEGABRAND

The megabrand, or "umbrella" brand, embraces numerous and diversified subbrand products. It tends to bypass intermediary symbolic powers and to directly represent all those items that are in any way connected with it. Its formation and continuation suppose strong financial power; the impossibility—with a few exceptions—of relying on aesthetic logic alone, owing to the heterogeneous nature of the products; the necessity to invent a new logic of global integration; and, last of all, the presence of a universe of meanings that extend to a vast territory. Depending on the survey consulted, the lists of megabrands vary slightly, but generally speaking they contain at least Nike, Virgin, Dannon, Marlboro, and Walt Disney.

The megabrand must construct a system of meanings that delineates a desirable world and, thereby, expands the number of clients and strengthens the intensity of client-brand relations. The only question we are going to explore—because it is an extreme case—is that of the relations of subordination between symbolic power and reality. In other words, does the belief that attaches to the megabrand extend to enabling it to surmount differences between product categories and to stamp them with the same qualification? Can the megabrand create for its worshippers, whose behavior it governs, a representation of reality that is desirable, in conformity with its goals, and different from the representations of others? Has the ideology of sport that Nike (with the longtime backing of Michael Jordan) managed to develop, embody, and propagate by playing on the cult of performance, perseverance, "pure sport," and so forth become a "desirable world" whose access is determined by possession of its products? Are the relations of adherence linked to the imaginary quasi worlds of the megabrands (Nike, sport prowess and Michael Jordan; Adidas and Madonna; Dannon and health; Timberland and nature; Marlboro and adventure) which would thus be endowed with a symbolic power (wielded on an international scale) to qualify goods and people—and to make the first desirable and cause the second to desire?

The source of this power is amazing, and it is shown by the following story. "When I am monitoring a written exam and I get bored, I make a list of the different tennis-shoe brands, I look at the feet of my pupils in primary school and I do the math. I usually come up with 100% tennis shoes. Then it is Nike and Adidas that score highest. The students not wearing "a brand" slink by, they are ashamed. On the other hand, if they are wearing brand socks, they roll up their sweats to show off the logo. . . . I try to talk about this with them. They explain to me quite knowledgeably that nobody tells them what to choose. So why do they like a T-shirt with a logo better than one without? What does a brand, a logo, a set of initials mean to them? Why Lacoste rather than Panzani? The answers are obviously vague because these are believers talking." Or: "In the continuum between the clothes and the hair, down to the tattoos and multiple piercings, the scarification and the brand seem to be the very latest. They say: these are my brands, my style, the personal thing that belongs only to me."[25]

There is nothing original in the twin movement of demarcation and unification by which the individual constructs his or her identity, except that, in the case in point, the process operates on an international scale

[25] M. Goyet, *Collèges de France* (Paris: Fayard, 2003), pp. 31–32; L. O'Neal Parker, "Brand identities," *The Washington Post*, 11 May 1998.

and revolves around a collective commercial actor. To be sure, one must be wary of the fantasies and the overwhelming power of megabrands cultivated—for opposite reasons—by professionals and opponents of the market system. Nevertheless, certain narratives seem to be powerful enough to fashion collective identities. This has to do with professional actors in the market place whose job it is to construct these beliefs. But it has just as much—and perhaps more—to do with the social actors. We fail to appreciate the intensity of the personal relationship consumers build with "their" brands. Furthermore, for many, the product does not represent the need it is supposed to satisfy. It is no longer a simple part of consumption, in the narrow sense of the term; it represents a means of gaining access to social dignity. What was once played out in the political field now occurs in the market place. Citizenship is acquired through brand ownership. We are no longer in the universe of pleasure or distinction, but in that of identity; no longer in the world of individual competition, but in that of collective action.

For certain segments of the population, the megabrand erases the distinction between singular and differentiated products. It is the megabrand, in itself, that stamps any given material support with the mark of singularity. And ordinary criticism of products loses its effectiveness because strong belief is immune to invalidation by either knowledge or reality. Examples exist but they remain few in number, since financial impact and technical sophistication are not enough without psychological and moral investment on the clients' part. When this integration is successful, reality is deprived of its power to convince.

• • •

The mega regime shares with the authenticity regime substantial devices and the primacy of quality competition over price competition; it differs from it by the increase in economic concentration, the rise of barriers to entry, and change in the scale of action; by the increased influence of commercial devices as compared to critical devices; by short- and mid-term high-profit seeking; by the rarefaction of names, judgment devices, products, and judgment criteria; and by the *reference to a global logic of aesthetics*. These differences explain that the markets of the mega regime share the tension between maintenance of singularities and pursuit of profit.

This tension is more or less acute, however. Despite persisting fears, blockbusters have not led to the disappearance of the *film d'auteur* or the "classical film," nor have they particularly departed from the originality model. Big luxury firms have opted to combine two different strategies, clienteles and product categories, under one power. Coexistence as it stands is not enough to guarantee the viability of this strategy. But as long as the responsibility for developing new products is left to creators, as long as brands do not stop defining themselves by the celebration of tradition and art (this is demonstrated today by the public support for contemporary painting after having played the different card of "artistic directors" the likes of Tom Ford, John Galliano, or Christian Lacroix), and as long as critical social circles as well as the elites form powerful and autonomous sociocultural groups, singularities are unlikely to disappear. The main danger could come from megabrands, but they cannot "reenchant" the world on whim. In every case, the search through collective beliefs produced by the symbolic power rooted in economic power can orient the market toward desingularization, but until now such changes have been limited.

Megafilms, luxury megafirms, and megabrands by no means exhaust the diversity of the mega regime. Moreover, as they are heterogeneous, one regime of coordination cannot completely explain their working. For each concrete market, the generality of the analysis would require the combined use of two or three regimes of coordination, as we will see later.

Nevertheless, three general conclusions can be formulated: (1) In spite of the size of the market and with some partial exceptions, the logic of aesthetics persists, even in the guise of the reference to aesthetics. It represents the common constraint under which the components of the regime are brought together. (2) The tension between the logics of aesthetics and profitability varies with each market: it is the weakest for megafilms and the strongest for megabrands, with the luxury industry in the middle. (3) Singularities continue to exist, which means that, even in the large market, actors' dispositions, substantial devices, and the interplay of cultural complexes can counterbalance the passion for short- and mid-term profits that would compel some desingularization.

## Chapter Twelve

# THE EXPERT-OPINION REGIME

THE EXPERT-OPINION regime is defined by a relation of delegation and a small market. It is a hybrid regime because it is based on formal devices transforming substantial choice criteria. The "prize" for the best novel, best film, and so forth picks out a singularity from other singularities; it does this only after a collective process of comparative evaluation of the specific product contents. This choice enables the consumer to buy a "good" product while sparing him the trouble of investing in knowledge, informa-

| Impersonal devices<br>Formal devices<br>Small market |
| :---: |
| *Passive and autonomous consumer* |
| (Conformity to)<br>expert logic |

tion, and time. Nevertheless, passivity does not exclude autonomy, which can eventually assert itself by rejection of the selection proposed by the delegate. Relying on an expert thus combines judgment on the contents with public presentation that focuses on the end result while keeping the arguments justifying this result under wraps: it is simply said to be the "best choice."

A priori, the prize system presents eminent advantages. And yet it intervenes only in an auxiliary form, sharing the explanation with other coordination regimes. The scope of the coordination regime is changing, though. It used to be modest, but in France as in other countries, with the appearance of a new public ranking by judgment devices based on expertise, it has begun to expand through the progressive inclusion of the *quasi markets* of hospitals and universities, which are characterized by competition, without prices.

Book or movie prizes, "concept stores," and quasi markets express a (conformity to) *expert* logic that reconciles juries, committees, and expert choices with the convenience that ensues from the use of formal devices.

## LITERARY PRIZES

Many justifications are advanced for literary prizes, and each involves a different interpretive perspective. We will look at the capacity of these prizes to consolidate or expand the market for books. For the past thirty years in France, reading habits and publishing have displayed opposite tendencies. While the proportion of nonreaders has remained constant at around one-third of the population and the proportion of "heavy" readers has fallen, in the same period, the number of new titles published each year has doubled. For publishers, this inflation is a way of increasing the likelihood of economic success; but at the same time it increases the opacity of the market, which is further exacerbated by the decline of average reading skills. A comparative examination of buying practices allows us to identify the means used to reduce the cognitive deficit.

Book purchases follow two models: while heavy readers buy their books everywhere except from book clubs, "occasional" readers flock to the supermarket shelves, bookshops, and book clubs. Embodied competence allows heavy readers to be mobile, independent of sales venues and mechanisms, while the restricted competence of the occasional readers leads them to rely on all of those devices that, in various forms and shapes—supermarket bins, word of mouth, regular selections of a small number of suggestions—help them make a choice.[1] There are other devices, but on the whole the cultural complex works according to a collusion rule, which keeps those who are not among the literati at a distance. But, apparently, the literary award remains independent from both partisan specific criteria and collusion with the usual readership.

Books, movies, music, theater—all have their prizes. But those in the literary world are the oldest and most numerous: more than fifteen hundred in France alone. Among the best known are the Goncourt, the Renaudot, the Medicis, the Femina, Interallié, and Académie française, in France, and the Pulitzer Prize, the National Book Award, the Man Booker Prize, and so on, in the English-speaking world.

The prize is the privileged device of the expertise regime. It rests on the authority of specialists in literature and the essay: writers, critics, and journalists, whose recognized competence qualifies them to make periodical selections (for the most part annually) of "good" books or the "best" book.[2] If the value of a work depends on the makeup of the jury, its orientation depends on a power struggle between two opposing demands, which were formulated to perfection by two members of the 2003 Goncourt jury: "The readers will be very disappointed by our choice," and "We have here a truly great writer." For one judge, the crowned book is supposed to be a pleasure to read for the majority of readers, while for the other, the prize is supposed to reward the author and thus link him or her directly with the grandeur of literature. This tension is not artificial, since the vigor of the criticism shows in the case of a prize deemed to be too "commercial," or on the contrary, as reflected by the

---

[1] In 2005, bookstores, large specialized stores, supermarkets, and book clubs represented 26.7, 21.7, 20.7, and 16.7 percent, respectively, of the total value of book sales. *Chiffres clés, 2007*, Ministère de la Culture et de la Communication, La Documentation Française.

[2] S. Ducas, "La reconnaissance littéraire: Littérature et prix littéraires" (doctoral diss., Sciences of Texts and Documents, Université de Paris VII, 1998).

mitigated success of certain films crowned by the Cannes Film Festival juries, which often defend a demanding conception of film.

The prize, or at least the *grand prix*, does not promise a "good" book; it promises the "best" book of the year. In justification of such an extravagant claim, the famous names on the jury are advanced, a collective choice is supposed to protect against arbitrariness, and the glorious names of the former prizewinners are recalled. But in a universe dominated by a plurality of aesthetic criteria, with the exception of the rare book that wins unanimous conviction, this promise is sustained only by the belief on the part of readers (or a portion of readers) that there are no better qualified judges than those whose profession is writing and reading and who are honestly dedicated to this impossible task. It is this shared representation that allows us to understand that past errors are frequently recalled in the form of names of writers who were unacknowledged by the judges and yet who subsequently turned out to be the best. The prize can serve as a collective reference only because a symbolic value is attributed to the jury and through it to the institution it represents and whose history sometimes stretches far into the past.

Once it has been awarded, the prize liberates the chosen book from the arguments and commentaries that had dogged it until then. No justification is given for the choice save, sometimes, a few brief lines. The work becomes mobile, ready to travel, open to a public sphere. In France, the setting, the awarding of the prize, the presence of the media, crowds, interviews, the celebration of the book and its author, anecdotes, petty scandals, excessive declarations, resignations—all go to make the prize a national happening, picturesque, exceptional, and periodical. Passions are declared, skepticism is expressed, and the unlucky contestants lose no time in calling into question both prize and jury. And yet, in spite of everything, trust in the prize system subsists, even if it has had its ups and downs.

The "great" literary prizes—beginning with the Goncourt—and the others, more recent and modest, offer a simple, almost routine, solution to radical quality uncertainty. Reputation and trust are the basis of a symbolic authority, measured in terms of the number of those who buy the prizewinning book. In itself the prize is a more or less powerful device for gaining an audience. It owes this capacity to the ambitions, the composition, and the past of the jury. The Goncourt is the promise of three hundred thousand copies sold, and the figure can even come to more than a million; the Renaudot represents one hundred thousand copies; the Femina, between fifty and one hundred thousand. No one scorns prizes, not authors, not publishers, and even less, readers. Or at least a certain category of readers: those who have enough respect for literature to not want to go wrong, and who, for various reasons, have few pertinent resources for making their own choice. For them, experts in culture are a guarantee of quality.

Prizes are a low-cost way of building the relationship between the universe of books and the hundreds of thousands—or more—of readers of good will. There is nothing automatic about this result, though. From time to time, those who habitually ratify the chosen works abandon a consent that seemed to be a given. Less ignorant and less dependent than they are held to be, and more autonomous than some would like them to be, they draw their own conclusions from the controversies surrounding the prize awards.[3] What is often presented as a ritual that, for some, is without consequences can provoke a loss of trust and refusal to buy the book.

Literary prizes, as well as the others, can be unfair without being worthless. They cannot construct a market by themselves, but they have a specific function. Year in, year out, they maintain the tie with those on the fringes of the authenticity market who would like to gain entry or, on the contrary, do not want to make a complete break with an old relationship and yet do not accept the obligation to gather information, compare, and judge. The advantages and disadvantages of literary prizes are the subject of endless discussion; but without the guarantee of quality that some persist in associating with literary juries, without a trust inseparable from the belief that jury members are inspired by the love of literature, it is not unthinkable that a portion of the occasional readership would disappear completely from the book world.

## TRENDSETTERS AND GATEKEEPERS

How does one come to be "in"? How can one be ahead of the times without remaining alone for too long? Such questions awaken an anxiety in whoever cannot live without being in tune with fashion and who follows the trends all the better for preceding them. In the world of fashion, where originality is the rule, where practices change rapidly (and such changes can be abrupt), where it is easy to blunder, where egos are easily ruffled, and where economic errors are costly, the competence necessary to select and consecrate avant-garde works matters. This is, in principle, the function of the "concept store"—a device charged with detecting new trends. The phenomenon existed before the term, and today concept stores are on the rise in France as elsewhere.

The concept store is defined not by a well-founded prophecy but by a self-fulfilling prophecy:[4] what is announced will happen. In this light it is

---

[3]H. Hamon and P. Rotman, *Les intellocrates: Expédition en haute intelligentsia* (Paris: Ramsay, 1981). A quarter of a century on, with a few name changes, this study of the attribution of literary prizes is still valid. See also E. Lemieux, *Le pouvoir intellectuel: Les nouveaux réseaux* (Paris: Denoël, 2003).

[4]G. Erner, *Victimes de la mode?* (Paris: La Découverte, 2004), p. 149.

understandable that many concept stores—in France and abroad—are not long-lived. Failure is hard to hide, and clients do not tend to forgive those who have cost them a blow to their self-esteem.

What does one find in a concept store? It sells a selection of "trendy" products—clothing, design items, art objects, beauty products, foods, books and CDs, furniture, hi-tech products, original objects and brand goods, and special and limited series. Such objects, though, would be nothing without the names of their creators (some well known, others promised to fame), who help each other face the famous clients who cannot do without big brand names but also need the "hype," and who must by no means be confused with the elite, their social adversary.

The concept store is at the same time a discoverer and a guarantee of the validity of its discoveries. It plays on names and signatures, on the relative scarcity of the objects, on their skillful display, and on a well-touted expertise. In principle it depends on women's magazines, fashion magazines, international art journals, and the mass media to put out the message.[5] But with the passage of time, the relationship has been reversed: the press, in all its diversity, is only too glad to receive and amplify the store's verdicts.

The concept store is thus the expression and the guide of its milieu, which acts as a formidable multiplier of knowledge and persuasion: in short, it is a trendsetter. The prediction of the next trend has all the more chance of coming true when it is validated by its potential deniers. Therefore not only ordinary customers but also professionals come to the boutique to discover—or at least scrutinize—the signs of a market in which it is inadvisable to be mistaken.

Does it look good? Does it look right? This twin uncertainty applies to both the aesthetic and the social values that weigh on avant-garde singularities and which can only be dispelled by validation from those intermediaries who possess both the appropriate aesthetic and sociocultural codes, and whose symbolic authority is such that their proposals and advice act as guides for those who want to avoid errors and therefore turn to the most unlikely of all competences: predicting the future.

## Public Quality-Rating Devices

Quasi markets are markets without prices and sometimes without profits. In some countries, like France, schools,[6] universities, and hospitals belong to the public sphere; their access is free or nearly so; and competition is

[5] "Les 400 lieux branchés de Paris: Les guides branchés," *Le nouvel observateur,* published annually.

[6] G. Felouzis and J. Perroton, "Les 'marchés scolaires': Une économie de la qualité," *Revue française de sociologie* 48, no. 4 (October–December 2007).

increasingly based on public quality-rating systems developed by experts and widely diffused by the mass media and the Internet. Such judgment devices serve as a basis for intensified competition between the organizational bodies that are attempting to occupy the top rungs of the rating scale and for the social struggle between the clients for access to the best-rated establishments, in other words those that offer the best personalized services. The effectiveness of the markets increases as the size of the units evaluated decreases: department, service, the individual.

When the stakes of the competition based on quality-rating devices are high, the effects on quasi markets are powerful. One can generalize the consequences identified by a pioneering study of American law-school ratings.[7] The central conclusion, which combines several findings, is that the presidents and managers of these schools cannot disregard their university's rank, since it dictates the "quality" of admissions, the "quality" of the teaching and research staff hired, and the size of the budget. In this case, their behavior follows a simple and informal rule: the greater the competition, the more the competing institutions tend to comply with the evaluation criteria underpinning their ratings. What over time might appear as mimicry is nothing of the kind: the decisions taken are highly rational since they determine the way talents and resources are distributed.

The fact that students and their families, like university heads, rely on these ratings has three major consequences. First, very small differences are magnified by being transformed into differences of rank. Second, part of the budget is used to finance the competition itself. And third, *competition favors compliance with the same game rule and therefore conformity to the same university practices* and, ultimately, restriction of the universities' autonomy.

What can these quasi markets be compared to? The answer lies in the type of rating used. It is a rating based on expertise, but it differs from the literary prize system and others since it bears on all of the entities in the area. It comes closer to a guide, except that usually there are several guides and therefore several different ratings. In reality, today, quite often quasi-market rating is different from all other devices used in the economics of singularities even though it deals with personalized services. The reason has to do with the monopoly given to a single criterion or a single configuration of criteria. Singularities require a plurality of logics of action. With a unique criterion, sooner or later competition obliges the collective actors to emulate the most efficient practice according to that criterion. It will be the rule of the "one best way." And as a result, standardization will tend to replace singularization.

[7] W. N. Espeland and M. Sauder, "Ranking and reactivity: How public measures recreate social worlds," *American Journal of Sociology* 113, no. 1 (July 2007): 1–40.

• • •

The expert-opinion regime is organized around judgment devices each of which, in its own domain, is charged with fulfilling exceptional functions—choosing the best book or movie or detecting tomorrow's fashions or rating collective activities. It combines relative qualification based on expertise, a small market, moderate profit, and expert logic, which means that conformity is asserted—not without problems—by the ratification of the delegates' choices. Above and beyond the contingencies of real life, the device promises the consumer easy and quick access to goods whose choice requires the mobilization of expert skills. And if conformity is the counterpart, it is not unconditional.

But a crucial difference separates expert-opinion markets from the large majority of present-day quasi markets and their equivalents: the first are multi-criteria and maintain singularities, while the second are uni-criterion and threaten them. Quasi markets will truly come into the economics of singularities only when different ratings built upon different evaluation criteria are allowed—*officially or de facto*—to compete and to offer several interpretations of the "best" practice. Shall we say, then, that the judgment devices for restaurants are infinitely more sophisticated and considerate of their object than are the present hospital and university ratings?

## Chapter Thirteen

# THE COMMON-OPINION REGIME

THE COMMON-OPINION coordination regime is defined by a large market and the consumer's delegation of power to a chart, which spares him the time
and effort of choosing. This formal device replaces
the absolute qualification of singularities linked to
substantial devices by rank and relative qualification.
Charts in the markets of cultural products carry
different names: *box office* for films, *best sellers* for
novels and essays, and *hit parade* or *Top 10/20/40/50*
for popular music. All use sales as a criterion for
ranking the products. Therefore, the adjustment between products, devices, and consumers obeys a logic of conformity with the representatives that is justified mainly by *convenience*. The effectiveness of the
chart thus logically presupposes a passive and heteronomous consumer.

| |
|---|
| Impersonal devices<br>Formal devices<br>Large market |
| *Passive and heteronomous consumer* |
| Conformity logic |

This coordination regime will serve to explain the workings of, for example,
the market of popular music, whose importance—above and beyond economic statistics—comes from a product that perpetuates or reinforces a youth-
ful passion and which is perhaps in the process of spreading to society as a
whole. In France, over two-thirds of young adults from fifteen to thirty-five
years of age tune in daily to music on the radio or on portable music players.[1]

In France, the catalogue of pop music lists some three hundred thousand
titles, among which are approximately thirty thousand new ones each year.
One may wonder about the ways consumers faced with such a bewildering
world can make reasonable choices. But the final market shows that 0.8 percent of the catalogue (2,260 titles) and 4.4 percent of the catalogue (12,777
titles) account for 75 percent and 90 percent, respectively, of the total sales.[2]
One may wonder, too, about the process that ends in such a highly concentrated total figure. How is such a head-spinning supply reduced to so few titles? How can the choices be reasonable? How can the market keep going or
expand with so low a proportion of economic successes?

---

[1] L. Muller, "Participation culturelle et sportive," Enquête 2003, INSEE.

[2] Unless otherwise indicated, the 2004 figures are taken from A. Nicolas' valuable studies
*La diversité musicale dans le paysage radiophonique, Rapport 2004* (Paris: Observatoire de
la Musique, 2005), and *Les marchés de la musique entegistrée, Rapport 2004* (Paris: Observatoire de la Musique, 2005).

The common-opinion regime should provide answers to these and other questions. Our study of the pop-music market will be done in two steps. First, in the present chapter, a simplified view of the reality will be presented to demonstrate that this concrete market is not far from the coordination regime model.[3] And in Chapter 18, the interpretation will be extended to deal with the issue of desingularization.

## SONGS

The encounter between an overabundant supply of titles, multiple musical genres, numerous artists, and an audience with very diverse musical preferences and which is, moreover, dispersed over a large territory represents such a gigantic number of combinations that, logically, it can only prevent reasonable choices. The first two problems to be resolved are, therefore, how to share that information and how to reduce it. Knowledge circulates through radio, television, and additional mass-media devices, not to mention networks. And between the products and the customers stand the charts.[4] Using a centralization process, the chart translates a multitude of scanned decentralized decisions taken by the buyers into a global hierarchical order: the Top 40 ranks each song title by the number of CDs sold during the week.[5]

The ranking system allows the buyer to move down and up, from the higher to the lower sales and from the best to the lowest quality. Such movement presupposes the validity of the chart, which relies on the common belief that symbolic value and economic value go hand in hand. Under such conditions, the chart is a particularly effective support for individual choice.

The strategic position and the peculiar influence of the chart are inseparable from the evolution in which the market has changed its scale of

[3] Since 2000, CD sales have dropped off sharply. Piracy and electronic trade are purportedly the main causes of this evolution although other interpretations have been formulated. But until now, this change has not modified the ways singularities are chosen. The musical supports may have changed, but the choices are not that different from one support to the other. For example, charts are still influential.

[4] In France, the national Hit Parade, created in 1968, was followed in 1983 by the Top 50, itself replaced in 1993. Today, the chart is under the control of the National Recording Professional Association (SNEP). This association rates the best-selling singles, albums, and compilations on the basis of figures taken from a sample of national record sellers. The information is based on cash-register sales recorded automatically without manual intervention. In the United States, the *Billboard* Hot 100 was created in 1958, and its information has been automatically registered since 1991.

[5] Depending on the circumstances, actors use the Top 100/50/40/30/20/ or 10. Unless otherwise indicated, we have used the Top 40.

action to become tightly organized around radio in the 1980s and around television in 2000.

## Radio

A few propositions may summarize an initial view of how the market works: (1) the most broadcast titles sell the most; (2) the Top lists bring together the most popular titles; (3) the most popular titles will be broadcast the most. But such circular reasoning hides the concrete ways through which popularity is constructed, and conflates identifying the filtering process that applies to plentiful entities with the ways the selection may become the expression of common opinion.

A realistic presentation of the pop-music market should begin by recalling two of its main characteristics: (1) airtime is a central and scarce economic asset; (2) the central economic competition happens between the *majors* (once five in number, there are now only four: Universal, Warner, EMI, Sony-BMG) and the independent firms; the former have systematically mobilized to control a larger share of the national and world markets.[6] Radio and TV are therefore strategic places where power struggles, even when invisible, are fierce. We therefore need to go back to our initial view and introduce some changes.

(1) To be over-broadcast (broadcast much more than the mean title), titles must get onto the playlist (the weekly program of songs to play), whose composition results from an intense and continuous struggle. (2) The shorter the playlist, the greater the broadcast inequality. (3) Advertising and promotion represent gigantic financial budgets and reinforce the probabilities that the relevant records will make it onto the playlist and then be "over-played" (get more spins that those allocated to other records). (4) Since they are the most sold, the Top 40 titles usually concentrate airtime and financial resources, and thus are the first to get better treatment. Consequently, the Top 40 now represent nearly two-thirds of the total number of titles broadcast, and the proportion is on the rise. (5) Compared with the independent firms, the majors can mobilize huge amounts of financial capital on the basis of their relative part in the producing of new titles, and therefore control a disproportionate share of airtime.

The functioning of the market explains that the ten best-selling artists, who are therefore in the Top 40 list, were among those whose titles were played more than four hundred times a year on radio, and whose financial investment in radio and TV promotion exceeded one million euros.[7] And

---

[6]The major recording labels (Universal, Warner, EMI, Sony-BMG) control 80 percent of the world market and (with distribution) 95 percent of the French market.

[7]A. Nicolas, *Les marchés de la musique entegistrée, Rapport 2007* (Paris: Observatoire de la Musique, 2007), pp. 26, 68–69.

although they produced 54 percent of new titles, the majors controlled 81 percent of radio airtime. The gap between the major labels and the independent firms suffices to explain why the first are driving the second out of the market.

## Television

Before 2000, television played only a minor role in the popular-music market.[8] Since then, as in other countries, French television has become the chief architect of a new production mode, with shows like *Popstar* and *Star Academy*.[9] The TV popular-music market has some particular features: over a period of several weeks or months, young fans and future artists participate in a show which draws a large audience; the new songs, written in haste, are made for simplicity; after a few weeks or months, the winners are "launched" directly on stage or on the record market; their recordings are massively promoted on radio and TV; the winners' success is both almost immediate and stunning; the new stars rocket to the top of the Top chart, thus benefiting from stronger promotion and increased likelihood of staying at the top; independent criticism goes unheard; and independent producers are increasingly marginalized.

The market of pop music designed for television is the product of a miracle formula combining high profits with low risk. Success stems from the mesh between two registers: the show put on by a handful of potential celebrities for a few million viewers who share the same ambition—to break into the celebrity universe—and a remarkable organization that has succeeded in integrating radio, television and recording companies, specialized tour organization, promotion campaigns, and the making and sale of records.

### ADJUSTMENT BY THE CHARTS

The Top chart is a *framework* that acts as a guideline, a competitive arena, and a playground. First, it is to the market of singularities what the price board is to the standard market, presenting to all a list of possible choices whose length is arbitrary: 50, 40, 30, or 10 slots. One could call it a

---

[8] TV exerted its influence on music through variety shows and advertising. The TV market irrupted in 1989 with the song "Lambada," the summer hit, which sold five million copies. These one-off, unequally successful, summer operations eventually paved the way for a more elaborate form of intervention.

[9] *Star Academy* has become the symbol of the TV reality show. It has been broadcasted by more than fifty countries. Although there have been some variations in the format and in the name according to the country, I have kept the best-known title as a generic term.

qualities board. Second, the chart is the result of two repeated processes: the drawing of a line between being and nonbeing—it is from the outer unknown that the newly visible titles come and into the same outer unknown that the old titles are banished; and the weekly delivery of an ordinal order based on registered sales and relayed by the media. Third, for those fascinated by this universe, the movement of titles and artists up and down the charts makes dramatic theater. For all these reasons, market actors *focus their attention* on the charts.

Officially, the Top is purely objective, as it is the faithful and contingent expression of the distribution of preferences recorded at the time of purchase, eschewing human intermediacy and gathering buyers' purchase judgments at the source: the Top produces a valid order. The question of trust should not arise since the fear of opportunism is eliminated by the automated techniques, by the respectability of the technical institutes charged with the data gathering, and by the guarantee following upon its repeated publication in the media, including the most respectable and respected magazines.

The chart has become a legitimate guide for individual choices. It neutralizes radical quality uncertainty and at the same time provides the kind of knowledge that authorizes individual judgments, on the condition that one accepts that aesthetic value and economic value are but two sides of the same reality. This homology is made possible only by the belief that assimilates the market to political democracy. Some consider this comparison to be arbitrary because it unduly extends the validity of the political model to a reality alien to it; for them, quantity cannot be converted into quality. For the others, on the contrary, the ranking of collective preferences is indispensable because worth can only be the product of the choice of all.

The equivalence rests on a three-pronged justification: no other mechanism allows a better transformation of sales volume into relative aesthetic value; no other mechanism allows better adjustment to the variations in collective taste; and no other mechanism permits such a quick and simple purchase decision. When the aggregation of individual wills constitutes the ranking and citizen-consumers recognize no higher authority than the *demos*, the distribution of purchases is assimilated to that of votes and results in the legitimate ranking of artistic values. The sum of the individual criteria constitutes a *common opinion*, which grounds the authority of the ranking and its transformation into a public guidepost. Since the chart is assimilated to a representative and enjoys the trust of the represented party, adjustment comes about in conformity with the chart; in other words, the consumer is supposed to be passive and homogeneous, to follow the chart, and to accept its artistic and/or economic criteria.

Like all rankings, the Top chart has remarkable advantages for the buyer. By merging artistic with economic positions and personal with collective choice logics, it reconciles three features usually considered to be contradictory: selection of the "best" singularities; lack of the buyer's knowledge, competence, and time; and rapidity of choice. The rest—the real sales—is no longer a matter of choice but of logistics.

•  •  •

The common-opinion regime works the most simply of all coordination regimes. Once consumers are assimilated to a collective entity whose purchases are faithfully reported by the charts and once consumers assimilate aesthetic value to sales volume, the economic coordination regime is set to go. And its effectiveness is undeniable.

The chart is central for the pop-music market because it builds and continually reinforces a grid of musical subdivisions—the genres—that encompasses the entire production, which thus becomes a common musical culture; it also helps to bring together music titles, radio, TV, advertising, and promotion, and therefore to build collective action; finally, it is a very convenient device for consumers. This effectiveness supposes that the symbolic authority of the chart is recognized, that the devices enjoy user trust, and that consumers make the expected choices. Such conformity is all the more probable when consumers do not have access to outside information that would eventually allow them to criticize the music produced by the market.

Although firms pursue profit, and consumers, pleasure, both are supposed to share the same judgment criteria. This is precisely what gives the former such powerful capacities to act on the latter. This coordination regime is all the more coherent when the intervention of the judgment devices is dominated by a relatively unitary economic and cultural power, when heterodox voices are few and barely audible, and when the charts provide a continual reminder of the majority will. Nevertheless, although the common-opinion regime appears strong, it is probably the most vulnerable of all coordination regimes. As we will see later, its workings and the conditions of its functioning explain why desingularization is a greater threat to this regime than to the other regimes.

PERSONALIZED GOODS and quasi-professional and professional services have one feature in common: they belong to markets that elude ordinary observation, since the exchanges are ensured through networks. The way these regimes of coordination are constructed can therefore only be different from that of regimes based on impersonal devices.

There are two stages in this construction: The first is devoted to the *network-market*, considered to be the basis of every market of personalized services. The second distinguishes three coordination regimes by their increasing distance from the simple network-market: the reticular regime, to which the professional regime adds control devices, and the interfirm regime adds organizational rules.[1]

[1] For lack of adequate empirical material, it is not possible to devote an entire chapter to interfirm relations. Any work on subcontracting relations and partnerships should look into the following questions: (1) How can firms protect themselves from relations of mutual dependence, which at the same time are the basis of cooperation and an open door to opportunism? (2) How can it be explained that the usual arrangements—shared codes of ethics, rules, contracts, and financial stimulants—fail to eliminate the possibility of error and/or cheating? (3) How can it be explained that formalization of relations combined with outside oversight by an independent authority—something provided by quality assurance—reduces risk but fails to eliminate it completely? (4) In practice, the solution is sought in the use of credible judgment devices. And we discover that, under these conditions, the most effective guarantees of the predictability of the interactions are still human beings as credible representatives of the partners to the cooperative undertaking.

# Chapter Fourteen

## THE NETWORK-MARKET

SEVERAL FEATURES characterize most markets of personalized products: among others, the absence of an official nomenclature of activities, the weak relevance of public signs, the partial or complete ban on personal advertising, which relegates practitioners' fees and particular qualities to secrecy, and the prohibition on collective fee schedules. They exclude the spontaneous encounter of supply and demand. These markets operate regularly because they are embedded in personal devices, which diversify into the *personal network*, the *trade network*, and the *practitioner network*.

The *personal network* embraces family, friends, and colleagues (persons with whom relations are less frequent, less familiar, and usually occur in the workplace), to which are often connected professional,[1] ideological, and other networks. The personal network is by far the most accessible, utilized, and important. All personal networks form spontaneously and outside the market, all are made up of interpersonal relations through which knowledge circulates. Whoever taps into the network can gather information, for example on singular products, and thus possess terms of comparison. The *trade network* is made up of sellers and buyers, whose interaction may lead to replacing distrust with trust and to exchanges based on credible knowledge of reciprocal behaviors. The *practitioner network* includes professionals whose interpersonal relations ensure the circulation of credible knowledge about their practices.

Just as the different impersonal devices allowed a classification of coordination regimes, so the relations between the three network categories should provide a basis for classifying coordination regimes of personalized services.

### THE PERSONAL NETWORK

Those connected to a personal network satisfy their need for knowledge by word of mouth. The persons mobilized are readily accessible and credible (because there is no reason for opportunism), and their help is free; but it

---

[1] For instance, the networks used by heads of firms to gather information on business advisers and consultants. See C. Sauviat, "Le conseil: Un 'marché réseau' singulier," in J. de Bandt and J. Gadrey (eds.), *Relations de service, marchés de services* (Paris: Editions du CNRS, 1994), pp. 241–262.

takes time to make the rounds to collect the pertinent information. The network generally intervenes locally, but it can also extend over great distances.

Stories, personal experiences, evaluations, names, prices, and advice are all useful and valuable information, since they allow comparison and a reasonable decision. The exchange of words has the major advantage of modulating the knowledge transmitted to take account of the request. The search for information usually comes to a fairly rapid end: after a few people have been consulted. Even if the format of the knowledge, the contexts of the experiences, and the details all favor comparison, they do not eliminate hesitation, especially when different information and advice come from several persons recognized as possessing the same degree of authority and competence. This network therefore does not exclude indecision and deliberation, but, on the whole, the choice is made simpler.

When it comes to the market of personalized products, recourse to the personal network is almost obligatory. This requirement cannot be explained solely by the absence of impersonal devices, because networks sometimes also intervene at the same time as the impersonal devices—when they exist—and because it does not help make sense of the persisting use of the network alone in old markets that, faced with costly and dangerous inefficiency, could have been reformed long ago. The presence of the network thus has to do with causes that are peculiar to it.

In the job market, *personal devices are more efficient than impersonal devices*. For upwardly mobile professionals, managers, and technicians, those who rely on networks—compared to those who use impersonal means (classified ads, spontaneous candidacies)—are more likely to have "better jobs." Furthermore, with respect to those who consult family and friends, the help of colleagues is more useful because they have broader and more diversified information. The personal device is thus more effective than the impersonal device, and the same is true of "weak" ties (workplace relations) as compared to "strong" ties (friends and family). This applies not only to the relevance of the job but also to the costs and time necessary to get one and explains the fact that personal networks are used even when the markets are equipped with impersonal judgment devices.[2]

Informing, describing, transmitting, interpreting, replying, proposing, arguing, calling back, and clarifying demand a rich and varied language: the tool best suited to this task is speech. Speech establishes an irreducible advantage. And network means speech. The device that ensures the cir-

---

[2] "Better jobs are found through contacts, and the best jobs, the ones with the highest pay and prestige and affording the greatest satisfaction to those in them, are more apt to be filled in this way." M. Granovetter, *Getting a Job* (Cambridge, MA: Harvard University Press, 1995), pp. 22, 40–46. See also W. W. Powell and L. Smith-Doerr, "Networks and economic life," in N. J. Smelser and R. Swedberg (eds.), *Handbook of Economic Sociology* (Princeton: Princeton University Press, 1994), pp. 372–376.

culation of speech is more effective than impersonal devices. To be sure, under the twin influences of the speaker's interpretation and the receiver's reinterpretation, knowledge undergoes a transformation without the final meaning being knowable in advance. But there, too, speech lends itself more readily to rectification: it is the most flexible and therefore most effective mechanism for exploring similarities and constructing convergences of meanings.

While this advantage holds for singularities,[3] it varies with the volume and the quality of the network members' cognitive resources, which are not unrelated to the socioprofessional makeup of the networks. It also varies with the users, their positions in the interpersonal relations,[4] their competence, and their commitment.

Since the personal network supplies knowledge, it also acts—usually without its members' awareness—as a competitive mechanism. The idiosyncratic speech circulating in this network circumscribes the range of possible choices, and the new information or advice that regularly replaces the old confirms the outcome of the economic battles between producers of the personalized services. Competition, in this case, is conducted via changes of judgment; these changes are probably slower than those occurring in a market endowed with public information. Since the network is invisible, the quality competition is invisible as well.

The personal network does away with ignorance and uncertainty concerning quality by turning the unfeasible, spontaneous, direct meeting of employer and employee or of practitioner and client into a triangular relationship that allows a satisfactory adjustment in the end. The representatives not only propose knowledge, they also stand behind it. This is standard practice in the market of professional services. Every choice is the expression of the joint action of network and actor.

## The Trade Network

Personalized products markets are embedded in trade networks; these have specific modes of action and effects. Mark Granovetter's general interpretation posits that uncertainty disappears when a market is embedded in seller-buyer networks whose relationship spontaneously gives rise to trust and therefore to predictable reciprocal behavior. To be sure, this network does not expand in a regular fashion, so that Homo eco-

---

[3] "In many important situations, one has to obtain information about rather unstandardized alternatives." Further on, the author notes the importance of the "particularism." Granovetter, *Getting a Job*, pp. 97, 101–102.

[4] S. Burt, *Structural Holes: The Social Structure of Competition* (Cambridge, MA: Harvard University Press: 1992).

nomicus can be found in primitive, as well as in modern, societies. The trade network is an intermediate social structure that is spontaneous, invisible, and omnipresent; as such it helps makes sense of the way the market regularly functions.

Here, embedding is relational. But how do we identify it? How can we tell that relations between vendors and clients entail both exchange and trust, that they are "personal"? For Granovetter three causes can help. The first is indistinguishable from interaction, but it is not so obvious that the simple intensity of interpersonal relations suffices to qualify it. The second adds a sharing of values inimical to self-interest. The third is defined in a short passage: "Departing from pure economic motives, continuing economic relations often become overlaid with social content that carries strong expectations of trust and abstention from opportunism."[5] Sharing the same symbolic reality therefore creates mutual trust.

The question of trust has still not been completely clarified, though. It is possible to accept that "personal relations" promote trust, with the proviso that not only is interaction alone not enough to produce such a result but that trust, particularly in the case of professional services, must come *before* personal interaction. Without an "advance on trust," without credit—in both senses of the word—the practitioner would have neither the time nor the opportunity to win his client's trust. In sum, interaction on its own is no guarantee that trust will arise, and trust can exist without seller-buyer interaction.[6] The notion of trade network therefore implies taking a close look at the various kinds of trust that come into play.

## THE PRACTITIONER NETWORK

Little work has been done on the practitioner network, which locates each professional in a more or less diverse and dense universe of interpersonal relations that circulate anecdotes, information, rumors, criticism, invitations, electoral campaigns, mobilizations, and so forth. The knowledge possessed by other practitioners is all the more useful because it allows realistic comparisons and thus eventually correction of practices in one direction or the other.

[5]M. Granovetter, "Economic action and social structure: The problem of embeddedness," *American Journal of Sociology* 3 (1985): 490.

[6]The incarnation of the trustworthy figure in sociological literature—"We can trust old Max"—rests on a reputation that, in a structured milieu, encompasses a growing number of persons for whom one's word is worth anything written. S. Macaulay, "Non-contractual relations in business: A preliminary study," *American Sociological Review* 28 (1963): 55–67.

For the practitioner network to be used in this way and to act to regulate prices and shared standards of behavior, those wanting to make comparisons need to have the same criteria of evaluation and judgment. They must also feel that these criteria are widely enough shared for the reference to be part of an order. Of course, disagreements can exist, for the profession has many dimensions. But outside periods of rapid change, an intersubjective agreement tends to come about that ensures the reproduction and even the extension of the network-market.

•  •  •

The effects of these three networks on the market are specific, as are the effects stemming from their interactions. *The network-market is defined by the intertwining of personal, trade, and practitioner networks.* It encompasses all of the resources necessary for a market of professionalized services to function in a lasting manner. Further, the flexibility of its components allows new configurations and thus makes the network-market all the more durable. It is the common platform from which rise the various architectures that compose the market of personalized services: the reticular regime, the professional regime, and the interfirm regime.

*Chapter Fifteen*

# THE RETICULAR COORDINATION REGIME

THE RETICULAR COORDINATION regime includes the markets of singularities whose functioning rests exclusively or mainly on the network-market. That leaves some diversity and explains the presence of three variants, which correspond respectively to the *conviction*, *miracle*, and *revelation* logics of coordination. We will present only the first two. The first is the closest to the analytical definition of the reticular regime (network-market only), and it will be applied to the violin market; the second hides the primacy given to networks and will be used for the market of private lessons; the third will be merely evoked at the end of the chapter.

## COORDINATION BY SHARED CONVICTIONS

The top-of-the-range violin is a singularity. For musicians, its qualities are crucial because they determine musical performance. This conviction is rooted both in experience and in a tenacious mythology embodied in the legendary musical quality of the

| Network-market |
|---|
| Conviction logic |

Stradivarius and a good number of early violins, in particular those made in Italy. The demand for a "good" violin is compelling. But the generic term *good* designates instruments that differ in the volume of the sound produced, precision, ease of play, correspondence with a type of music, sound quality, and fit with the musician's body. The many configurations of the instrument's qualities mirror the multiplicity of the clients' logics of action. For a musician, the choice is personalized, and the instrument unique.

How can a musician find the desired instrument? Opportunities are rare. Violins are usually sold through the network, although some are auctioned. And their price—especially for eighteenth-century instruments—is particularly high. The musician is usually either obliged to buy a new, ready-made instrument or, more often, to commission one. In the latter case, the uncertainty becomes radical: it bears on the mutual understanding between the client and the violinmaker; on a craft—which does not exclude unforeseen technical hazards; and on the deferral of the evaluation, since a definitive judgment on the musical quality of the instrument can be made only after a long period of repeated controls following the purchase.[1]

Priority of qualities, incommensurability, and uncertainty—everything is present. And as usual, everything revolves around the question: how can one embark on the choice of an object to which one attaches so much importance—and which is expensive as well—when its true character, even after purchase, will not be known for some time? And, as usual, the solution calls for replacing the search for the "right" violin by the search for the "right" violinmaker, since he (or she) is the one who makes, adjusts, and looks after the violin. He is the one who possesses the technical and musical knowledge and skill that create an asymmetry of competence between himself and his clients. He is the one who sets the price of the instruments he sells and the services he provides. He is the one who personalizes the instruments and thus plays a role in the musicians' professional careers. He and he alone guarantees his work and the future career of the instrument.[2]

The choice of the "right" violinmaker is all the more crucial for being largely irreversible. It is all the more complicated because his skill and talent are not matters of public information. Musicians (in the broad sense of the term) turn to their professional personal networks, since it is they that ensure the informal circulation of concrete knowledge resulting from the accumulation of individual experiences. The choice is full of dangers, for unlike the lawyer's or the doctor's clients, musicians enjoy no particular protection. The profession of violinmaker has no conditions of access, no diplomas, no official and obligatory training, no code of ethics, and no professional disciplinary board. The professional associations have no power over their members. In sum, the discretionary power of the violinmaker is not restricted by the state, a school, or the profession.

In view of the possibility of error and opportunism, the personal network takes on a decisive value, not only because of the knowledge it circulates but also because of the power of dissuasion it derives as the embodiment of a relatively small professional milieu: the profession as a body looms large behind the individual. This does not mean that the market relies exclusively, or even primarily, on a mixture of knowledge and threats—even implicit ones. Such reliance would not really explain the rarity of opportunistic behaviors and the generality of practices similar to those of the traditional regulated professions. How can we understand that a craft behaves like a profession although it looks much very like a network-market?

[1] F. Peltier, "L'innovation dans la facture instrumentale" (doctoral diss., Ecole des Mines, Paris, 1994).

[2] The inseparable relationship between the product and the producer is valid for personalized goods as well as for services.

The causes lie in the trust sustained by a common project and a long-standing coproduction (which does not exclude asymmetrical competences) as well as in a shared belonging to the world of the arts. Violinmakers and their clients often form duos engaged in long professional paths; they share an artistic project which, in the case of the violinmaker, is incarnated in the demands of professional pride. These individual choices and forms of cooperation create lineages that are embodied as socially recognized models of success.[3]

The strong mutual trust that inhabits the project shared by violinmaker and violinist structures the violin market. It can be seen at certain specific articulations of their interactions: the musician's delegation of his power to the craftsman's skill; the conviction that technical discussions are not opportunistic strategies for raising the price; the reputation of the violinmaker, which does not necessarily translate into profit; and the sharing of the artist's career. This trust causes cooperation to prevail over conflicting interests, and the question of price to recede behind the singular qualities engaged in any artistic venture.

The market of top-of-the-range violins eschews impersonal judgment devices (with the exception of a few instruments used by the violinmaker for technical evaluations); it also eschews rules. Even though it is characterized by a number of forms of uncertainty, it operates essentially through intertwining personal and trade networks.

To explain the solidity of this market in a world dominated by self-interest, to explain the continued presence of a logic of excellence that turns every piece into a measure of professional qualities, another force must be at work. It must tip the scales in favor of the future, must give full weight to symbolic rewards, must transform the exchange relationship into one of coproduction—all of which suppose prior mutual construction of a collective entity that builds its strength and unity on passion and belief: music as a way of life and the shared love of art.

The network-market alone cannot ensure the survival of the violin market; it also needs passions and beliefs—let us them call "convictions"—to which the actors adhere sufficiently to render all other guarantees of re-

---

[3] "How does one find someone to make a violin? . . . It was only when I finally had a whole instrument, a violin that wanted looking after, that a true relationship grew up with André Lévi—my teacher Gérard Poulet's violinmaker—that was comparable to the relationship one may have with one's physician." Amanda Favier, violinist. "How can one describe the relationship between the violinist and his violinmaker? It is a relationship of trust that has to do with the nature of the instrument, simple and apparently fragile, but a solo instrument with a rich musical potential. Furthermore the instrument is often old and needs to be kept in shape. . . . What about modern violins? For its first twenty years a violin is unstable because its components (wood, glue, and varnish) are still young. Its maker is the best person to follow its evolution. . . . It should be said that a very small minority of violinmakers are competent experts." André Lévi, violinmaker, *Journal du Conservatoire* 32 (December 1998).

ciprocal behavior useless. It is because convictions structure both the trade and the personal networks that no trace of control devices and other expressions of a collective action principle can be seen, that no rule intrudes from outside to reduce quality uncertainty, and that the violin market seems to be self-regulating. Shared convictions are not a secondary consideration: it is the surplus that ensures the market's durability. If the immaterial reality that holds the actors together were to be altered, violinmakers would have to adopt the same collective guarantees as the traditional professions.

## COORDINATION BY BELIEF IN MIRACLE WORKERS

Coordination by belief in miracle workers concerns ambiguous professional services. The validity and dependability of their promises are not obvious to those who purchase such services, even though their value may not really be suspect. Such forms of am-

| Network-market |
|---|
| Miracle logic |

biguity do not necessarily apply to exceptional practices, as we see from the market of private tutoring, a longstanding and ever growing practice.

For many struggling pupils and for a fraction of good students in the secondary schools and colleges who want to better their relative advantage, private lessons are believed to improve performance. At school, parents and students quickly learned that children's grades depended on the quality of the teacher; therefore, in the private-tuition market, the search is for a "good" tutor. Definitions may vary, but not expectations. One criterion wins out over all others: a good tutor raises grades.

How does one go about finding a good tutor? The supply is visible in the form of impersonal judgment devices: a notice in the shop, an ad in the free press or on other supports, flyers tacked on university bulletin boards, advertising, information on the Internet. A large majority of the offerings are university students, and they use the same ranking system—a combination of diplomas and fees—which in principle reflects the hierarchy of competences.[4]

This public device is validated by both those who give the lessons and those who take or purchase them. It dispels the opacity of the market. It establishes the relative level of "teachers'" competences by the relative level of the diplomas.[5] Yet the device has a limited effect, since the majority

---

[4] For reasons of simplicity, the analysis does not include private schools, which, though rapidly expanding, account for only a portion of tutors and also recruit according to the same grid of diplomas and competences.

[5] "Far from being a matter of private supply and demand, the fee for private lessons is more a question of social organization based on rules and norms." E. Ghillebaert, "Le marché particulier des leçons particulières" (doctoral diss., Faculté des Sciences économiques et sociales, Lille, 1995), p. 60.

of potential clients have recourse to networks; and, as a consequence, other parents' or students' recommendations become more important than diplomas. The public device sets the hourly fee, but only those unable to tap into a "good" network use it to choose a "good" teacher.

To put it another way, a priori the diploma hierarchy lends itself remarkably well to the simultaneous appreciation of competences and prices. But no objective study substantiates this equivalence. For France at least, nothing is known about the differential teaching effectiveness according to diplomas. Critical observations concerning the validity of ranking by diploma and/or competence are a dime a dozen. Without this skepticism, certified teachers should have a decisive competitive edge, but this is not the case. And above all, the recruitment of private tutors should use public devices exclusively, and yet the majority are recruited through networks.[6] In this case, recruitment relies on individual evaluations, which do not necessarily coincide with the diploma level. Quality uncertainty therefore predominates.

Moreover, this uncertainty is not removed when other evaluation criteria are used. Nothing is objectively known about the outcome of tutoring on grades. No statistics, no studies, if such exist, are raised as arguments.[7] Students' qualitative judgments can legitimately come into play, but only after an indefinite time, usually much later. As a result, the criteria for evaluating tutors often shift from their educational competence to their human qualities, insofar as these are intuitively seen as a necessary if not sufficient condition for success. In sum, educational competence—as the capacity to implement skills or methods that improve school performances—is sought by everyone, but no one knows how to gauge it, so clients are obliged to rely essentially on word of mouth.

The market of private lessons, which does not seem difficult to interpret, is actually organized around an enigma: How does one reconcile classification of competences based on a hierarchy of diplomas and/or hourly fees with a practice that, insofar as it is possible, relies on the network? How can it be that the logic of impersonal judgment devices and that of personal judgment devices are so far apart? Why this double register by which clients deny the very thing they validate?

[6] A sample of students in Lille shows that 80 percent have had direct or indirect recourse to the network, but the sample is small. Ibid. A survey made in England shows that over half of students used the network, 13 percent the ads, and 8 percent an agency. J. Ireson and K. Rushforth, *Mapping and Evaluating Shadow Education* (University of London: Institute of Education, 2005).

[7] D. Glasman and G. Collonges (*Cours particuliers et construction social de la scolarité* [Paris: CNDP, 1994], pp. 160–164) are somewhat optimistic, but their study is based on the "opinions" of students and parents and not on grades. Moreover, they agree that "it is important to measure the role played by this advantage [private lessons], which is minor and not very determining compared with the others [advantages]." R. Establet, *L'école est-elle rentable?* (Paris: Presses Universitaires de France, 1987).

Recourse to private tutoring goes hand in hand with a strong belief in the efficacy of pedagogical competence. That people do not know how to recognize it does not mean it does not exist. The network should enable its identification. One repercussion of this belief is that teachers whose competence is equated with their diplomas and who are recruited on the public market benefit from only moderate trust. This trust is apparently fragile because there is no guarantee that it would pass a fairly strict test; and yet it is less fragile than one might think because the facts that would disprove a teacher's presumed quality intervene rarely and belatedly. Nevertheless, existing practices do not forbid the hope of encountering the person with the particular pedagogical gift capable of "working miracles." The actors oscillate between academic competence and pedagogical competence; between the hierarchy of diplomas and the hierarchy of talents; between impersonal public devices and invisible personal devices.

The market is indeed organized around the miracle worker. It is this figure that justifies recourse to the network in the hope of discovering its incarnation. Hiring a tutor thus becomes a lottery that leaves the client wavering between hope and disappointment while adjusting to the reality on the ground.

Democratization of schooling reinforces the intensity of the competition and gives rise to generalized anxiety. In this case, no means of satisfying students' professional and social ambitions can be neglected. To do so would be to disqualify the investment in advance. We believe, even though we know we have few reasons to believe. When choosing to believe rather than not to believe, however, the actors must construct a rational justification for their choice. They may find it in the public ranking that combines competence, diplomas, and hourly fee. But this meritocratic belief is too vulnerable to justify the market on its own. The belief in *natural pedagogical dispositions* takes the lead when an opportunity arises. The priority of the network over the impersonal device in fact indicates simultaneously that the market of miracle workers is close to the network-market, that the hierarchy of teaching competence counts more than the hierarchy of diplomas, and that therefore absolute belief matters more than moderate belief. But they go together.

The interplay of the two beliefs maintains the ambiguity of the reality. The market rests on a collective illusion, on a magical practice used to ward off social misfortune. Without belief—even tainted with skepticism—in impersonal devices, there would be no market; and without absolute trust in pedagogical gifts, and therefore in the network, nothing says that trust in public devices alone would be enough to make the market work. The two are complementary. The global logic of the market divides into two strands according to opportunity. It plays on certified merit when there is no other possibility, and on excellence—embodied in the search for a savior—when reality seems to hold out the means to turn belief into a reality principle. This oscillation explains at one and the same time that a great diversity of teaching practices are accepted by parents and students, that the active search for the "right" relationship continues, and that disappointments result in resignation rather than in complaints. The notion of *miracle logic* tries to convey the alternation between the two frames of action.

The fact that moderate trust/belief and absolute trust/belief are not only present but are even growing, with no demand for elucidation, is part of the particularism of this market; it is not impossible that, even if private lessons do not usually improve the academic situation of students in difficulty, they at least prove to the students, and to the parents themselves, that everything has been done to avoid failure. Indeed, perhaps they exist only to make it easier to accept the unacceptable.

Coordination by the search for a miracle worker does not seem to comply with the pure requirement of the network-market. If we have nevertheless placed it in the reticular coordination regime, it is because, in spite of the existence of impersonal devices, the essential plays out in networks. The conciliation between trade and personal networks supposes that public devices may be used for setting the prices, but for the selection of private "teachers," they come into competition with personal networks, even though they are—almost without exception—unable to prevail, for the ideal comprises merits that their actual performance necessarily lacks.

• • •

Far from being an exception, the private tutoring market is one of the "markets of lesser evils": it lies halfway between markets providing valid services and the third variant of the reticular regime: markets of revelation—clairvoyance, astrology, card reading, sorcery, and so forth—whose signs of quality are as dubious as the realities they are supposed to ensure.

The network-market underpins the regime of coordination based on shared convictions and on the search for a miracle worker. The difference between the two is that the first completely ignores impersonal devices while the second gives them some room. But, in isolation, the network-market lacks the resources to ensure its own longevity. It takes more than knowledge to establish a durable market. The repetition of exchange relations cannot be a matter of habit or self-interest alone. Symbolic forces are needed that are powerful enough to neutralize distrust and opportunism. When impersonal devices are lacking, or when they are of limited efficiency, then passions and beliefs are absolutely necessary.

## Chapter Sixteen

# THE PROFESSIONAL COORDINATION REGIME

THE NOTION OF *professions* refers to various groups—from doctors, dentists, lawyers, and architects to the diverse categories of business consultants—which "produce" and sell personalized services. They could not do this were they not embedded in specific devices: self-government, regulation, codes of ethics, disciplinary bodies, and the network-market. For proponents of neoclassical economics, these devices are incongruous and harmful, since they hinder competition: without them, professional services would be better and cheaper. The viewpoint I present here is just the opposite: *without specific devices, there would be no professions, and without professions, there would be no personalized services.*

| Network-market Control devices |
|---|
| Excellence logic |

What characterizes the professions?[1] Where do they begin and where do they leave off? These questions sum up several decades of debates within the sociology of professions. The results have taken more the form of compromises than of choices between alternatives. The professional model continues to occupy an eminent position, even though the degree of agreement on its definition is moderate, and even though it is recognized as not being valid either for all countries or for all times in the same country.

The present analysis focuses not on the profession as such but on the *personalized service*. It intends to determine the elements that ensure that this service is produced and will remain on the market. The reticular regime, based on personalized services, has already helped us identify professional groups whose solidity depends on a combination of the network-market and beliefs and/or passions. But the regulated professions represent a much more complex reality, especially when they are characterized by developed technical and social differentiation. A direct study could not go very far, and therefore a new step is necessary to simplify this reality, following the same procedure that has already been employed. We will

---

[1] One definition among others: "A profession . . . is an occupation that regulates itself through systematic, required training and collegial discipline; that has a base in technical, specialized knowledge; and that has a service rather than profit orientation enshrined in its code of ethics." P. Starr, *The Social Transformation of American Medicine* (New York: Basic Books, 1982), p. 15. For a general discussion, see C. Dubar and P. Tripier, *Sociologie des professions* (Paris: A. Colin, 1998).

elaborate the variants of the professional regime, which are also coordination regimes.

The starting point is the typical relationship between the practitioner and the client, which should be interpreted as a relation of delegation embedded in symbolic reality.[2] The practitioner is a representative whose (implicit or explicit) mandate is to act on his client's behalf, and, in return, the client is supposed to adopt a position of dependency, give his trust, and expect the initial pact to be respected. This relationship establishes a balance of rights and duties which, when institutionalized, is projected into the long term. The professions thus share a particular form of social organization, a historical legacy that in the past has served in the personalized use of knowledge and skills.

Personalized service is associated at one and the same time with a *form of collective action* based on cooperation between the representative and the person he represents, with the practitioner's *discretionary power* over his client, with *mutual trust*, and with a *transaction relationship*. The intensity of these relations varies such that the profession may be defined by the management of a system of tensions. It is as though, in order to accomplish his task, the practitioner could go in one direction but not to the point of jeopardizing the opposite term. He can act in concert with the represented party, but not to the point of fusing their interests; and vice versa he can pursue his own interests, but not to the point of jeopardizing the initial pact. He can try to expand his discretionary power, but not to the point of jeopardizing mutual trust; and again vice versa, he must not allow trust to endanger his obligation to act. Depending on the activities and the times, the balance changes, but maintenance of the system gives the professions a great capacity for adaptation.

These dimensions, combined with the network-market, should enable us to construct the variants of the professional coordination regime. Once these are worked out, we will then check the relevance of this classification against the results of a survey on lawyers' clients.

## Professional Regime Variants

Service relations and control devices are the two central features of professional services. The first deals with the relations between practitioners and their clients; the second concerns the means used to balance the risks incurred by the clients with the degree of trust available, and thereby to prevent "market failure." The classification of the variants of the professional regime is the result of combining the two dimensions

[2] On the relation of delegation, see chapter 5, section 1, of this volume.

## The Service Relation

*Service relation* is a generic term for the "tailor-made" interventions practiced on individual or collective actors. In everyday language, the personalized service is "sold" and "bought," but this is only a metaphor, since, in order to benefit from a personalized service, one must recruit and remunerate the producer. When the client considers the stakes to be important and when at the same time the product is inseparable from its producer, the client's demand focuses on the "good" or "right" practitioner. He looks for and hires an expert and dedicated capacity for action, even though at the time he partially, and sometimes totally, ignores the difficulties involved, the specific means to be used, and the results that can be obtained.

The service relation is often an ongoing process of production and sale. Depending on the activity and the profession, it can begin and end with a single intervention, or it can go on for weeks, months, and sometimes years. The notions of purchase and sale are ill-suited to a kind of transaction defined by a promise, by a variable deferred evaluation gap, and by the predominance of uncertainty.

With the relation of delegation, the representative is distinguished from the party represented by an asymmetry of knowledge, which is also an asymmetry of power. For reasons of efficacy, he exercises broad discretionary power. This concept, borrowed from the vocabulary of sociology, is at once useful and dangerous: useful because it underscores the practitioner's capacities of self-organization for "producing" the best personalized service; dangerous because the layperson easily confuses it with arbitrary or illegitimate action. But, a priori, none of these terms is relevant: discretionary power exists for technical reasons and presupposes at least tacit consent on the client's part.

Figure 2 provides a visual representation of the power relations between the professional and his client as defined by two orthogonal dimensions, representing, on one hand, the varying power of the professional and, on the other, the varying power of the client. Power relationships correspond to the space delimited by the practitioners' intervention, ranging from autonomy to subordination, and by the clients' commitment, which ranges from consenting passivity to dominating activity. According to their relative positions, one may distinguish schematically three main types of power relations. When practitioner autonomy and client passivity are both at their height, the relation is characterized by professional discretionary power. When the relative positions are inverse—practitioner autonomy is the smallest and client activity is the greatest—the relation is defined by professional subordination. In the middle, we have balanced power. The figure does not exhaust the possibilities, as professional and

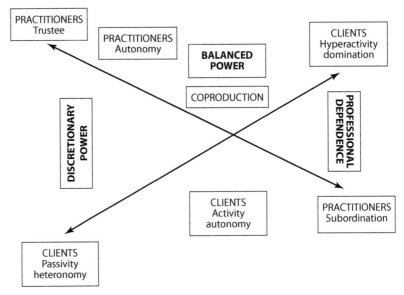

Figure 2. Relations of Power/Knowledge between Practitioners and Their Clients

client can both claim discretionary power or can both refuse autonomy. But these last cases are rare.[3]

### ON DISCRETIONARY POWER

The classical model of the profession is organized around discretionary power, which varies between a maximum and a minimum as the practitioner's autonomy and the client's passivity increase or diminish.

Discretionary power is sometimes given an economic meaning. Some analysts assimilate it to profit maximization, and according to them, autonomy could only serve this one end because it is impossible to go against human nature as embodied in Homo economicus. There is not much we can say to counter what is taken for granted. Nevertheless, although no one claims that professionals do not care about high incomes—even as high as possible—and, in spite of its shrinking domain, the idea of disinterested behavior remains pertinent, not as a claim to practitioners' altruism, but to explain that they do not necessarily carry self-interest to the

[3]The present analysis is limited to the classical service relation and the private service relation. *Professional dependence* is in principle excluded, since it directly contradicts the professions' conditions of existence. While such inversion of power is relatively rare, it can nevertheless be found in the case, for example, of economically vulnerable doctors when intense competition makes them subject to their patients' power and leads them to use heterodox practices. Likewise, big firms have the power to impose new forms of management that impinge on the integrity of personalized professional services. For the moment, though, these situations form a small minority. In the case of doctors, neoclassical econo-

extreme.[4] This principle is recalled here not because it is written in the code of ethics, but because it is associated with the notion of "fair price" and because it defines a diversified set of discrete practices.

When the distance between the practitioner and the client is maximal, the practitioner is not only autonomous, he or she must act as a *guardian*. The term is used to designate tutelage practices, which give certain professions, under specific conditions, not only the power but also the duty to defend the interests of their client, even against his or her wishes. It means, for example, that the doctor's task—and to a lesser degree that of the lawyer and a few other professionals—is not to satisfy a demand but to solve the peculiar real "problem" of a person or a collectivity. The need to act as a trustee reveals the secret truth about the professions: they are not exclusively determined by demand; they do not exist solely to satisfy their clients: their action is also governed by the public good. For the doctor this requirement is still respected, but for lawyers and other professions, it is in decline.

Discretionary power is to be confused neither with profit seeking nor with moralization or goodwill; it is a sphere of action granted to representatives in order to make their action more effective. Discretionary power is linked to a craft. In principle, when it is supported by trust, it creates the conditions favorable to the most effective "tailor-made" interventions. This trust is personal, impersonal, or both. The first results from social interactions in the merchant-network; the second exists prior to the encounter between practitioner and client and usually stems from a general belief in the profession's dedication to the public good. Impersonal trust occupies a crucial position when there are few occasions to call upon a type of practitioner: with it, trust is given without knowing who is receiving it. But it has often been noted that such a "trustworthy discretionary power" opens up the greatest opportunities for "breach of trust," for "malfeasance"; the client thus runs great risks.

### ON COPRODUCTION

It is in the relationship between business consultants and firms that coproduction has acquired its full meaning as a system of interactions whereby practitioners and their clients, because their knowledge and power are balanced, work together to create a personalized service. The practitio-

---

mists have developed the theory of "induction of demand by supply," which, were it demonstrated (which it has not been), would justify controlling doctors in order to counteract the absence of competition. S. Bejean, *Économie du système de santé* (Paris: Economica, 1994). The patients' capacity to impose their prescription demands on their doctor in the wake of intense competition is perhaps a more important phenomenon, which points up the contradiction between personalized service and the dynamics of competition.

[4] L. Karpik, *French Lawyers: A Study in Collective Action 1274–1994*, trans. Nora Scott (Oxford: Oxford University Press, 1999), pp. 105–111, 148–154.

ner's discretionary power can, in this case, play a modest role, with the same also being true for the visibility and evaluation of his contribution.

Such cooperation is supposed to result in greater efficiency, but this is not always the case. Behind a neutral formulation, coproduction in fact includes the possibility of antagonistic cooperation, in which the professional, defending his autonomy of intervention and protecting the limits of personal initiative, becomes hostile to the client's intervention. The term coproduction therefore designates both more efficient systems of global cooperation—at the cost of some loss of independence on all sides—and more conflictual systems of cooperation

## Control Devices

Professions are characterized by a combination of control devices that are more or less sophisticated, respected, and efficient. Moreover, such devices do not form a monolithic category: they are unequally present, depending on the profession and the historical period.

Although the usual interpretation of the expansion of these devices is the search by professions for an economic rent, and although this aim may exist, in fact, even a cursory observation of past and present history shows that the main cause lies somewhere else. To maintain its continuity, to avoid market failure, professions used (and still use) control devices to keep the clients' risks proportionate to the available collective trust. Another cause has been recently added: the control of work quality. Both categories of devices are quite different; they work differently and should be examined separately.

### PROFESSIONAL-MORALITY CONTROL DEVICES

The greater the practitioners' discretionary power, the greater the clients' trust must be to overcome the risks associated with radical quality uncertainty. When the service relationship is marked by numerous unexpected accidents, when numerous disappointments follow opportunistic practices, when social judgment deals more and more badly with a profession, distrust arises and threatens the foundations and the very organization of the profession.

It is then time to alleviate the *fiduciary deficit* either by augmenting the volume of trust available or by reducing the clients' risks. The first solution is sought through collective commitments to improve the quality of services, or through communication campaigns to enhance the profession's image. But these interventions take time, are costly, and their effectiveness is doubtful. The second solution, the one that is usually retained, consists in creating and implementing control devices in order to bring the practitioners' discretionary power into line with the available volume of client trust. The code of ethics, in association or not with a disciplinary body, contains the practitioners' explicit obligations to clients and more generally to the public. It may be enlarged and may be more strictly enforced until distrust is reduced, if not completely eliminated.

This evolution has obeyed two general rules: (1) the more social value that global society attributes to collective activities, the better protected the public should be; and (2) the greater the information asymmetry between practitioners and clients, the more powerful the control devices should be. Because society has considered their activities to be among the most important and because the information asymmetry between practitioners and clients has been the greatest, the health-care and legal professions have the densest and strictest universe of control devices, whereas the opposite was long true for business consultants, as a consequence of a much smaller difference between the knowledge possessed by consultants and that held by heads of firms. But, today, under the impact of growing distrust, even business consultants, at least part of them, are following the same strategy. It is now their turn to create a more or less dense set of control devices.

In present-day France, a set of combined causes—mainly history, discretionary power, and fiduciary deficit—explains that the number of the control devices tends to diminish down the line from doctors to the regulated health professions (dentists, pharmacists, veterinarians) and then to the legal professions (lawyers, attorneys), architects, and finally to business consultants.

### WORK CONTROL DEVICES

For the longest-standing professions, setting quality standards has long amounted to setting a minimum quality through mandatory diplomas, and sometimes professional training, and by reserving the monopoly of the practice for those having fulfilled the official conditions of access to the profession. With the extension of codes of ethics, these constraints circumscribe a mode of action that largely respects the independence of both the individual and the body, which means above all, respecting the practitioner's autonomy at work.[5] For a long time, the working domain was protected against external intrusions, but that has now changed.

Although a few professionals have voluntarily submitted to the constraints of quality assurance in order to benefit, in the competitive struggle, from quality certification by an independent authority, it is above all the state that has sparked a change of an altogether different magnitude by intervening directly in the content of the professional practices, as

---

[5] "I have defined professionalism as the occupational control of work." E. Freidson, *Professionalism: The Third Logic* (Chicago: University of Chicago Press, 2001), p. 179.

shown by the example of clinical medicine in France. Several reforms—
each time prompted by the quest for improved care quality and the desire
to reduce expenditures on public health care—were worked out, proposed, fought about, sometimes rejected, and sometimes accepted. Simply put: the repeated conflicts between the state, public agencies, and the
medical personnel have focused essentially on the definition and application of guidelines for professional practices.[6] The doctors' opposition
was generally grounded in the defense of individual and collective independence. Indeed, there is no issue more central than the autonomy of
professional practices, since it is the very condition of personalized care
and, thereby, the very condition of the profession's existence. But independence has become an all-purpose argument. To explain the practitioners' resistance, another principle must be added, less visible even for
professionals themselves: *professional pride.*

In universes of action that ignore direct hierarchical, technical, or disciplinary control, professional pride acts as an embodied normative device,
a principle of commitment rooted in the practitioner's identity and guided
by the demands of "good" quality. It is a historical, moral and social, and
individual and collective construction. While of course not the exclusive
prerogative of professionals, this principle is more crucial for them because, until now, work quality has depended on the practitioner alone.

The conflict stems from the meeting of, or the heterogeneity of, medical practices, something that is tracked down and rooted out by rationalization techniques. But, far from being considered a fault, diversity is on
the contrary (within certain limits) demanded by practitioners, who see it
as a sign of personalized practices, which, in situations of uncertainty,
make it possible to take into account the diversity of the cases, persons,
and situations. Professional pride varies in intensity, but it is a large
enough component of the professional's identity to withstand those who
would impose bounds on the conditions of its exercise. In this perspective, mandatory practice guidelines may ignite professional resistance.[7]

According to the degree of trust extended by the public and by the
state, professional power and professional pride are the causes of the
existence of two categories of devices that have different modes of functioning: one imposes the same obligations on everyone, while the other

[6]M. Robelet, "Réformes du système de santé et mobilisation éthique des médecins: Un
regard sociologique sur l'éthique des professions," in P. Batifoulier and M. Gadreau (eds.),
*Éthique médicale et politique de santé* (Paris: Economica, 2005), pp. 145–165.

[7]The desire of the state to alter the control devices and at the same time obtain professionals' adherence can give rise to long-lasting conflictual relations. See L. Karpik, "Ethique,
fierté et qualités professionneles," in P. Batifoulier and M. Gadreau (eds.), *Éthique médicale
et politique de santé* (Paris: Economica, 2005), pp. 167–179; and Robelet, "Réformes du
système de santé."

justifies the relative heterogeneity of practices. One calls on protection of similarity, while the other guarantees diversity.

• • •

Until the past few decades, professional self-government and the state have acted on service quality by means of relatively stable and general rules and on the norms governing practices with clients by introducing more professional ethics devices. In both cases, the autonomy of the working situation was respected. For physicians, and more generally the health professions, it is no longer the case, for two concurrent reasons: their practices are linked with science and their interventions are costly for the public budget. Regulation by the public authority therefore entered the "work domain," because the professional power either refused to step in or found itself powerless to do so. For the other professions, on the whole, the traditional balance between the types of control devices has remained constant and can be studied as usual, but this probably will not last.

## Legal-Services Coordination Regime Variants

As in a large number of countries, the market of French lawyers is for the most part impenetrable. Public information is very limited, but we know that the legal market is fairly heterogeneous.[8] Without direct investigation, it is practically impossible to gain accurate and systematic knowledge, but even with this knowledge, the problem of its analysis remains completely open. We propose to use coordination regimes as an explanatory tool.

The unequal distribution of knowledge and power between professionals and consumers and the unequal distribution of control devices are associated. As a result, the professional coordination regime displays two variants, defined by two different configurations: the *public variant* combines *discretionary power*, a strong universe of control devices, the network-market, and personal and impersonal trust; and the *private variant*, which is associated with *balanced power*, combines a weak universe of control devices, reliance on the personal and practitioner networks, and personal trust alone. In both cases, quality competition pre-

---

[8] For a general presentation and analysis of the French legal market, see A. Boigeol and L. Willemez, "Fighting for survival: Unification, differentiation and representation of the French Bar B," in W. Felstiner (ed.), *Reorganization and Resistance: Legal Professions Confront a Changing World* (Oxford: Hart Publishing, 2005), pp. 41–66; Karpik, *French Lawyers*, pp. 157–190.

vails over price competition, and in both cases excellence logic is the working rationale. But from one case to the other, meanings are somewhat modified.

The validity of the distinction between the two variants of professional regimes and, at least indirectly, the validity of the general classification of coordination regimes will be put to the test with the analysis of a survey on individual and small-firm clients who have been asked about their lawyer's characteristics and their relations with him. The questions have been formulated carefully to fit into the perspective of the economics of singularities, and the results are shown in Table 4.

Taking all the answers together, we see that: (1) nine out of ten clients consider that having a "good" lawyer has an important or very important impact on the outcome of the case; (2) fewer than one in ten chose their lawyer because he charged the lowest fee; and (3) three out of four chose their lawyer on the basis of information from the personal network. The search for a "good" singularity, the predominance of quality competition over price competition, the centrality of the personal network—we are indeed in the universe of singularities.[9]

Since the devices and practices that go into each coordination regime obey a particular logic and since all of the components are interdependent, it does not matter where we start the analysis. Let us therefore begin with trust. Trust is defined by various combinations of personal trust and impersonal trust. Crossing these two dimensions leads to four possibilities and a correlative distribution of the clients between *twofold trust, personal trust* alone, *impersonal trust* alone, *absence of trust*. The other survey data have been broken down on the basis of their associations with the four forms of trust. The lines in italics show the responses, and the lines in parentheses give the corresponding analysis. The four cases presented in Table 4 are called, respectively, the *price market* (1 out of 10 clients), the *public variant* (6 out of 10 clients), the *private variant* (2 out of 10 clients), and the *authoritarian market* (1 out of 10 clients).

The central questions are: Are the data distributed randomly? Can some regularities be linked to specific causes or do they belong to different coordination regimes? For the latter, it is necessary to show for each coordination regime, first, that there are four types of affinities between devices, practices, and trust, and second, that these affinities are theoreti-

---

[9]The INSEE (Institut National de la Statistique et des Etudes Statistiques) survey was carried out in two waves (November 1996 and February 1997). Conducted on a nationwide sample of 4,109 persons, it identified 660 people who had engaged a lawyer. Those respondents were then interviewed. The survey was conducted in the context of the "Enquête mensuelle de conjoncture auprès des ménages" [Monthly household survey of the conjuncture] carried out by the Department of Consumer Prices, Household Resources, and Household Living Conditions.

TABLE 4
Economic Coordination Regimes: Legal Clients
(% of client sample)

| | Impersonal Trust | Absence of Impersonal Trust |
|---|---|---|
| Personal trust | Having a "good" lawyer is important (singularity and effectiveness of the representative) | The lawyer's legal competence is important (primacy of qualities) |
| | Least references to minimum fee (primacy of qualities) | "To be kept informed" (coproduction) |
| | The greatest recourse to the personal network (search for information for reasonable choice) | Recourse to the personal network (search for reasonable choice) |
| | Primacy of lawyer's human qualities (recognition of knowledge asymmetry) | Personal trust alone |
| | | Personal financing (merchant networks) |
| | **Public Variant** (58%) (n = 383) | **Private Variant** (19%) (n = 125) |
| Absence of personal trust | No demand for specific legal competence (rejection of professional competence) | Having a "good" lawyer is not important (rejection of discretionary power) |
| | Random selection of lawyer (interchangeability of lawyers) | Criticism of lawyers: authoritarianism, lack of dedication, opportunism (rejection) |
| | Most references to minimum fee (primacy of price competition) | |
| | **Price Market** (10%) (n = 66) | **Authoritarian Market** (13%) (n = 86) |

cally meaningful: that they represent four more or less coherent regimes of coordination.

One in ten clients on the *price-market* is characterized by the "choice" of a lawyer without any specific legal competence, who was selected either at random or because he or she charged the lowest fee. This configuration may look surprising for a lawyers market, but it is less so when we know that two-thirds of these clients are engaged in divorce proceedings, usually by mutual consent, and the others are asking mainly for simple contracts. When the legal service is simple, predictable, and relatively standardized or standardizable, the clients regard lawyers as being interchangeable, since they have all had the same basic training, which should be sufficient to do satisfactorily what the client is asking. If they are interchangeable, it is no more illogical to look for the cheapest lawyer than to choose one at random. Personal trust is not necessary, but impersonal trust is, as it is considered as a measure of the effectiveness of the bar association in protecting the clients from lawyers' opportunistic behavior.

If they were given the chance to speak, lawyers would not fail to contest the central view justifying these practices, namely: that their activity is routine. Thus, for specific practices, the qualification of the legal services may become conflictual. "Socio-logically" speaking, when services are no longer personalized (or considered to be so by clients), when services belong to the universe of standardized/differentiated products, or when they are the equivalent of those found in the standard market, price competition will predominate, and the analysis should be performed using neoclassical economic theory.

The *public variant* is characterized by the search for a "good" lawyer, belief in the lawyer's dedication and effectiveness, use of the personal network, weakest association with the lowest fee, and reference not only to personal trust but also to the impersonal trust that is extended in advance to all members of the profession and so makes it possible for them to defend clients who are strangers. Six out of ten clients come under this heading, which fulfills the classical conditions for the effective coordination of personalized services: validity of the relation of delegation, validity of the control mechanisms, validity of the personal network, and twofold trust.

With the *private variant*, many of the clients (but fewer than in the preceding category) recognize the importance of a "good" lawyer, and at the same time more of them stress the need to be "kept informed" of their case: their relationship comes under the heading of "coproduction," or whatever comes the closest to it. These clients differ from their public counterpart by the absence of impersonal trust in the institution.

With the demand for technical legal competence, which concerns more particularly certain fields of law—especially commercial—than others, clients aim to create and maintain a relation of cooperation that is exclusively and unconditionally devoted to the defense of their interests. The overall logic is that of the exclusive relation characteristic of the corporate lawyers market. The absence of impersonal trust means not so much opposition to the profession as a collective body as indifference to collective guarantees; this is borne out by personal financing, the demand for dedication, and in exchange, personal trust in the lawyer as well as the use of not only the personal but also the trade networks. Clients actually tend to pressure their lawyers to draw a line between their craft and the profession; they come down on the side of the market because the form of dedication they understand best is remunerated dedication.

Few clients are *totally lacking in trust* (1 in 10). And the expression of this judgment is a whole set of accusations—inefficiency, authoritarianism, lack of dedication, opportunism—incurred mainly by lawyers assigned to individuals by insurance companies, banks, and so forth. How is it that clients who are brought together in this category are composed mainly of malcontents? The answer could be that the network-market does not come into play here, that these clients have not chosen their lawyers, they do not pay them and have no control over them. Because these clients are probably faced with manifestations of authoritarianism/indifference, their rejection of lawyers is the expression of their generalized powerlessness. It is the first time these clients appear as a specific category. And the authoritarian market is an ambiguous reality. It will take some time, and more detailed data, to solidly decide if we have to consider these clients' judgments as the products of the private-variant desingularization process or as the birth of a new regime of coordination that would only partially belong to the market.

· · ·

The analysis of each coordination regime could be taken further, but some conclusions can already be formulated: (1) The legal market is composed of four unequally distributed regimes of coordination. (2) Each of these regimes manifests a specific modality of product-client adjustment and, therefore, a peculiar working logic. (3) Each of these regimes appears under specific conditions. (4) The two dominant regimes are the public and the private variants; as peculiar realities, they are not far from the analytical models, and together they represent eight out of ten lawyers chosen by the clients. (5) As far as we can see, a new coordination regime—the authoritarian variant—has appeared, which is linked to the growth of legal insurance. (6) A fraction of the profession practices desingularized services, and as a consequence, the exchange is part of the standard market. (7) The method of analysis used here makes it possible to evaluate the respective weights of the coordination regimes within the profession.

The same approach can be appropriately applied to other markets of singularities. It is possible to extrapolate from the legal-market analysis because the diverse modalities of concrete adjustment between products, devices, and consumers fit the regimes of coordination quite well and because the heterogeneity of the singularities markets expresses the coexistence, interaction, and relative weights of the coordination regimes at work; therefore, *the classification of the coordination regimes explains the way markets of singularities work in reality.*

## Chapter Seventeen

# PRICES

THE ECONOMICS of singularities requires a new theory of price. The present analysis is a first step in that direction. It is limited in two ways. On the one hand, price is taken in a *narrow sense*: the cost (of production, transaction, search) is assumed to be given, and therefore the object of study concerns only the variation in the surplus realized by the producer and/or seller. On the other hand, the explanation of price variations is restricted to two causes only: relative quality and relative scarcity. Other causes exist but they will not be taken into account here.[1] Our aim is to build a unitary reasoning that will integrate the independent and the combined effects of relative quality and relative scarcity of products in price formation. Even restricted in this manner, though, our objective may seem rash; but above all, it is inevitable.

The impossibility of explaining price differences by the relation between supply and demand alone, which results from the primacy of quality competition over price competition, is not exceptional. For instance, the Sefrou market in Morocco is depicted as "a tumbling chaos"; exchange there is a complex process, given "the multiplicity of units . . . the inhomogeneity of goods, price dispersion . . . the amorphousness of business reputation"—and of course the quality uncertainty.[2] Information is scarce,

---

[1] Among the other causes affecting prices and which would probably be relevant in explaining the prices of singularities are (1) *network effects* (see W. Baker, "The social structure of a national securities market," *American Journal of Sociology* 89 [1984]: 775–811; and B. Uzzi and R. Lancaster, "Embeddedness and price formation in corporate law market," *American Sociological Review* 69, no. 3 [2004]: 319–344); (2) *comparison with competitors* (see S. Barrey, "Formation et calcul des prix: Le travail de tarification dans la grande distribution," *Sociologie du travail* 142 [2006]); (3) *judgment criteria and power relations* (see B. G. Carruthers, *City of Capital* [Princeton: Princeton University Press, 1996]; and V. Yakubovich, M. Granovetter, and P. McGuire, "Electric charges: The social construction of rate systems," *Theory and Society* 34, no. 5–6 [2005]: 579–612); (4) *collective representations* (see V. Zelizer, *Pricing the Priceless Child: The Changing Social Value of Children* [New York: Basic Books, 1985]); (5) *uncertainty* (see M. R. Kehoe, "Quality uncertainty and price in monopoly markets," *The Journal of Industrial Economics* 44, no. 1 [1996]: 25–32); (6) *reputation* (see J. M. Podolny, "A status-based model of market competition," *American Journal of Sociology* 98, no. 4 [1993]: 839–872. The list is not exhaustive.

[2] C. Geertz, "Suq: the bazaar economy in Sefrou," in C. Geertz, H. Geertz, and L. Rosen (eds.), *Meaning and Order in Moroccan Society: Three Essays in Cultural Analysis* (Cambridge: Cambridge University Press, 1979), pp. 123–310; pp. 197, 217, 221. See also C. Geertz, "The bazaar economy: Information and search in peasant marketing," *American Economic Review* May (1978): 28–32.

as is trust. How is it, then, that goods that are literally incomparable, owing to the many unobservable variations in their quality, have a price. This apparent disorder can be made sense of only through the action of two central devices: "customer loyalty," which ensures the distribution of customers among the merchants, and the only device that is important here: "bargaining."

Bargaining not only allows the client to drive down the price, it works also as a "particular mode of information search," since it gives the merchant a tool for setting the prices of a broad universe of products. By playing like a tenacious virtuoso on all of the calculable and calculated variables of the commodity—both qualitative and quantitative—the bargaining partners/antagonists determine the price of every state of the product, and thus compose a detailed scale of prices that can then be applied to the various forms of the products. The pricing system thus rests on an unexpected and ingenious mechanism that protects the incomparability of the products, creates the conditions of the seller's profit seeking, and maintains the customer's trust.

To analyze pricing on the markets of singularities, four problems must be resolved. First, we must lend visibility and intelligibility to the relationship between qualities and prices and, more specifically, we must verify the general principle that states, the greater the qualities, the higher the prices. However obvious this relationship may seem, it is no easier to study for that. There exists no tool that can be taken as the common criterion for ordering the general qualities of the singularities. And so we must look for the actual procedures that have been and still are being used by the economic actors. And then we must assess their consistency and make sure they are effective, which implies that they are socially valid. Even once these difficulties are resolved, others may arise, for example, from the multiplicity of partially contradictory rankings or from the impossibility of discovering the particular procedures through which is formed the strong association between qualities and prices that may be observed in certain markets. Nevertheless, we need to know them in order to establish the relations of *concordance* between relative qualities and relative prices.

Second, we must explain why, under certain conditions, the price differentials corresponding to the interval between quality ranks can vary widely, depending on whether the singularities are close to or far from the top of the quality hierarchy. These *relations of disproportion* express the substitution of a linear relationship by a nonlinear one, and they show the "excess" that is so often linked to the symbolic logic of markets of singularities and which induces spectacular changes in the way these markets operate.

Third, we have to show that, even when "quality ordering" and the supply-and-demand relationship interact, it is possible to evaluate their relative and combined influences on pricing; this amounts to demonstrating that the law of supply and demand participates in the economic relationship governed by the primacy of competition by quality. And, fourth, we need to discover the determined relations, if any, between the pricing procedures and the regimes of coordination.

The distinction between the *relation of concordance* and the *relation of disproportion* will organize the study. Each type of relation will be discussed and connected as much and as systematically as possible to concrete reality, which means in this case using the few rare and valuable relevant studies that already exist.

## CONCORDANCE

It would be simple in the market of singularities to study the relationship between qualities and prices if the first were ranked, as the second are; all that would remain to be done would be to calculate the strength of the association between the two dimensions. But these conditions exist for only a fraction of singularities. For the others, one has to find the substitute procedures that de facto act on pricing. Thus, a central distinction should be made between two forms of quality ordering: *ranking* and *gradation*. In the first case, the products occupy, according to their qualities, distinctive and clear positions in a hierarchy; this not the case with the second distinction, where the same product may occupy different positions on multiple vertical arrangements and as a result will be part of a confused global vertical picture. We will show that ranking is related mainly to price, and gradation to sales volume.

### Qualities and Prices

The concordance relationship is not about absolute economic values, it concerns the relative positions, and that involves *quality ranking* and the *price scale*. For this relation to exist, the quality ranking must satisfy two requirements: unequivocal meanings of the qualities and a common viewpoint that leads to the sharing of the evaluation criterion and to the possibility of comparing singularities.

The correlation between these two dimensions may vary but, all other things being equal, the stronger it is, the higher the probabilities are that the singularities will occupy the same position on the quality ranking and on the price scale. When several quality rankings are in competition, the price scale will depend on their relative strength. This perspective orients the successive presentation of studies of prices on three different markets—American university professors, French lawyers, and contemporary painters—to which we have added a more elaborate analysis of the market of fine wines. For the sake of simplicity, the selected markets are characterized by a predominant ranking, without the need to bring in the modifications stemming from competing but secondary orderings.

AMERICAN UNIVERSITY PROFESSORS

The salary of American university professors is set at the time of hiring by means of two different procedures.[3] For *senior* professors, it depends both on peer judgment and on the negotiating margins that the various universities have. It rises with the candidate's reputation, and its differentials increase as the candidate's fame approaches star status.[4] For *junior* professors, with a few exceptions, the salary does not depend directly on individual talent but on the relative position of the hiring university department in the prestige hierarchy of the same specialty departments.

FRENCH LAWYERS

French lawyers use the *hourly fee* as the unit of measure of economic value, and the market uses three very unequally ways of setting this fee.[5] The first is a public social judgment, which is crystallized in an excellence authority embodied in a few celebrities of the bar who receive very high fees, whereas, at the opposite end of the hierarchy, a small fraction of lawyers whose skills are considered by their clients to be interchangeable will, for this reason, find their fees imposed by a highly competitive market.

The second and largely dominant practice takes the form of self-evaluation based on professional hierarchy. This practice is almost inevitable when public information on the principal characteristics of the market—and prices to begin with—is lacking. For professionals, setting their price is a source of torment and worry; it is a problem. Like their clients, lawyers need a reference in order to evaluate the economic value of their service.

The practical solution lies in the practitioner network; it ensures the circulation of fine-tuned, individualized, personalized knowledge of the professional behaviors practiced and prices charged by colleagues; it en-

---

[3] C. Musselin, *Le marché des universitaires: France, Allemagne, États-Unis* (Paris: Presses de Sciences-Po, 2005), pp. 223–352.

[4] "The market for top economists is starting to look like those for movie stars, basketball players and bond traders." S. Nasar, "New breed of college all-star: Columbia pays top dollar for economics heavy hitter," *New York Times*, 8 April 1998, p. D1.

[5] L. Karpik, *French Lawyers: A Study in Collective Action, 1274–1994* trans. Nora Scott (Oxford: Oxford University Press, 1999), pp. 165–169.

ables the realistic comparisons needed to set an hourly fee that corresponds to one's relative professional value. Nor is it indispensable to have access to the full scale of hourly rates in order to get one's bearings: comparisons are most frequently made within the hierarchical segment often shared by colleagues who meet often and know each other well. Comparison makes it possible to dispel indetermination: it gives an idea of the "fair price," the concept which regulates the practice and corresponds to the "surplus" befitting a given professional position.

This comparison is not without rules. It is guided by known and socially recognized criteria considered to be relevant for assessing professional excellence: experience, kind of business, and for business lawyers and those dealing with individuals, the size of the law firm and the type of clientele, respectively. The generalized use of these three criteria attests that lawyers share the same conception of professional value. Of course, this interpretive frame is neither fully shared nor perfectly rigorous. It contains variations from one lawyer to another, so that comparisons do not guarantee that the judgments will mesh perfectly. It would be pointless to attempt to identify opportunistic practices, for self-evaluation is nothing more than an aid to decision making, and in the end, it is the client who validates (or not) the choice made by his or her lawyer. Imperfection exists, but it makes little difference to a comparison that includes an inevitable share of approximation.

Third, the importance of the stakes, especially in the case of business law firms, should logically give rise to intense price competition. It exists, to be sure—and is stronger or weaker depending the period—in particular through the use of the concrete, but by no means automatic, mechanism of "cutting rates." This discreet practice is explained by the fact that the hourly fee is assimilated simultaneously to a remuneration and to a measure of professional value. The result is that lawyers are not inclined to openly lower their rates, since to do so would be deliberately to affirm a professional dequalification.

Furthermore, competition between legal firms should not be assimilated to a war of all against all: it goes on within more-or-less informal compartmentalized legal-firms universes whose quality is supposed to be different. As a result of clients distributing their "cases" among lawyers in accordance with their type of legal practice and the hourly rates that go with it, and inasmuch as client practices are relatively convergent, the market is divided into universes of legal firms which are informally defined but nevertheless arranged according to quality. The effective competition takes place between firms from the same universe, and the "cut rates," when they exist, do not descend to the hourly rates charged by firms in the next category down. Not only does higher quality command higher fees, but the fee differentials also increase as the firms near the top of the quality scale. It is thus the "practitioner network" that represents the main tool for "revealing" and preserving—while (slowly) changing—the relation of concordance between the competence hierarchy and the price scale.

Depending on whether *contemporary painters* are little or well known, the pricing of their paintings obeys different mechanisms. In Amsterdam, the prices that art dealers set for the works of little-known artists, far from resulting exclusively or mainly from comparison with other painters, correspond to strategies that fluctuate between daring and caution. The *art of pricing* encompasses not only technical expertise and interpersonal skills, but also conceptions about the evolution of artists and the art world as reflected in the diversity of professional strategies. Over time, however, economic value becomes increasingly associated with "institutional recognition."[6]

Beginning in the 1970s, under the influence of an increasingly international market and the growing numbers of connoisseurs and semi-laymen, together with speculative practices, the equipment of the art market was reinforced so as to reduce buyers' cognitive deficit and the misadventures and misfortunes that inevitably ensued. Christie's, Sotheby's, and Philips, the three multinational auction houses, acquired teams of experts and guarantee mechanisms. More systematically, *Kunstkompass* draws up an annual list, based on several institutional criteria, of the top one hundred artists in the world of contemporary painting.[7] But the term "top" can be misleading: the ranks are not set by common opinion but by experts using specific institutional criteria. Each year, therefore, the hierarchy of talents, which is supposed to be linked to the hierarchy of prices, is set by a collective aesthetic authority. The statistical correspondence is only partial, but the guide intervenes actively to strengthen it by means of buying advice to its readers.

The guide has drawn numerous criticisms.[8] But in a market characterized by radical uncertainty and an often considerable cognitive deficit, it has become indispensable to art-lovers wanting to make reasoned purchases. Since it is based on concordance, it makes pricing intelligible. Beyond minor variations, serious discrepancies between the guide's list and market reality can only reveal a major aesthetic conflict, one of the pos-

---

[6] O. Velthuis, *Talking Prices: Symbolic Meanings of the Market for Contemporary Art* (Princeton: Princeton University Press, 2005), pp. 107–115, 117.

[7] A. Quemin, "L'illusion de l'abolition des frontières dans le monde de l'art international: La place des pays 'périphériques' à l'ère de la 'globalisation et du métissage,'" *Sociologie et sociétés* 34, no. 2 (2002): 15–40.

[8] R. Moulin, *L'artiste, l'institution et le marché* (Paris: Flammarion, 1992), pp. 77–80.

sible consequences of which would be doubt as to the guide's symbolic authority and a resulting loss of its influence on buyers.

### THE MARKET OF FINE WINES

Prices in the market of fine wines are the product of (1) an *aesthetic authority* based on a specific form of expertise and mainly embodied in wine guides, (2) *collective self-evaluations* as a particular form of cooperation between the producer and the practitioner networks, and (3) the *competitive market* driven by impersonal forces. The present analysis will deal exclusively with the first two, which are complementary.

There is nothing new about the existence of a judgment authority operating in the fine-wines market, independently of supply and demand: it exists and has long existed in the Bordeaux region in the form of the *classement de 1855*, which originally resulted from a conversion of prices into ranks and subsequently came to be considered as a hierarchy of qualities preserved over a long period by a profession with enough authority to protect it from being disorganized by the workings of the market.

Insofar as wine criticism defined itself by opposition to the traditional authorities, it embodied a new and independent form of judgment authority based on expertise, whose assessments, carried and diffused by numerous devices (journals, newspapers, guides), acted as collective signposts for consumers. For a long time these authorities were modest and pluralist, sometimes contradictory, and gave rise to only partial disagreement and minor tussles over rankings; and these were generally settled by the market.

Contemporary market evolution is characterized by the symbolic and economic rise of the guide. The better known it becomes, the more users trust it; and the more it is used by professionals and customers, the more it indirectly imposes prices by building rankings through ratings.[9] For a long time—in France as well as in most other countries—several guides competed, but they exerted an unequal influence on prices. For some years, however, the situation has become exceptional since one guide has overshadowed all others.[10]

---

[9] B. Benjamin and J. Podolny, "Status, quality and social order in the California wine industry," *Administrative Science Quarterly* 44 (1999): 563–589; B-H. Ling and L. Lockshin, "Components of wine prices for Australian wine: How winery reputation, wine quality, region, vintage, and winery size contribute to the price of varietal wines," *Australasian Marketing Journal* 11, no. 3 (2003): 19–32; E. Oczkowski, "A hedonic price function for Australian premium wine," *Australian Journal of Agricultural Economics* 38 (1994): 93–110.

[10] This was not without a debate on the relative influence of the *classement de 1855* and the Parker guide. See V. A. Ginsburgh, "Techniques de production, réputation et qualité des vins: Essais économétriques sur les vins rouges du haut Médoc," *Les arts du vin* (Bruxelles: Le Crédit Communal, 1995).

*Parker's Wine Buyer's Guide* proved its primacy in the most concrete way: by the fact that every year more and more producers of Bordeaux wines waited to see the ratings published in the new guide before setting their prices. This influence is inseparable from the strategic international position the Parker guide has managed to capture by combining a reputation grounded in long-recognized oenological competence with advice to wine sellers and clients in a rapidly expanding American market. The guide then went on gradually to acquire the *symbolic authority* that *indirectly* turned it into a *pricemaker*. This mutation was complete when the prices on the market tended to align themselves on the guide's ranking, that is, when the price scale tended to follow the quality hierarchy set by the guide, all the more for the wines near the top of the quality hierarchy.

*Collective self-evaluation* concerns a few high-end qualities and more middle-of-the range ones: it is invisible since it is produced by practitioner networks made up of peers and sales professionals, and sometimes exporters, who trust each other, talk to each other, exchange judgments, and create a discourse on the qualities and flaws of the year's wines that circulates within the network and enables everyone to find their bearings and set their prices, although this does not mean that they ignore the Parker guide.[11] In fact, the influences of these two judgment devices overlap in part, hinder each other at times, and reinforce each other in most cases.

The guide's authority is not recognized by all actors of the market. Some winegrowers on the fringes engage in individual strategies that circumvent the guide's judgments through personal promotion. Others tend to keep their prices stable over the middle term and to ignore the guide's verdicts, even though they may have risen a few places in its list, so as to ensure customers' loyalty.[12] Lastly, wines from newly developed regions can momentarily adopt other strategies. Yet such heterodox practices are not enough to cast doubt on a symbolic authority that extends well beyond the most famous regions of Bordeaux and Burgundy. These pricing procedures clearly show that forces *independent of market equilibrium* also determine prices.

In the case of fine wines, econometric studies show that prices are associated not only with relative qualities but also with demand, supply, and vintage (which can be assimilated to increasing scarcity of supply). This confirms the influence of the law of supply and demand. Generally speaking, the stronger the relation of concordance, the less independent the influence of supply and demand. But changes of position in the quality ranking can lead to rapid upsets. When a product rating goes up, the new equilibrium is not very hard to find. But when it undergoes a relative

[11] Y. Chiffoleau and C. Laporte, "Price formation: The Burgundy wine market," *Revue française de sociologie* 47 (2006): 157–182 (supplement).
    [12] Ibid., pp. 177–178.

decline (following the rise of direct competitors) or an absolute fall (following a lower rating), the contrary is true: it puts winegrowers in a perilous position.

If winemakers lower their prices, customers will interpret it as the signal that confirms the guide's judgment of the wine's inferior quality: this can only prompt a durable loss of clients, in accordance with a process that is the opposite of that predicted by mainstream economics. If they maintain their prices—which is the measure they prefer as the logical expression of a price downward rigidity whose strength and continuity are rooted in the use of price to measure professional and social value— they will nevertheless lose part of their clientele and find themselves in overproduction. More or less secret pragmatic means can be used to artificially reduce supply (stocking, distillation), but recapturing the clientele and returning to market equilibrium are long and complicated processes that sometimes go wrong.

Depending on the situations, the dynamics of the quality ranking and that of the market equilibrium can either reinforce or hinder each other, take on greater or lesser relative importance, and reinforce the tendency of prices to rise or fall. Clearly, *it is up to the market equilibrium to adjust to the quality evaluation.* The actors have some room for maneuver, but within limits that are all the narrower the smaller the vineyards and the further they are from the top of the quality rating.

• • •

These analyses are mutually substantiating and allow us to formulate the following propositions: (1) experts as human beings and as guides, peer networks, self-evaluation, and practitioners' networks, among other arrangements,[13] are used as devices for constructing quality rankings; (2) relative qualities and relative prices are linked by a relation of concordance, which may vary in strength, but in the specific examples examined, strength was rather strong; (3) the relation of concordance is found in markets of singularities using aesthetic criteria as well as criteria of excellence, which means that it will be found in the authenticity as well as in the professional coordination regimes; (4) downward mobility in the quality ranking shows the independent effect of the relationship between supply and demand, because it may provoke lasting market disequilibria that affect prices; (5) the supply/demand relationship is subordinated to quality ranking; and (6) price-formation theory could and should include the independent and combined effects of quality ranking and of market disequilibria.

[13] For a more complicated process, see P. François, "The market for early music concerts," *Revue française de sociologie* 47 (2006): 183–209 (supplement).

The price scale measures simultaneously the relative scarcity and the relative qualities of the products. But this observation may express two very different situations. In neoclassical theory, the two values are inevitably conflated, since they are projected on the same dimension, hence the criticism levied by Stiglitz, for whom to evaluate quality by price is irrational because it keeps the law of supply and demand from operating.[14] But what holds for neoclassical theory does not necessarily apply to the economics of singularities because relative qualities, supply/demand relations, and prices are expressed by mutually independent dimensions.

The study of the lawyer market has already shown that judgment devices, such as control devices, mandatory diplomas, networks, and trust, far from hobbling free quality competition and thus leading to market closure and monopolistic practices, should instead be considered as the necessary means to ensure a rational functioning of this market.[15] This proposition may be extended to prices, since they can be taken as independent effects of relative qualities as well as of relative scarcity—or of both together.

## Qualities and Quantities

How can prices be set when quality rankings are not sufficiently visible or coherent or general or stable to be known and recognized? Such is the case of the book market, for example, with its numerous critics, its many mass-media supports, its numerous famous or obscure literary prizes, its strong inequality in promotion capacities, and its countless reader networks, not to mention the numerous books that are neither listed nor evaluated. The combined effects of these devices produce *quality gradation lists* that are shorter or longer, numerous, most often vague or different, or even contradictory, thus creating multiple confusing states of "order." They therefore cannot serve as a basis for setting prices, and yet market forces must respect them, since "nobody knows" beforehand the commitments, interactions, and movements that might produce the next best seller. In such a situation, the solution lies in a general configuration of practices, which include (1) neutralization of the effects of qualities on prices; (2) outsourcing of the symbolic value judgments, and (3) evaluation of the relative quality through sales volume.

Neutralization of the effects of qualities on prices means that singular products are separated from their symbolic value and assimilated to differentiated or to interchangeable products. For instance, book prices or the price of a seat at the movies are independent of the symbolic value of

---

[14] J. Stiglitz, "The causes and consequences of the dependence of quality on price," *Journal of Economic Literature* 25 (1987): 1–48.

[15] Karpik, *French Lawyers*, p. 178.

the works. They are tied to the reality that creates the singularity—the industrial support—without being fused with it. In the book market, prices vary with the categories of books, with the collections or the thickness of the volume; and in the movie market admission prices differ according to the category and location of the theater. Price differences usually stem from general decisions referring to categories, countries, or periods of time. In both of these markets, as well as in analogous ones, price is part of a collective regulation without being a sign of quality.

This practice entails a number of advantages when success is not assured, when it depends on an initial moment—the launch of a film or a book—during which the quality judgments are formed that dictate the later course of the demand. Stable prices ensure visibility and quick adaptation, providing nothing happens to stop the book becoming a best seller, or the film, a hit. In markets where radical uncertainty predominates, producers/sellers must believe that it is possible each time to capture the national or world markets and thus make large and even fabulous profits. They must therefore believe that *the volume of sales* will more than compensate the neutralization of prices. Such a logic implies big markets, large-scale diffusion, and great symbolic power embodied in names and brands—all of which are in principle characteristic of both the mega regime and the common-opinion regime.

• • •

The relationship between qualities, quantities, and prices is dictated by the relations between *forms of ordering* and *production capacities*. When quality ranking is combined with fixed production capacity, relative qualities will mainly affect prices. And when combined with flexible production capacity, relative qualities may affect prices as well as sales volume, although, as we will show below, the two logics are not all that easy to accord. When quality gradation is combined with flexible production capacity, relative qualities will be measured primarily by the volume of sales. And when quality gradation is combined with rigid production capacity, the market may become fragmented. Whatever the case, in one form or another, in the market of singularities, *relative qualities are transcribed into relative prices and/or relative volumes of sales.*

### DISPROPORTION

Why do price differentials increase when singularities approach the top of the quality ranking? Why can the same phenomenon be observed in the volume of sales? This relation of disproportion is striking in its magnitude, in the diversity of its forms, in its extension, and at the same time, in the difficulty of determining its causes and limits. We will present and discuss some suggested explanations and then formulate and develop a hypothesis that is rooted in the symbolic logic of the markets of singularities. This leads us to distinguish between relations of disproportion as they apply to prices or to volumes.

## Disproportion of Prices

Huge differences in earnings separate stars from other human beings. And, as a result of the substitution of a linear relationship by a nonlinear one in the relation between relative qualities and relative prices, the "winner takes all." Sherwin Rosen inaugurated the analysis of the phenomenon in an article devoted to the *economics of superstars*. For Rosen, the superstar phenomenon designates the small number of highly talented individuals who can only with difficulty be substituted for each other, who receive "extraordinary" salaries, who concentrate production in their activity (film, fashion, sports),[16] and who, when the technical and economic conditions are right, draw huge audiences and attract huge numbers of clients from a distance. Superstars have thus become the supports of planetary economic successes in the markets of cultural products, entertainment, and luxury goods. Of course their influence cannot be separated from the collective enterprises of which they are a part and which conjoin, on a grand scale, talents, capital, promotion, and distribution. In most cases these heterogeneous assets coalesce only around a name that has global recognition, and the personal influence of the star cannot be confused with the firm's means of action.

Might the scarcity of irreplaceable talents explain the extraordinary earnings of superstars? The formula for large-scale economic success would thus be deciphered: it would lie in the combination of hard-to-replace talent and a consumer technology coupled with commercial efficiency, and it would justify the increasing differences in salary the closer a person gets to star status.[17] This rule would create a high concentration of earnings and profit, not to mention tight market control. The thesis has drawn criticism. On the one hand, when it comes to talent, how does one identify the superior qualities that define it? How, if one takes an objectivist view of reality, does one go about comparing what is defined

---

[16] "Relatively small numbers of people earn enormous amounts of money and seem to dominate the fields in which they are engaged." S. Rosen, "The economics of superstars," *American Economic Review* 71 (December 1981): 845.

[17] "Rewards and the probability of success appear to rise more than proportionately with talent and ability." S. Rosen, "The economics of superstars," *The American Scholar* 52, no. 4 (1983).

as incomparable? How does one determine the threshold of the "small differences in talent" that produce such huge effects? On the other hand, some critics suggested replacing talent by "chance" or shared culture.[18]

My criticism is of another nature. It originates in the observation that similar phenomena can be seen in very different markets of singularities. In the market of artworks, of course, but also in the market of fine wines.[19] And therefore the list of superstars should include the few great wines which, compared with the rest, are assimilated to rare, original works belonging to the world of luxury goods and therefore near the price of priceless works.[20] On a more modest scale, it should also include the "great" lawyers or the "top" academic talents in American markets. In other words, *disproportion* is a widespread phenomenon, and the search for specific causes must give way to the search for an explanation that applies to all cases.

How are we to understand the phenomenon and its generality? Disproportion of prices results from a collective mobilization of the quality judgments made by actors engaged in cultural struggles and who, over sometimes long periods, manage to singularize the products and to endow some with exceptional properties. When the Parker guide says that great wines are works of art and/or luxury products, the author is not talking about their nature but about the enormous collective, material, and symbolic work of singularization that has gone into them and in which the guide, too, had a hand; he is talking about the psychological, professional, and material investments as well as the dynamism of the cultural complex. It is the commitment and the mobilization of the devotees, producers, art connoisseurs, and speculators that produce, in the art and culture markets, the twin movement of elevation and separation by which products become unique. The increasing disproportion in the price intervals is both part of this transformation and its consecration. Through its visibility, the market of fine wines openly displays processes that are more discreet in other markets but that are also organized around enhancing

---

[18]Respectively, G. MacDonald, "The economics of rising stars," *American Economic Review* 78, no. 1 (1988): 155–166; and M. Adler, "Stardom and talent," *American Economic Review* 75, no. 1 (1985): 208–212.

[19]G. V. Jones and K.-H. Storchmann, "Wine market prices and investment under uncertainty: An econometric model for Bordeaux Crus Classés," *Agricultural Economics* 26 (2001): 115–133.

[20]Rather than listing prices, this story, which happened in London on a July evening in 2001, and which made the rounds, is worth a demonstration. A few senior employees of an English bank decided on a well-lubricated dinner; they ordered a Château-Pétrus 1945 (£11,600/€14,335/$20,420), a Château-Pétrus 1946 (£9,400/€11,633/$16,579), a Château-Pétrus 1947 (£12,300/€15,220/$17,575), and a Château-Yquem 1900 (£9,200/€11,385/$16,220), which, with the mineral water and two beers, came to a total of £44,000/€54,450/$62,720). P. Georges, "Le Petrus jusqu'à la lie," *Le Monde*, 27 February 2002, p. 38; exchange rate of 5 September 2008.

the value of the "best" in that particular activity. Yet the generality of these concrete practices does not explain them.

The rule of disproportion is a modality of action. It is a formal rule in the sense that it is indifferent to the nature of the singularities. Its purpose is to symbolically and materially resolve the central contradiction affecting singularities: How to avoid commensuration while occupying a position on a price scale? How to ward off the threat of equivalence that necessarily comes with any hierarchy? To be sure, the multiplicity of judgment criteria shows that singularity can always be requalified, that no rank or price is definitive, and that, barring destruction, incommensurability cannot disappear for good. Nevertheless, in the language of money, a linear relationship between prices means that the intervals between the positions in the quality ranking are themselves equal and that we are in a system of equivalence.

It is this threat that the disproportion of prices keeps at bay. Disproportion between prices is a reminder that ranking creates an order of incommensurable entities. It shows that, when it comes to the economics of singularities, ranking is at once inevitable and absurd. It is a fiction. Disproportion is the "solution" to a general problem that the economics of singularities cannot avoid: how to symbolically and materially impose the sign of an irreducible difference where exchange assumes that no difference is irreducible.

In the symbolic logic that dominates markets of singularities, inequalities in the remuneration intervals institute a reality that the pricing mechanism tends to efface: incomparability. Whenever price differences are of such a magnitude that they make it impossible to see product ranking as based on equivalences, the *disproportion reestablishes incommensurability*. After having proposed this interpretation in the French edition of my book, I discovered the same explanation in the work of Olav Velthuis who, via Zelizer, makes reference to Simmel![21] The interpretation is therefore less original than I had thought, but, on the other hand, it is more credible!

### Disproportion of Quantities

Disproportionate relationships find another spectacular expression in the huge economic success of films like *Titanic* or *Jurassic Park*. How can we explain this? The cause usually invoked is the new strategy of film pro-

---

[21] "The price mechanism reinforces rather than just undermines the incommensurability of art." Velthuis, *Talking Prices* p. 173; "Money value in very great sums contains an element of rarity which makes it more individual and less interchangeable. . . . These sums install a good, . . . with fantastic possibilities that transcend the definiteness of numbers." G. Simmel, The *Philosophy of Money* (Routledge: London 1900, 1999), p. 515.

duction based on excess, on the concentration of symbolic, financial, and material resources, and on the extension of its distribution to the global market—it is the blockbuster model, the gigantic superproduction model supposed to bring in no less gigantic profits.[22]

The blockbuster promise is more a belief than a reality as, upon close examination, this strategy is no more likely than others to produce a hit. There is one exception to this observation: the star. In a market necessarily characterized by radical quality uncertainty, the star is a "universal" symbolic authority capable of orienting spectator/consumer choices from afar; in this case, the star acts as a magnetic judgment device. On his or her own or through what he or she guarantees, the star holds out the promise of "a good" or "the best" singularity. For some, the star acts as a guideline for choosing, for others, as a mechanism for reducing risk. As a result, the star guarantees collective economic success.[23]

And yet the star's real effectiveness is more limited than is commonly thought. The presence of stars does not increase the chances of success; but in association with big budgets, it manages to counterbalance the consequence of unfavorable critical judgments. And if star-laden films earn on average more than others, this relation holds for only a small number of stars, and above all, the profit rate for films is the same, stars or not, because the surplus goes to the stars.[24] Moreover, the huge outlay can become a source of vulnerability: most blockbusters lose money or barely cover expenses; the big profits are concentrated in a mere handful of films.[25]

The blockbuster strategy cannot avoid the "nobody knows" principle. The "hit" is both always expected and always a surprise. Not only can it not be predicted, even the probabilities of success cannot be increased. According to conventional economic rationality, the many and resounding film failures should have led either to an increase in theater admission prices or to the disappearance of investors. Yet none of this has happened. Belief is built on the denial of reality, but in the face of radical uncertainty, voluntarism is a limited asset. Nevertheless, the "hit" is not an irrational phenomenon, and it does not escape analysis.

When market size grows, when a wealth of decisions are made in a short period of time, as in financial crises, mimesis seems the obvious

[22] Traditional production, on the other hand, managed to produce and diffuse superproductions from *Ben Hur* to *Gone with the Wind*.

[23] Fr. Benhamou, *L'économie du star-system* (Paris: Odile Jacob, 2002).

[24] S. Basuroy, S. Chaterjee, and S. A. Ravid, "How critical are critical reviews? The box-office effects of film critics, star power, and budgets," *Journal of Marketing* 67, no. 4 (2003): 103–117; S. A. Ravid, "Information, blockbusters, and stars: A study of the film industry," *The Journal of Business* 72, no. 4 (1999): 463–492.

[25] L. Menand, "Is the blockbuster the end of cinema?" *The New Yorker*, 7 February 2005.

explanation. Herein lies the full importance of De Vany's demonstration that, even with an extreme reality unfavorable to the thesis, individual autonomy remains central and drives collective action.[26] In other words, *judgment matters a lot and imitation very little*. It reinforces the economics of singularities which, calling on the notions of judgment, forms of commitment, judgment struggles and judgment devices, connects choices—even those made on a grand scale—with the interaction between individual actors and judgment devices.

Following De Vany's model, we may insist on three results: (1) The fate of the major success does not depend on consumer imitation. It depends on dense and expanding interactions between the commitment and mobilization of consumers/clients; on the circulation of judgments of quality—"qualities" create the audience; and on the active intervention of a growing number of judgment devices, which expand with no foreseeable limits if given enough time. (2) In a market characterized by radical uncertainty, the star, the film critic, and the viewer networks, as well as promotion, of course, have some power over people's judgment; but the central factor is the density of the interactions between people and devices. (3) This way of constituting an audience leads globally to a highly unequal distribution of takings and profit: 20 percent of the products make 80 percent of the market's global earnings, and between 5 and 20 percent of the products concentrate 80 percent of the market's global profits.

The *hit market* concentrates all of the elements that make up markets of singularities: radical uncertainty, incommensurability, personal and impersonal judgment devices, quality judgments, commitment, and, in some cases, mobilization of the actors, struggles over judgment, and inequality of symbolic and material powers. However, it does not follow that all markets of singularities are, or can even become, hit markets, though many already are, at least partially. Such a market has to be constructed. Nor does it follow that the only valid rankings are the latest in date, although they may have begun somewhere within the gradations, because many valid quality rankings are based on criteria other than economic success.

The relations between qualities and the hit market show several characteristics: (1) The hit is the product of a collective action based on the voluntary and enthusiastic mobilization of individual actors and of judgment devices. (2) The enormous differences in the financial successes of films crystallize incommensurability in the form of myths, which are all the more memorable for being constantly recalled to mind. (3) The relation of disproportion should appear in the mega and the common-opinion

[26] A. De Vany, *Hollywood Economics: How Extreme Uncertainty Shapes the Film Industry* (London: Routledge, 2004), pp. 9, 60–63.

regimes, since both deal with large markets, but a difference distinguishes them: contrary to the first, the second is organized around the chart and may simultaneously link qualities to price and sales volume.

• • •

To begin constructing an initial explanation of price formation, we have had to distinguish between ranking and gradation, and between concordance and disproportion. We have had to integrate the types of authority that affect prices, the degrees of clients' mobilization and interaction with the judgment devices that drive the increase of the sales volumes, the production capacity, and the price rigidity. And finally we have had to integrate the relationship between supply and demand as well as the more or less lasting market disequilibrium.

The analysis can be summarized in three propositions: (1) The combinations of the forms of quality orderings and of production capacities open onto two different paths, which may or may not be combined, for rewarding qualities: prices and volumes. (2) The primacy of quality competition over price competition finds its expression in the primacy of relative qualities over market-equilibrium adjustment. (3) Symbolic logic asserts itself, here as elsewhere, through "excesses," which take the form of disproportionate differences in earnings, thus revealing that, in the market of singularities, exchange products are incommensurable products.

The theory is unitary because it simultaneously integrates relative quality and relative scarcity, because it deals with the structural changes of the market (and especially the evolution from the conventional market to the "hit" market), and, finally, because it should be applicable to all markets of singularities.

# PART FOUR

# Finale

## Chapter Eighteen

# THE HISTORICITY OF SINGULARITIES

DESPITE SUSTAINED expansion over the last thirty or forty years, the universe of singularities is still haunted by the specter of its own disappearance. Although it may be expressed differently at different times, the topic of that vulnerability is still with us. It belongs to the debates over the future of high culture that go back to the second half of the nineteenth century but whose contemporary starting point was a book chapter by Max Horkheimer and Theodor Adorno on the "culture industry,"[1] a notion that was unfamiliar at the time and that connoted for the authors a "regression of Reason." According to their arguments, although it is subject to the marketing imperative of "standardization," the mass production of cultural goods (movies, radio, jazz, magazines) is fated to win out over "high culture." This efficacy is all the more irresistible because the economic struggle occurs in "mass societies" where individuals, separated from their collective belonging, have become mere interchangeable atoms dedicated to the consumption of equally interchangeable cultural goods. Because the phenomena of mass-culture goods and mass consumerism go hand in hand in democracies, they pave the way for barbarity. For all its notoriety, their text, which is the cornerstone of the critical tradition, is not devoid of confusion: for instance, the entertainment culture and standardization can both be a threat to high culture, yet there is no reason to conflate the two.

The issue was still dominant in the United States during the 1950s–1960s: since mass culture was entertaining and prolific, democratic and homogeneous, it could only drive out high culture and thus become the constituent reality of mass society.[2] In the 1960s–1970s, the criticism extended to a consumer society that looked from then on as if it were driven by social distinction.[3] Far from being qualified by their specific

---

[1] M. Horkheimer and T. Adorno, "The culture industry: Enlightenment as mass deception," *Dialectic of Enlightenment: Philosophical Fragments* (Stanford: Stanford University Press, 2002), pp. 94–136.

[2] N. Jacobs (ed.), *Culture for the Millions? Mass Media in Modern Democracy* (Princeton: J. N. Van Nostrand, 1961); E. Larrabee and R. Meyersohn (eds.), *Mass Leisure* (Glencoe: The Free Press, 1958); D. MacDonald, "A theory of mass culture," in B. Rosenberg and D. M. White (eds.), *Mass Culture* (Glencoe: The Free Press, 1957), pp. 59–73.

[3] J. Baudrillard, *The Consumer Society: Myths and Structures* (Thousand Oaks, CA: Sage, 1970, 1998); P. Bourdieu, *Distinction : A Social Critique of the Judgement of Taste* (London: Routledge & Kegan Paul), 1979, 1984.

contents, cultural goods were defined by the social status of their pos-
sessors. High culture derived its prestige from the fact that it had been
appropriated by the dominant classes, with the result that mass culture
lost not only its originality but also its capacity to arouse pleasure.[4] However, rearranging the interpretive frame in this way does not alter the
general thesis, namely: that the entertainment culture can only eliminate
high culture, and the market can only bring about the regression of civilization. The concern is still with us.

Ethnographers were no less pessimistic.[5] Early on, Claude Lévi-Strauss
announced, "Mankind has opted for monoculture; it is in the process of
creating a mass civilization."[6] More recently, Kopytoff saw commoditization as being well advanced, and he considered cultural goods to be an
endangered species because their reserves were on the way to extinction.[7]
The rejection of the "commoditization of culture" in the 1980s grew with
the fear that the stocks of singularities were vanishing.[8]

Just when this second interpretation began to seem obvious, it was
countered by the anthropologist Arjun Appadurai,[9] whose complex analysis is organized around two main arguments: (1) Singular goods (or as he
says, "commodities"), considered to be unique or as classes of culturally
valued singularities, are found both inside and outside the market. The
idea that the market leads to the dequalification of culture is therefore no
longer a given: it must be demonstrated. (2) And while he acknowledges
that "the central problem of today's global interactions is the tension
between cultural homogenization and cultural heterogenization," he

---

[4] Baudrillard, *Consumer Society*, pp. 109, 134.

[5] "In general "Western" consumption goods were viewed as a loss of culture and threat
to the anthropological object of study." D. Miller, "Consumption studies as the transformation of anthropology," in D. Miller (ed.), *Acknowledging Consumption* (London: Routledge, 1995), p. 264.

[6] C. Lévi-Strauss, *Tristes Tropiques*, trans. John and Doreen Weightman, (New York:
Penguin Books, 1973), p. 38.

[7] "The extensive commoditization we associate with capitalism is thus not a feature of
capitalism per se, but of the exchange technology that, historically, was associated with it
and that set dramatically wider limits to maximum feasible commoditization." I. Kopytoff,
"The cultural biography of things: commoditization as process," in A. Appadurai (ed.), *The
Social Life of Things: Commodities in Cultural Perspective* (Cambridge: Cambridge University Press, 1986), p. 72.

[8] "Now the economy has turned its attention to the last remaining independent sphere of
human activity: the culture itself. Cultural rituals, community events, social gatherings, the
arts, sports and games, social movements, and civic engagements all are being encroached
upon by the commercial sphere." J. Rifkin, *The Age of Access: The New Culture of Hyper-
capitalism, Where All of Life Is a Paid-for Experience* (New York: J. P. Tarcher/Putnam,
2000), p.10.

[9] A. Appadurai, "Introduction: Commodities and the politics of value," in Appadurai,
*Social Life of Things*, pp. 3–63.

concludes that "globalization is not the story of cultural homogenization."[10] The justification of this thesis lies in people's interpretative capacities, in the creative presence of a collective imaginary that represents an ability to invent something out of nothing, to constantly re-create difference. By dropping the two assumptions of antinomy between market and culture and of the necessity of cultural homogenization, Appadurai stands the whole critical tradition on its head.

These debates have left us with two lines of conflicting interpretations based on the twofold distinction between high culture and entertainment culture, between diversity and standardization, which can easily be combined. Whichever side is taken, the level of analysis is the same: it is global. Therefore each thesis is more impressionistic than demonstrative (given the scale of the interpretation, it could hardly be otherwise), and neither provides the tools that would facilitate access to somewhat more solid truths. The evolution of the economics of singularities thus once more becomes problematic. But the debate is inescapable; for, when it comes to singularities, we find it expressed over and over, among others, when *films d'auteur* are faced with blockbusters, when American lawyers feel threatened by "deprofessionalization," or when appellation wines (AOC) must contend with brand wines.

What seems important is not to choose between the two interpretations but to move to another level of analysis that would give us safer means to identify the specific form and conditions of evolution. It is here that coordination regimes, as an analytical tool, can be of help. The scale of their action is restricted and their combinations are a way to handle the changes in the concrete markets. Coordination regimes should be as useful in studying desingularization as they have been for singularization, although the first is a more or less visible—that is to say, a more or less elusive—process whereby the singular product trades its originality for uniformity and is turned into a differentiated or even a standardized product.

The present analysis therefore bears on the changes that dequalify singularities. There is, however, no question of picking product categories that would lend themselves more readily than others to this transformation. Instead, we will attempt to discover under what particular conditions one or another of the coordination regimes maintains the universe of singularities—or operates in reverse and regularly brings about the very thing it was until then preventing.

This analysis will be dedicated primarily to two concrete evolutions. The first is more an attempt at, than a real process of (although it still may become one), desingularization, but it shows clearly under what conditions

[10] A. Appadurai, *Modernity at Large: Cultural Dimensions of Globalization* (Minneapolis: University Minnesota Press, 1996), pp. 32, 11.

an unexpected political change may appear and transform singularities; it is exemplified by the professions in Europe. The second evolution is a real change. It deals with the market of popular music and therefore with the common-opinion regime. The extended study of this market will look at the conditions that bring the maintenance of singularities and the market logic into direct conflict.

But a general interpretation that would be relevant for all singularities cannot be excluded a priori. Thus, before dealing with these two specific processes, we will consider the question of general evolution. Can we detect a change that is equally valid for all markets of singularities? And as a result, is it possible to study singularities without appealing to coordination regimes? This investigation will concentrate on the question of the product-renewal rule.

## The Rule of Product Renewal

Since the 1970s, the world economy has been driven by two trends: the unification of market places and the proliferation of commodities. Globalization is the extension of a very old process of the expansion of flows of merchandise in the international market, which soared in the nineteenth century only to be engulfed by the First World War and the 1929 Crash. At present, under the impact of the international division of labor, of increasingly powerful multinationals, of evermore intense economic struggles, and of a profit-seeking logic that tends to prevail everywhere, economic connections are multiplying, national borders are opening up, and India and China—without which there would be no globalization—are coming to play a growing role in international economics. Globalization is advancing but, with the exception of finance, it is far from being complete.

With the expansion of this common exchange space comes a new way of relating to time: the pace of product renewal has shifted gears. The change began in the 1960s, at a time when a multifaceted crisis was threatening the affluent society: labor's criticism of Taylorism and Fordism reached fever pitch, a growing portion of consumers rejected standardized products, and overproduction loomed. At this juncture, competition by differentiation teamed up with price competition, and the universe of new products expanded. In the presence of diversified, turbulent markets, the industrial equipment was forced to change; it became more and more flexible, while the forms of organization changed as well: the hierarchical firm gave way to the multidivisional firm, and then to the network-firm. The Fordism model lost ground.

The multiplication of symbolic goods and services sparked far-reaching cultural changes, of which singularities were a part. But we cannot color in their territory on a world map, no more than we can measure their rate of development, since they are buried in the universe of differentiation. Nevertheless, our ignorance could be at least partially dispelled if, based on what we already know about the economics of singularities, we could distinguish what it *does not share* with the other forms of coordination. We need to outline the general features of the *economics of novelty*, which includes differentiated, as well as singular, products and has spawned numerous social-science interpretations, and we must evaluate how pertinent they are for the economics of singularities. It is thus through an a contrario interpretation that the particularism of the economics of singularities may be singled out.

## The Economics of Novelty

The economics of novelty is characterized by evermore widespread and rapid differentiation. The intensification of product renewal stems from the changes brought to the creation and qualification of products. Innovation, marketing, packaging, and advertising are now the components of rationalized processes of differentiation. A growing number of market professionals command an increasing amount of knowledge and skill, and intervene in all phases of the industrial and commercial process. Upstream from production, they conceive the new products and integrate the techniques of anticipating consumer choices and behaviors; between production and sales, they stabilize the characteristics that have been adjusted to the consumers; and in the end market, they deploy devices for channeling and seducing customers in the supermarkets and malls. The scope of this change is under debate: for some, it is a simple accentuation of already existing trends,[11] while for others it is a complete break with the past.[12] But there is broad, if not general, agreement that the pace of product renewal has been picking up rapidly, while consumption has become increasingly ephemeral.[13]

## The Economics of Singularities

Does the tendential law governing the economics of novelty apply to all (or almost all) end products and therefore to the economics of singularities?

We can immediately exclude the reticular and the professional regimes, as both are alien to this form of competition. The authenticity regime,

[11] A. Giddens, *The Consequences of Modernity* (Stanford: Stanford University Press, 1990).

[12] Appadurai, *Modernity at Large*, pp. 32, 11.

[13] See G. Lipovetsky, *The Empire of Fashion: Dressing French Democracy* (Princeton: Princeton University Press, 1987, 2002); G. Lipovetsky and S. Charles, *Hypermodern Times* (Cambridge: Polity Press, 2005); P. Veltz, *Le nouveau monde industriel* (Paris: Gallimard, 2000).

characterized by the proliferation of singularities, by the most direct
reference to the artistic model, and by the widest diversity of choice logics, also features the greatest diversity of temporal relations. Moreover
the *tendency to oppose change*, which ensures unlimited reproduction of
the same singularity—except for eventual variations in packaging and
publicity—is integral to typical products because it is the source of their
differential economic advantage. Names (AOC, labels) which are the legal
guarantee of monopoly, are included in the specific terms and specifications
of requirements and are enforced by watchdog bodies in order to produce a commodity durably distinguished from the rest by a typical taste.
The product is unique, incomparable; everything must be done to protect
it.[14] Doing so implies strict constraints aimed at preventing the emergence of differences that might destroy the link with the past. The act of
qualifying is therefore aimed at curbing innovation, which might under-
mine justification of the differential economic advantage. Thus the authenticity regime contains nearly all rates of change, from the slowest to
the fastest. Until now, the expert-opinion regime has behaved mainly like
an offshoot of the authenticity regime.

The mega regime, with the shift in market size, its big corporations
whose fixed capital imposes a new scale of production and sales, its goal
of short- and medium-term profits, and its huge promotion budgets, together with the simplification of the symbolic universe of the market
through brands and megabrands, is under pressure to renew its products
rapidly. Nevertheless, the pace of renewal varies with the products and
the clienteles. In the luxury industry, aside from the fact that competition
among the big firms is fairly moderate, the past still has an economic
value, as can be seen in the lasting appeal of the Hermes scarf and the
Vuitton handbag. Films are a typical example of the ambiguity that characterizes *ephemeral consumption*: the average film run has been halved in
the space of a few years (from six to three weeks). The success that was
once gradually built up over time and that punctuated the trajectory of so
many movies, and more generally of so many cultural productions, has
recently been replaced by "guillotine verdicts" that come down after
only two or three weeks. Even word of mouth is outpaced. With the
number of movies increasing more rapidly than the number of theaters,
the managers may decide to replace one film by another at a higher point
on the weekly curve of profitability. In this case, ephemeral consumption is not the product of decisions taken by consumers, it is the consequence of economic choices made by the owners and managers of movie

---

[14] M.-T. Letablier and C. Delfosse, "Genèse d'une convention de qualité: Cas des appela-
tions d'origine fromagère," in G. Allaire and R. Boter (eds.), *La grande transformation de
l'agriculture* (Paris: INRA Editions/Economica, 1995), pp. 97–118; M-T. Letablier and F.
Nicolas, "Genèse de la typicité," *Science des aliments* 14 (1994): 541–556.

houses.[15] The mega regime is not homogeneous. It contains many rates of change and numerous principles of preservation, which connect through the substantial devices of the regime to lineages that belong to the cultural frameworks shared by the sellers, buyers, and critics involved in the regime, and therefore obstruct the pure and simple autonomization of economic logic.

Finally, the common-opinion regime already operates in numerous markets of singularities and is expanding daily; moreover, it contains the most curbs on the continuity of singularities. Because the limits are not attached to products and because the devices are formal and the market is large, it is this regime that is the most inclined to the rapid renewal of products.

By now we have come far enough to be able to say that *the general propositions applicable to the economics of novelty are not, on the whole, valid for the economics of singularities*. The particularism of the economics of singularities does not lie solely in the multiplicity of its temporal relations; its effects are much more radical: if the history of differentiation revolves around Fordism, the economics of singularities belongs to another historical space altogether.

When it comes to luxury apparel, jewelry, books, or the services of a lawyer, the production lineages go far back in time and are completely other. Made up of small workshop companies with their traditional skills and flexible organization, luxury firms are defined by quality production, by products that are made to order or in small series, and by elitist markets targeted at the upper-class and well-heeled middle-class consumer.[16] The handcraft system looked down on the assembly-line model, even though it was called upon to satisfy increasingly broad markets. The existence of "industrial districts" showed, first in Italy and then further abroad, that it was possible to combine small and middle-size businesses concentrated in the same territory, machine tools, and sophisticated qualifications into a production system wielding "flexible specialization" and reactivity, and alternating limited and large series.[17] In the 1980s, industry

---

[15] More modest facts also show that, under certain conditions, "moral" limits are imposed on a product renewal based on the recycling of products. For example, the coloring of black-and-white films, having sparked strong reactions, was dropped. Also, the remastering of old classical music or jazz recordings inspired serious fears and led to minimalist practices. The strength of these rejections comes from the originality model and from respect for the rule of closure it dictates: what is finished should not be tinkered with.

[16] "From the standpoint of value, the model is dominated especially by criteria of quality, a quality not comparable from one good or market to another. It is this quality that, when injected into the wider aura of a social order to be preserved, legitimizes the communitarian protection of artisans." P. Veltz, *Le nouveau monde industriel* (Paris: Le Débat/Gallimard, 2000), p. 45.

[17] M. Piore and C. F. Sabel, *Les chemins de la propsérité: De la production de masse à la spécialisation souple* (Paris: Hachette, 1989), p. 342; and *The Second Industrial Divide: Possibilities for Prosperity* (New York: Basic Books, 1986).

and craft tended to join forces for certain categories of singular products; as a result, it became difficult to establish unequivocal relations between product categories and systems of production. This development did not affect all products, though. Alongside the goods that subsequently fell into the industrial system, numerous singular products and all personalized professional services remained solidly associated with craft skills and concern for the person.

*The historicity of the economics of singularities remains to be constructed, however.* It should not be confused purely and simply with the prevailing conception of an industrial history built around Fordism; it differs in its objects and its implementation. It can no more be separated from the creation and production of singularities than from the use of judgment devices that ensure economic exchange, or from the clienteles committed to the search for originality, for personalized goods and services as well as to the recognition of its identity.

## DESINGULARIZATION OF PERSONALIZED SERVICES

A priori the professional-services market does not exclude the dynamics of desingularization. Yet having systematically compared several professions on the basis of "cognitive rationalization" and "institutional rationalization/formalization," Jean Gadrey concludes that, for France, standardization of the professions is improbable and that professional organizations are relatively capable of successfully combating attempts at its application.[18] To introduce some diversity into the terms of the comparison, we will examine successively the influence of the market and that of the state.

### Market, Professional Firms, and Desingularization

A sociohistorical analysis of American lawyers allows us to identify the consequences of market evolution on practitioners' services through the effects of firm size. It is mainly in this profession, with the exception of the audit sector, that big firms have developed, and lawyers have for some time shown themselves to be extremely sensitive to the risk of their practices becoming dequalified.

The first wave of concentration, which began at the turn of the twentieth century and continued into the 1960s, fuelled fears of "proletarianization." At this time, the ethnographic-sociological study, *The Wall*

---

[18] J. Gadrey, "La modernisation des services professionnels," *Revue française de sociologie* 2 (1994): 172–173.

*Street Lawyer*, paved the way to understanding the "professional organization."[19] Contrary to the public bureaucracy and the corporation bureaucracy, the organizational form found in Wall Street legal firms was characterized chiefly by work autonomy, collegial power, a limited number of rules, and external control exercised by the profession through codes of ethics, in other words by a set of techniques adapted to maintaining professional services. Twenty years later, the megafirms made their appearance, and again fears—this time of "deprofessionalization"—arose and then subsided.[20] Since the turn of the present century, the largest firms have grown from two or three hundred lawyers to over a thousand, the organizational structure and functioning has become more complex and more constraining, and "the corporate firm" has partially replaced the "Wall Street firm." Nevertheless, the lawyers in the large private firms, even when compared to the solo lawyers, have retained at least a moderate professional autonomy in the delivery of personalized services.[21]

The same interpretation can be applied to legal megafirms, large hospitals, big corporate consulting firms, and architectural firms, in sum wherever services are personalized. Although some desingularization may appear,[22] bigger size is not necessarily accompanied by a rationalization of the organization that might destroy the two conditions necessary for maintaining personalized services, namely: discretionary power and a personal relationship with the client. The large professional firms had

[19] E. O. Smigel, *The Wall Street Lawyer: Professional Organization Man?* (Bloomington: Indiana University Press, 1964).

[20] M. Galanter and T. Palay, "The transformation of the large law firm," in R. L. Nelson, D. M. Trubek, and R. L. Solomon (eds.), *Lawyers' Ideals and Lawyers' Practices: Transformation in the American Legal Profession* (Ithaca, NY: Cornell University Press, 1992), pp. 52–116; E. Lazéga, *The Collegial Phenomenon* (Oxford: Oxford University Press, 2001); R. L. Nelson, *Partners with Power: Social Transformation of the Large Law Firm* (Berkeley: University of California Press, 1988).

[21] The picture is complicated because professional autonomy is a multidimensional notion that varies with organizational constraints as well as with the power of the clients. Those two dimensions, in turn, vary together with the size of the legal firms, and that relation prevents disentangling their specific effects on professional autonomy. See J. P. Heinz, R. L. Nelson, R. Sandefur, and E. O. Laumann (eds.), *Urban Lawyers: The New Social Structure of the Bar* (Chicago: University of Chicago Press, 2005), pp. 98–139; R. Nelson and L. Dansefur, "Professional dominance to organizational dominance," in W. Felstiner (ed.), *Reorganization and Resistance: Legal Professions Confront a Changing World* (Oxford: Oxford University Press, 2005), pp. 313–42.

[22] In the case of lawyers, one of the mechanisms consists in the breaking down of cases into subsets distributed among the different legal firms. For doctors practicing in private hospitals, another mechanism is the reduction of the consultation time. K.S. Cook and R. M. Kramer, "Trust and distrust in patient-physicians relationships: Perceived determinants of high- and low-trust relationships in managed-care settings," in R. M. Kramer and K. S. Cook (eds.), *Trust and Distrust in Organizations: Dilemmas and Approaches* (New York: Russell Sage Foundation, 2004), pp. 65–98.

found a form of organization, bearing at once on the distribution of internal power and on the relations between the professionals and their clients, that made it possible to maintain the production of "tailor-made" services, albeit not without some distortions and conflicts. The conditions for this continuity even through partial transformations are also maintained because the cultural complexes, which largely overlap with the university and academic research, have a strong influence on the renewal of knowledge and practices.

### Mainstream Economics, Political Action, and Desingularization

For neoclassical theory, the control devices used by the professions exist purely for the purpose of creating and appropriating an economic rent. Therefore professions are assimilated to economic entities that multiply the obstacles to free competition in order to exploit their clients. Formulated and reformulated, before and after the 1960s, this reasoning has remained basically unchanged.[23] It would thus serve to justify a systematic policy of dismantling the professional regulation.

When it came to fighting the regulation of professions, the European Commission did not limit its justifications to neoclassical theory in general; it also based them directly on the findings of a large-scale economic study that was conducted in 2000 on six professions (lawyers, accountants, *notaires*, architects, pharmacists, and engineers) by a team of economists and that compared the degrees of regulation of these professions with the relative prices of their services in European Union countries.[24] The official general finding was that the stronger the regulation, the lower consumers' well-being. In other words, the practitioners' gain is the clients' loss.[25] The usual proposition of neoclassical economic theory was again confirmed. As a result, the Commission's policy of imposing deregulation of the professions to bring down prices and favor economic

[23] The literature on this subject is plentiful and repetitive. Milton Friedman, in *Capitalism and Freedom* (Chicago: University of Chicago Press, 1962), was one of the first to formulate most of these arguments, sometimes in an extreme form.

[24] M. Monti, "Competition in professional services: New lights and new challenges," (Berlin, 21 March 2003); N. Kroes, "Commissioner's opening speech to the EPI Jury committee on 20 November 2005," http://*www.ec.europa.eu/competition/speeches/text*. The first author is a former European Commissioner for Competition (1999–2004), and the second author has held the same position since 2005.

[25] "This result supports the hypothesis arising out of contra-regulation theories, namely that economic benefits are being gained by highly regulated professions at the expense of consumer welfare." (I. Paterson, M. Fink, A. Ogus, et al., *Economic Impact of Regulation in the Field of Liberal Professions in Different Member States: Regulation of Professional Services* (Vienna: Institute for Advanced Studies, 2003), 3 vols., vol. 1, p. 127.

growth could be put to work.[26] Clearly, political action was, at least publicly, based almost exclusively on what were held to be scientific truths. Science and politics were inextricably intertwined. The strategic position of this research justifies some critical examination.[27]

An essential feature that characterizes this study was the indeterminate nature of the object studied, a consequence of the ways the two main notions are defined. First, professional services are considered, historically, as the activities of people who exercise liberal professions; they are also distinguished from services in general by their high quality: "There is . . . no basis for questioning the high quality and essential values of existing professional services, *regardless* of the presence of high or low levels of regulation";[28] and, at the same time, this particularism is deliberately ignored.[29]

But with the notion of "liberal profession," which is the basis of the comparison, the authors are interested not in the peculiar form of social organization which, for specific activities, appeared at the beginning of the eighteenth century and is found almost everywhere, but only in direct or indirect self-regulation. They are using it not to propose a specific interpretation but as an equivalent of the notion of "regulated occupations," which applies to a great diversity of occupations.

Moreover, professional services are supposed to be of high quality; but of course there are variations and even strong variations between professionals. When consumers are looking for a "good" or the "right" professional and sometimes making a great effort to find him or her, they know full well that the types and the quality of the professional services are unequally distributed. Nevertheless, no tool is used by the research group to deal with quality. The study begins with two substitutions and one conspicuous absence: service in general replaces professional services, regulated bodies replace liberal professions, and the notion of quality is absent.

Better services cost more. If one takes into account this rather trivial proposition advanced in the study, it becomes impossible to decide whether the differences in national prices are to be explained by differences in the degrees of professional regulation or by differences in the

[26] The Commission did not adopt the radical version of deregulation. In an argument too long to feature here, it limited its intervention to generalizing the regulation of each profession at the lowest level found in the countries under comparison.

[27] For the present discussion I have avoided dealing with the technical and statistical part of this study, which also offers up some curious practices.

[28] Paterson, Fink, Ogus, et al., *Economic Impact*, vol. 1, p. 7.

[29] "In spite of the supposed and existing 'special' character of liberal professions, in respect of their relationship with clients, and responsibilities vis-à-vis the system of law, and/or governments, the approach taken here is primarily to regard the professions in their role as actors—in equal treatment along with other branches." Ibid.

quality of the service. To counter such an argument, the authors are obliged to make a desperate assumption: they state that the quality of the services is relatively homogeneous throughout the countries of Europe.[30] Under this condition, price differences can only be attributed to differences in the degree of regulation. That is the condition that had to be satisfied for the general finding to exist. But the authors do not have the faintest idea of the distribution of qualities among the different countries, and all the more so because they do not have any precise conception of service quality. In fact, a somewhat operational definition of a professional service—a personalized service as opposed to a standardized or differentiated service—shows for French lawyers (and this observation can probably be generalized) that the legal profession's services are diverse, that the nature and degree of this diversity vary from one regional bar to the next, and that the differences between the European bars should be even greater. The authors' assumption is therefore perfectly arbitrary.

Even on this limited basis, one may conclude at least that the research group has not demonstrated what it wrote it had. And the results are too problematic for the study to serve as a basis for European policy. In reality, the situation is even worse. The Commission has often given as examples two spontaneously decided reforms that were oriented toward deregulation. One concerns the abolition of solicitors' monopoly on conveyance services in Great Britain, and the second deals with the deregulation of the profession of *notaire* in the Netherlands. Both were supposed to build a more efficient market with lower prices: exactly the contrary happened.[31] There may be good theoretical reasons for that, but until now they have not been exposed.

The Vienna study is not the first, nor is it the last, to have derived such "results" but what makes it different is the fact that a whole policy has been based on its "findings." Its limits stem from a theoretical framework that lacks the conceptual resources to qualify professional services and the interpretative resources to account for their variations. As we have already said, for the neoclassical theory, self-government, control devices, network, trust, and so forth are seen as obstacles to free competition; while for the economics of singularities, these devices make it possible to

---

[30] This postulate is so important for justifying the results that it serves as a framework for the text: "It seems fair to point out that the study does not deal with the quality and range of services provided in member states—no information is available—so this is assumed to be homogeneous enough for a fair comparison of economic outcomes to be made." Ibid., vol. 1, pp. 5, 127).

[31] See OECD (Organization for Economic Cooperation and Development), *Competitive Restrictions in Legal Professions*, 2007, http://www.oecd.org/dataoecd/12/38/40080343.pdf.

dispel the opacity of the market, to avoid opportunism, and to establish quality competition. Far from threatening the market, these devices keep it from self-destructing.[32] The stakes are high, because from this perspective, professions without control devices would not be able to maintain personalized services, and by blindly following the neoclassical theory, the *European Commission is defining and enforcing a general policy that favors the standardization of professional services.* The economics of singularities excludes neither monopolistic practices nor the need to combat them, but particular counteractions should take care not to destroy precious human skills.[33]

To be sure, the danger should probably not be overestimated insofar as these governments are facing consumers and producers who have a vested interest in maintaining markets of singularities. Nevertheless, since this intervention is only at its beginning, it would be helpful to abandon received wisdom and instead turn to arguments and means adapted to the specific reality of personalized services.

Paradoxically, it was the U.S. Supreme Court that led the way several decades ago. To justify the famous 1977 decision rescinding the traditional ban on lawyers advertising their services, the Court, far from referring to the general reasoning of neoclassical theory, developed, among others, two arguments: first, advertising prices cannot deceive the consumer insofar as the services are standardized, and second, in the case of routine services, advertising should not drive down quality because in such cases, standardized services are often preferable to the half-hearted services of certain lawyers.[34] By basing its ruling on the distinction between *routine* service and *unique* service, the Court was able to avoid confusing two categories of professional services and two markets, even if it did not carry this difference to its logical conclusion.

---

[32] A historical reading of French professional regulation shows clearly that it usually stems from the government's desire to maintain public order, which means essentially protecting, rather than exploiting, consumers. That was the case for the French legal bar at the end of the seventeenth century, and it is still the case for the recent organization of the profession of psychotherapists by the law of 19 August 2004, which, far from being market oriented, is explicitly aimed at "protecting the public" by creating a profession regulated by law with access conditions based on mandatory certification.

[33] The profession of lawyer, like other professions, cannot be defined by the market alone. Its organization is also the result of exercising a political function of defense of individual liberties, whose history in Europe goes back to the eighteenth century and which, in more or less recent times, has become constitutive of the profession in a great number of countries throughout the world. See T. Halliday, L. Karpik, and M. Feeley, *Fighting for Freedom. Comparative Studies of the Legal Complex and Political Liberalism* (Oxford: Hart Publishing, 2007).

[34] *Bates v. State Bar of Arizona*, 433 U.S. 350 (1977), http://caselaw.lp.findlaw.com/scripts/getcase.pl?navby=case&court=us&vol=433&page=350.

## Desingularization of Pop Music

The probability of desingularization is greater with large markets than with small ones, and greater with formal devices than with substantial devices or with networks. The probability is therefore the greatest in the case of the common-opinion regime, which has both features. And among the concrete markets that make up this coordination regime, some much more than others show signs of this evolution: this is the case today of popular music. We will therefore extend the study of this market so as to identify the conditions that bring the maintenance of singularities and the regime logic into contradiction.

There is nothing more subjective than musical judgment, especially when it comes to popular songs, for which there is no aesthetic authority that might act as the caretaker of creation, originality, orthodoxy, and quality. Nor is there anything more difficult than to gain an overview, since the music is in constant flux and imperceptible changes in the state of these products occur over time, so the terms of reference fade from memory. And yet there are many signs that change has occurred. Whether we look at surveys and reports or the numerous forums and blogs or the reactions of the many experts, journalists, or music lovers, no other cultural industry in the United States or France comes anywhere near displaying such a large amount of virulent criticism articulated around the opposition between originality and standardization (the term most used). It began long before the dispute over "piracy," and it has become such a central question that even the most orthodox economic view can no longer ignore it, since the decline in aesthetic value directly threatens the record companies' economic value.[35]

How should we go about delimiting the changing universe of desingularized products? In the domain of paintings, with the "chromos," those "impoverished pictorial works," "those interchangeable pictures, products of a conventional, fossilized craftsmanship that cultural actors, whatever their area, unanimously exclude from the universe of art,"[36] (almost) all of the conditions are met. Production is carried out on a large scale, likeness is compatible with miniscule differentiations, and the paintings are bought by wholesalers and resold, cheaply, at markets and in department stores. And yet even at this level, at least in the discourse, the artistic process is already underway. It would probably be possible to see an analogous opposition between a popular mystery collection like

---

[35] "These days they rarely develop new artists into long-lasting acts, relying instead on short-term hits promoted in mainstream media. . . . Music bosses agree that the majors have a creative problem. . . . Even Wall Street analysts are questioning quality." "Music's brighter future," *The Economist*, 28 October 2004.

[36] R. Moulin, *L'artiste, l'institution et le marché* (Paris: Flammarion, 1992).

the French Fleuve Noir or the Harlequin romances and the "universe of literature."

As in the other domains, in every era, greater or fewer numbers of talented artists set themselves apart from desingularized products. But in popular music, the boundary is fuzzier, owing to the considerable corpus and its elusive meanings. Desingularization is thus an object of study that can only be constructed at the maximum distance from subjectivity, which makes method a central question. While in the case of painting, classical music, or literature, reference to famous masterpieces or to the conventions that define "true art" can offer at least indirect aid, nothing of the kind exists for popular music. That is in fact why we chose this market: to propose an interpretation based on a particularly ambiguous concrete reality.

In the common-opinion coordination regime, where the market of popular-music recordings mainly operates, desingularization is a specific and multi-faceted evolution that involves three different processes—*impoverishment*, *standardization*, and *dequalification*—which are, moreover, necessarily linked to a threat to the symbolic authority of the *chart*. The first term points up a collective practice of reducing originality, which progressively leaves more and more triviality, conformity, formatting, and clichés. The second term is an image widely used by critics, which means uniformization, redundancy, imitation, repetition, homogeneousness—everything that favors interchangeability. Not that the songs are identical, but they are sufficiently alike for their differences not to be regarded as meaningful. The third term indicates a product transformation that amounts to a loss of identity and establishes the conditions favorable to the two previous processes. And the fourth term deals with the central interlinking device that is the operator of the desingularization evolution. Of course it is easier to study impoverishment, dequalification, and chart changes, since that can be done through indirect signs, than it is to study "standardization," since in that case we have to deal directly with the specificity of the music.

### Musical Impoverishment

A few American sociological studies have dealt with the tendency of popular music toward impoverishment, especially in relation to the market's structure. The findings do not converge, but then the authors used different ways of defining and evaluating musical quality.[37] The study by Peterson

---

[37] W. Hamlen, "Superstardom in popular music: Empirical evidence," *Review of Economics and Statistics* 73 (2001): 729–733; P. D. Lopes, "Innovation and diversity in the popular music industry, 1969 to 1990," *American Sociological Review* 57, no. 1 (1992): 56–71; P. J. Alexander, "Entropy and popular culture: Product diversity in the popular music recording industry," *American Sociological Review* 61, no. 1 (1996): 171–174.

and Berger, which we will take as a starting point, deals with the period from 1948 to 1973 in the United States, when the pop-music market was marked by swings between concentration and deconcentration.[38] Comparison of the various points of the economic cycle shows that the homogeneity of musical products increased with the rate of economic concentration. These variations were clearly expressed in the make-up of the Top 10: in times of economic concentration, the positions were monopolized by the four biggest record companies; in times of deconcentration, they were split between the majors and independent firms.

The interpretation rests on the strategies of the majors and on market access. In times of economic concentration, nothing keeps the big companies from putting out numerous quality songs, which could explain their grip on the Top 10. But examination of their policies shows that, in reality, during these periods, the oligopolies devote themselves to strengthening their hold on the market by gaining control of the radio stations and airtime. So the composition of the Top 10 does not reflect an artistic reality; it measures economic power. In such periods, the reduced competition favors the expansion of imitation. The musical space is populated with minimally differentiated entities. Music renewal springs only from the collapse of market entry barriers and the breakthrough of new companies, new artists, and new musical genres, whose titles soon make it into the Top 10. To sum up: originality varies according to the relative position of the independent firms in the pop-music market.

Can such reasoning be applied to the French market? In the past, the record industry has twice shown these swings between concentration and deconcentration; but since the 1970s, and especially since the 1980s, horizontal and vertical concentration have become stronger: the Big Six were replaced by the Big Five and then by the Big Four (Universal Music, EMI, Warner Music, and Sony-BMG), takeovers of innovative independent firms have become more frequent, and control of the music chain, from production and diffusion down to final distribution, has also increased. Thus we should find signs of the impoverishment process.

To study the degree of market closure, we could compare the evolution of the number of pop-music novelties that the majors and independents have created. But such a calculation would not be vey helpful, as it deals with catalogs and not with market access. In contrast, the relationship between music and radio is much more realistic, since we know that the most aired titles are also the most sold.

Especially since the 1990s, with the concentration of radio stations, a small number of commercial music stations targeted at teenagers and

[38] R. Peterson and D. V. Berger, "Cycles in symbol production: The case of popular music," *American Sociological Review* 40, no. 2 (1975): 158–173.

young adults (the main purchasers of CDs) have become the obligatory gateway to the final market. The independence of the music stations could have led them to seek out—at least some of the time—artists exploring new paths so as to diversify the musical supply. But they made the opposite choice, and the cause is not hard to find. Because radio airtime is scarce, the majors succeeded, on the one hand, in controlling a disproportionate share of radio time by means of marketing, advertising, and very big promotional budgets, and, on the other hand, in gaining the capacity to influence the composition of playlists, by restricting the number of songs chosen and played, obtaining, as a result, as many spins as possible concentrated on as few titles as possible. All of which meant that those songs would climb up the chart, that their rank would become a new asset, and that they would be played even more often. All these moves and interventions were justified by market control and by an ardent quest for hits.

The relationship between the majors, mass marketing, over-broadcasting, and the top tunes are summarized for France by these 2007 figures:[39] (1) The new titles produced by the majors represented 54 percent of all new titles and 81 percent of the total airtime (for the independent firms, the corresponding figures are 45 percent and 17 percent). (2) The Top 10 records and 95 percent of the Top 100 records were produced by the majors labels. (3) Nine record titles that had been played on radio more than four hundred times and had benefited from a promotion budget superior to one million euros were among the Top 10.

Because the same strategy is found more or less everywhere,[40] the consequences come as no surprise: the independents' share of the airtime and of the Top charts could only dwindle, and as a result, in France, the independent firms' share of the music-record market declined from 23 percent in 1990 to 13 percent in 1995 and to 8 percent in 2005.[41] The independent producers, who are the main discoverers and producers of new talents and new musical styles, have been gradually marginalized. In France, as in the United States, concentration has reduced the sources of originality and brought musical impoverishment.[42]

---

[39] A. Nicolas, *Les marchés de la musique enregistrée, Rapport 2007* (Paris: Observatoire de la Musique, 2008).

[40] For the United States, see the detailed inventory of the relations between the majors and the radio stations in *Attorney General of the State of New York in the Matter of Warner Music Group Corp*, 22 November 2005, http://www.oag.state.ny.us/media_center/2005/nov/nov22a_05.html.

[41] N. Curien and F. Moreau, *L'industrie du disque* (Paris: La Découverte, 2006), p. 42.

[42] "But we should in fact blame concentration, which had the immediate effect of impoverishing the supply and trivializing the product. Standardization of the record, application of uniform mass-marketing techniques made the record more an industrial than a cultural product. We have forgotten that the record buyer is not just another consumer. He or she is

## *Music Reality and Standardization*

Standardization has always existed. Popular music was sometimes called "rubbish." Bad vocalists and simplistic lyrics and tunes have always been true of a fraction of the musical output. The novelty therefore lies not in the continuation but in the expansion of the phenomenon. With *Star Academy* and other musical reality shows, TV has largely dispelled the ambiguity previously maintained by music producers and broadcasters. They have always said what they were going to do and then done it. In France, this discourse went unheard for some time because *Star Academy*, which was its main exponent, broke with the reference to the artistic model. Although this TV program was received with criticism that was at the same time virulent and ineffective, it escaped the denunciation of its failings and imperfections because it claimed another model.

*Star Academy* showed that it was not a utopian dream to produce one or several celebrities in the space of a few weeks or months. It has demonstrated publicly that famous artists—too expensive and not necessarily tractable—could be replaced by younger ones who were more dependent and whose short-term profits were also greater than those of the bulk of their elders.[43] The new "artist" does not come out of the traditional lineage and is not aiming to fit the classical pattern of originality, inspiration, or message; furthermore, no one is asking him or her to do so. The fact is that audience identification with the artist is not based on difference but on likeness. Some distance can be introduced, but very little, so as not to produce an effect of otherness. The figure of the artist is thus defined in negative terms—neither a dandy nor an esthete, neither romantic nor inspired nor gaudy—all of which breaks with countless myths. The new artist should be an average person.

The same demands are made of the songs. Nothing must jostle consensus, communion, or sharing with the audience. From this standpoint, remakes of old favorites and new works obey a single rule: "Do not disturb." Critics may argue about the lack of aesthetic value, the absence of originality, or the repetition, or worse; but they are missing the point. The new "object" is judged on other criteria. Basically these songs are not meant to "say" anything. They belong to a universe of works that are made fast, consumed fast, discarded fast, and fast forgotten. This is

---

someone who enjoys making discoveries, someone who is not to be tricked." P. Zelnik, CEO of "Naïve" (an independent firm) and president of UPFI (Independent French Producers Association), *Le Point*, 31 October 2003: 108.

[43] The same process can be seen in the United States. In this entertainment economy, concepts and marketing have become so big that the artists are increasingly regarded as an element of publicity. To regain control of their unpredictable stars, studios are also increasingly trying to use celebrities as a replaceable commodity. D. Carr, "In pop culture, concepts are outshining stars," *New York Times/Le Monde*, 29–30 June 2003.

the universe of the interchangeable commodity that is often indicated by the term *standardization*.

Such a requalification of both the work and the artist is not evident: the process is inseparable from the power of television and its special relationship with the audience. Before the future artist is launched, he or she builds a relationship with his or her audience, after which, future performances cannot differ radically from the initial ones; time is too short. The very real difference lies elsewhere. Insofar as the audience, following a skillfully orchestrated social drama, identifies with the reality-show celebrity and with the standardized songs, and is swept along by a collective desire for upward mobility and the power of TV, the singer sells millions of records and shoots to the top of the Top 50. She or he becomes famous but does not necessarily achieve the status that protects her or him from a fickle producer or audience.

Fame is a cultural construction; celebrity is the product of a versatile public opinion. The star existed in a remote space, beyond the reach of ordinary humans; the celebrity exists only through a proximity that makes him or her like the rest of us, and therefore vulnerable. Nevertheless, for a time at least, celebrity is what counts. In fact, the star still exists, with her godlike powers, with his capacity to disregard normally binding rules; but it is not a human celebrity, it is the device that produces this celebrity: television.

With music reality shows, desingularization is no longer a heterodox process; it is an organized practice. Songs are no longer made to be listened to; the audience shares an experience and keeps a memory. It was by simultaneously reconstructing the product and the audience that television brought about the shift and made itself immune to competition and indifferent to criticism. Thus television succeeded, at least for a time, in controlling the uncontrollable: economic success. Unlike the official conception of the major music producers, television is radically agnostic about musical quality and, therefore, can aim to maximize returns in the short run. Minimal differences, interchangeability and idolization of the normal, and mass promotion: the artist and the song are now defined solely by the conditions of economic success. Music reality shows have never been very important in terms of sales but they used to be important for what they expressed, for the debates they aroused and especially for the influence they exerted on other music as they lifted the taboo based on the value of the originality model. Standardization became a more common practice.

### Mass Sales and Dequalification

Since the1980s, the majors have chosen to increase their short-term profits by expanding their sales. The main vehicles of that strategy have been the supermarkets. From the late 1980s on, the majors practiced a twin-pronged policy based on two alliances: one with the specialized music stores and the other with the supermarkets, whose pop-music market share leapt from 40 percent to 50–60 percent, only to fall back in recent years under the impact of price competition from the discount stores.

In principle, the pop-music market looks like the book or the movie market, and we would therefore expect to find the same pattern: relatively stable prices, search for sales maximization, and a strong mutual autonomy between them. But this is not the case. Some commercial practices are the same, but not the configurations of measures, as we will show by examining the price disorder, two different ways of sales maximization and, finally, the transformation of the product.

For a long time, CD prices have, according to experts and clients, comprised a chaotic reality.[44] Price dispersion is as great as price volatility. Such "disorder" does not come about by chance. It is too exceptional and too lasting not to be deliberate. One might think that such a mess forbids any comparison between the price lists used by the majors.[45] One might also think that it gives managers a free hand to formulate a pragmatic musical policy. Whatever the case may be, it is through such a policy that the majors sought greater short-term profits.[46] This maximization was imperative. And it became even stronger when the majors, having been swallowed up by multimedia conglomerates, found themselves all the more obliged to respect this financial imperative because their power within the conglomerate was limited (unlike the case of the movie industry), because the usual relationship between artistic and economic criteria had been stood on its head, because marketing and finances were the backbone of the conglomerate, and because the future directors of the main companies started out as heads of branches, where they imposed the short-term profit criterion on which they themselves would be judged. This requirement has meant two different sales strategies: The regular one, practiced in the music stores, and the other one, less familiar, in the general chains stores.

The latter were chosen to expand the volume of sales, and the CDs gained access to the general public by means of a dequalification policy. This transformation was brought about through two major practices: one

[44] "The pricing policy managed by or inflicted by the profession is increasingly incoherent and extremely volatile. . . . The problem isn't so much price in itself. . . . It's the inconsistency of the pricing policy that is more troubling since it offers no readibility, no promotional and artistic ranking that the consumer might understand." Nicolas, *Les marchés*, p. 6.

[45] "The incitation to differentiate products decreases when firms do not compete in prices," J. Tirole, *The Theory of Industrial Organization* (Cambridge, MA: MIT Press, 1988), p. 287.

[46] Like all international firms, the recording majors have seen the constraints on short-term returns, which are defined by the international bosses, gradually tighten." A. Cocquebert, *Le financement de l'industrie du disque* (Paris: Ministère de la Culture, 2005), p. 5.

within the stores and the other between them. From the very beginning, the selling of records was based on short lists of references, concentration on Top titles, a large number of compilations, shelf location between anything and anything, hit CDs in piles at the endcaps, and absence of customer assistance in the form of signs and sales clerks. All of which should logically produce random choices. But although it was invisible, the Top chart had a strong influence. And an apparent erratic price policy was at work: prices differed from one CD to another and changed from one week to the next, usually but not always high prices for novelties, very low prices for numerous "special deals," and quite often the use of CDs as a loss leader. On such a scale, these commercial practices could only produce two main consequences. On the one hand, the meaning of "right" price disappeared, leaving space for global suspicion. On the other hand, the pop-music CD (the following is also true for classical CDs) as an expression of the cultural product, whether "good" or "bad" (that was not the issue as all of them were equally considered), was treated as a *good without qualities*—pure commodity, an interchangeable commodity. It lost its identity, its symbolic worth. The equivalence between a CD and a pot of yogurt became a commonplace. And by the same token the consumer, too, was dequalified.

This process was further reinforced by external competition. Because the supermarkets benefited from privileged prices from the majors, they were able to eliminate local record stores, which often concentrated competent, knowledgeable enthusiasts, who were sources of personal advice and criticism for their clients and were actors whose influence reached through networks far into society. With their disappearance, the record as a singularity was weakened.

The dequalification process was all the more conducive to impoverishment and/or standardization because it demonstrated that music was largely unprotected. Pop music is a minor art and has not given rise to a lively written culture: there are no institutions devoted to celebrating popular music and artists, to making sense of their history, to situating popular song with regard to society, and above all, to leading the debate—current in all other areas—on quality or qualities. In France, with a few rare exceptions—mainly jazz and rock—criticism and trade journals are almost nonexistent. The cultural complex was and still is weak. In the absence of aesthetic counterpowers, the CD was a weak adversary.

### The Chart and Convenience

Only one force could have compromised this strategy, and more generally this evolution, and that was the clientele. But the chart, or more precisely a certain use of the chart, together with the weak cultural complex, prevented that eventual action. Not everyone who buys popular music uses charts, and not everyone who uses charts relies on them as their only source of knowledge. Of those who limit themselves to charts, some even have the competence to make their own choices, but the majority cling to a combination of ranking and genre. There is nothing illogical in this conformity since passivity and heteronomy are the features of consumer commitment which correspond to the requirements of the specific formal devices that operate within the common-opinion regime. They are not psychological attributes but reasonable behaviors. But this presupposes that the delegate sticks to its mandate.

For the common-opinion regime, the chart is a crucial judgment device. As Anand and Peterson rightly emphasize,[47] by procuring information, it helps people make sense of the market, and by acting as a focal point for the producers, artists, mass-media professionals, and consumers, it creates a "unified field." But unity may take several forms. The chart is a valuable help to customers who find themselves lost amid the relentless proliferation of new musical titles. Its justification is *convenience of choice*, which often comes down to the collective obsession with saving time. In the name of a recognized legitimate authority, the chart makes it possible to reconcile lack of knowledge, competence, and time with reasonable choices. For many, such an advantage is irresistible.

It is useful to the producers too, since it gives them, in real time, useful information on rapidly changing tastes. It is especially useful because it is open to "manipulation."[48] The term here designates neither the tricks that have disappeared with the bar code nor payola practices (pay-to-play), but the strategic means by which the chart proclaims, insofar as possible, the public measures of success in order to benefit again from the resources that may improve that success. In other words, the chart is among the tools that foster closure of a worldwide oligopolistic market—the restriction in the number of the works, the concentration of advertisement and promotion on fewer titles—by excluding all those that, for different reasons, are adversaries: the music stores and the independent firms. The goal is not only to make hits but, more structurally, to build a hit market.

## A Digression: Classical Music and Desingularization

It would be all too easy to explain the evolution of pop music by the very fact that it is pop music. It is therefore useful to make a brief comparison with the evolution of classical recordings, especially since they are produced and distributed by the same corporations. For a long time, the

---

[47]N. Anand and R. Peterson, "When market information constitutes fields: Sensemaking of markets in the commercial music industry," *Organization Science* 11, no. 3 (2000):270–284.

[48] "All labels share the common objective of advancing the circulation of record labels' product to the listening public. In each case, music consumers remain unaware of the extent

classical-music department enjoyed a special status: it was considered prestigious, and the financial constraints were not too strong. Then history sprang a completely unexpected event: the Three Tenors in Concert recording, which teamed up famous voices of the 1990s—José Carreras, Placido Domingo, and Luciano Pavarotti—sold over ten million copies. This phenomenal success produced a radical revision of the commercial conception of the classical recording.

For the majors, it demonstrated that classical music, like pop music, could become a hit market, and so it was reconstructed in this way. All the means and practices used for pop music were also applied to classical music: market concentration, exclusion of the independent firms, alliance with supermarkets, special deals, and loss leaders: in other words, impoverishment and dequalification. Only the chart was missing, but not completely, because best-seller lists appeared in the stores, supermarkets, and in advertisements. Standardization took hold in the forms of light classical music, numerous compilations, and now ring tones. Of course, one may only be delighted that the music of the "divine" Mozart brings in fabulous amounts from ring tones and other comparable uses.

After nearly fifteen years, this policy of building a mass market for classical recordings can be evaluated: it is a complete failure.[49] Classical music hits can be counted on the fingers of one hand, and global sales have fallen sharply. After having amounted to 15 percent of total recorded music, earnings have fallen—depending on the category and the country—to between 3 and 5 percent; and closer to 3 percent than to 5 percent if we exclude "light classical music" and the countless compilations.

Numerous essays and analyses have been devoted to this evolution, and their conclusions are contradictory: for some, the 3 percent represent the durable fraction of the clientele interested in classical music, while for others the same 3 percent are only a stage on the way to an inevitable disappearance.[50] In all events, with the exception of a few stars, the majors have shown a growing indifference toward the contemporary situation of

---

to which radio programming and records' popularity statistics are being manipulated and compromised ." *Attorney General of the State of New York in the Matter of Warner Music Group Corp*, 22 November 2005.

[49] Economic failure is an ambiguous notion. Here it designates the decline of the share of classical-recording sales in global record-market profits. This is summed up by the title of an American article: "Dear music industry, Low quality = low demand." Nevertheless, the profit decline is perhaps not as dramatic as it officially looks. See for example, the price for which Warner Group was sold to the Thomas H. Lee Partners fund, which was interested only in the possibility of getting the most money out of the operation. "They were no more interested in music than a born-again Christian is in pornography." "Warner Music Group et ses critiques," *Music Reporter Daily*, Tuesday 15 March 2005.

[50] L. Bricard, *Vingt préconisations pour la survie des disques de musique classique* (Paris: Ministère de la Culture et de la Communication, 2005); J. Lee, "A requiem for classical music," *Regional Review* 14 (2003).

the music. Classical music is about the subtle art of interpretation; that is why the different versions of a same work are not interchangeable. Sometimes the differences are minimal, sometimes they are essential. Each epoch or each artist may have a different interpretation. But funding for recording classical music has now been sharply cut, and relations with living classical music have been severely weakened. Refusal to invest and produce and desingularization are the two faces of the same history.

•  •  •

Is singularity preserved in culture and lost in the market? The book began with this question, to which a documented answer can now be offered: *the fall from singularity to commodity is not necessary*, but when it does happen *the explanation does not require us to deal with such global realities as culture, capitalism, or the market.*

Singularity is maintained in markets with the authenticity regime and in markets relying on personal devices, although desingularization may appear at the fringes without jeopardizing the global operating logics. In the professional regime, it is only the deregulating action of a political authority that could impose such an alteration. This evolution may be present in the markets of the mega regime, though for the moment we are unable to specify the general conditions under which it would appear. It is thus within the markets of the common-opinion regime that desingularization is most likely to appear and develop.

Although the movie and book markets, both of which may have one foot in the common-opinion regime, seem close to the pop-music market, they are not. Whereas the universe of popular music has little cultural autonomy, film criticism, even if it no longer enjoys the authority it did in the 1970s, is plentiful, pluralist, and influential. It has the support of a large share of regular moviegoers and a good number of professionals. The same is even truer for the book market. Here, too, criticism, in the name of one or several autonomous aesthetic logics, continues to wield a diversified influence in specialized journals, in magazines and newspapers, and in the media. Here, too, criticism has the support of numerous readers. In both cases, cultural complexes concentrate a symbolic power based on an autonomous aesthetic conception that places some limitations on the effectiveness of the charts.

That is only one cause among others, which explains why desingularization reaches its full-blown form in the popular-music market. For oligopolistic power, in addition to keeping competition weak, has managed here better than in any other market we have examined to neutralize all of the forces that elsewhere serve more or less as a counterweight: local-store networks, independent creative companies, the cultural complex, and the clientele. Under these conditions, the majors are free to increase their profit through desingularization.

When recording professionals reminisce, the 1980s appear as a "happy" time: "independents" could still get airtime, there was real diversity in the music, and financial constraints were moderate. Although these recollections should be taken with caution, they nevertheless indicate the changes that have been produced in the last two or three decades period by the growing interweaving of impoverishment, standardization, and dequalification. To describe and explain the dynamics through which singularities are eliminated, it is not necessary to invoke global changes and conflicts: the coordination regimes give us the tools to elaborate interpretations of specific changes, based on particular causes and conditions.

The Internet and digital music have not yet developed to the extent that the market's working rules have changed in any fundamental way.[51] Therefore it was not necessary to mention them. But this should change when the Internet becomes linked to the promise of a vast expansion of singularities. That is the central meaning of the economic model called the Long Tail, proposed by C. Anderson. As a result of the infinite and almost costless space available on the Internet and of the ease of downloading, millions of musical references, old and new, known and unknown, will become available. And since it is as profitable to sell a large number of titles to a few clients as it is to sell a few titles to a large number of people, "the cultural benefit of all of this is much more diversity, reversing the blanding effects of a century of distribution scarcity and ending the tyranny of the hit."[52]

Unfortunately, this is only half true. It takes more than technology to solve social or cultural problems. Is it realistic, for example, to believe that, as people "wander further from the beaten path, they [will] discover their taste is not as mainstream as they thought (or as they had been led to believe by marketing, a lack of alternatives, and a hit-driven culture)"? How many people will "wander" through very long lists of titles? How will they make choices from among the unknown? This difficulty was later discovered by the author: "a long tail without good filters is just noise." In fact, the paradox of the Long Tail is that, taken alone, it could only reinforce the search for "hits" or "semi-hits," because the more numerous the choices and the greater the cognitive deficit, the more people will use convenient devices for making choices. The Long Tail can keep its promises only if it is combined with sophisticated and trustworthy judgment devices—which brings us back to the economics of singularities.

[51] In France, the rate of digital-music sales has grown moderately: from 2.2 percent in 2002 to 6.4 percent of the global music market in 2007.

[52] C. Anderson, "The long tail," *Wired Magazine*, October 2004, http://www.wired.com. The quotations are from C. Anderson's blog.

What do we do with the desingularization threat? If the goal of the music-recording corporations is to achieve a two-digit, short-term profit rate, and if to achieve that goal, they have to maintain or even reinforce the desingularization process, what can be done? In the 1950s, Walter Legge, a music producer at EMI, recorded a series of operas that are still among the most outstanding interpretations. At the time, the clientele, in absolute numbers, was infinitely smaller than today, and profitability was low and calculated over the long term. There were fewer clients and lower returns, but a passion for music existed that overcame all obstacles and created its audience. But what can be done when the holders of economic power do not respect or love their own products? What counterpower will have the duty and the strength to protect society against the process of desingularization ?

One could stop with that question. But there is an answer, although it is not the only one: At least one authority could become such a counterpower if it were prepared to extend the conception of its action. After all, singularities come within the market, and competition by qualities stands side by side with competition by price. Therefore, why should not the same regulatory authorities that are in charge of maintaining free competition and low prices also maintain the integrity of singularities? Some theoretical and practical adjustments will be required, but the goal of a well-functioning market justifies the fight against both desingularization and economic rent.[53]

[53] History keeps repeating itself. I have just read for the first time for classical music something that has long been linked with pop music: "uniformity is threatening . . . indifferent soloists and standardized orchestras . . . an uniform quality. So goes the world." B. Dermoncourt, "Music tastes" (editorial), *Classica* no. 116 (October 2009). This process needs of course to be checked.

## Chapter Nineteen

# CONCLUSION

## ECONOMICS OF SINGULARITIES AND
## DEMOCRATIC INDIVIDUALISM

IT IS IN JUDGMENT that the economics of singularities finds its unity and on the coordination regimes that it bases its explanatory power. Each regime of coordination is defined by a distinctive global logic, which is expressed in the adjustment between a particular qualified singular product, a particular category of judgment devices, and a particular form of consumer commitment. Taken together, the coordination regimes explain the workings of all concrete markets. Nor would the theory be any less coherent were variants to be added to the coordination regimes, provided they were constructed according to the same approach.

The explanation of market functioning rests on a unitary conceptualization: notions are interdependent, and their precise meaning can be defined only through their interrelations. It rests also on three general principles: first, reference to the coordination regimes as abstract models is the general explanatory principle of reality; second, depending on whether the concrete markets are homogeneous or not, the explanation of their operation depends on one or more coordination regimes; and third, the relationship between markets and coordination regimes is not built around types of products but around types of qualified products; as a result, the "same" product may be found in two or more coordination regimes.

The analysis has been limited to the *market*, which means *transactions*, but it should not be inferred that a general rule exists which clearly defines the boundaries. In fact, use of the economics of singularities can be extended, but not according to a general rule that would add, for example, all organizations or political systems or cultural institutions. The enlargement procedure is specific to the theory. It is governed by the answer given to the following question: Is it possible to identify a universe of singularities? The positive answer explains that some quasi markets have been added and this could also be the case, for example, for judges, even though they belong to organizations. In both cases, singularities are involved, and even if the present tools have to be partially transformed, we assume that fundamental problems and fundamental characteristics are shared, and that the reasoning should largely be the same. Decisions should be made not on the basis of general rules, however, but on a case-by-case basis and, moreover, their fruitfulness has to be demonstrated. As a result, the enlargement, if any, cannot be reliably delimited in advance.

A research program is usually associated with a theoretical perspective, but priorities and research strategies can be diverse. Therefore I will merely single out two issues. The first priority is to study the competitive integration and the effects of the multiple judgment devices of specific concrete markets of singularities. Such analysis also concerns knowledge of the effects of the imbalance between the personal and the impersonal judgment devices on the market. Although the study of networks has been the major theoretical advance in economic sociology, and although it is still central, it now seems time to turn our attention to both types of judgment devices and to rectify what may become a distorted view of social reality. In this instance, the main obstacle is perhaps less theoretical than methodological and technical: How are we to observe and identify the effects of configurations of competing impersonal judgment devices whose scales and means of action are highly diverse? The second issue is obvious: We need to enlarge the verification of the validity of the regimes of coordination. Several concrete studies have already been explained by regimes of coordination, but, as the survey of the French lawyers market showed, it is not only a matter of increasing the number of markets; more specific data and, as a result, more elaborated analysis are also needed.

•  •  •

To conclude, I would like to address the relationship between the economics of singularities and democratic individualism. This brings us back to a classic problem—the relationship between the market and social forces—and it seems a good way to recall that the market is a historical reality and cannot be separated from social structure.[1]

## ON INDIVIDUALISM

After three or four decades of major change, individualism, according to the prevailing representation, is now clearly associated with a cultural configuration that includes the pursuit of pleasure, a passion for things, the primacy of the ephemeral, and boundless desire. It is theoretically as compatible with the demands of capitalism's extended development as it

[1] For a critical review, see V. Zelizer, "Culture and consumption," in N. Smelser and R. Swedberg (eds.), *Handbook of Economic Sociology* (Princeton: Princeton University Press, 2005), pp. 331–354.

is with the demands for integration in societies that, increasingly oblivious of the traditional cultures and the major ideologies of the twentieth century, have generalized hedonism as their sole common horizon. Such would be the fate shared by developed societies. But before taking a stand on what looks like a new philosophy of history, some clarifications have to be brought to the notion and evolution of democratic individualism.

The contemporary individual, as scrutinized by the most exacting observers, is defined by two often-mentioned features: personal self-fulfillment and interpersonal relations. Self-fulfillment means that the value of a person's action is not measured by the changes he or she makes in the world, for which it was once right and good to sacrifice all (this was the figure of the militant activist), but by the realization of a personal existence that can and should be a creative work.[2] Responsibility for this accomplishment is incumbent on the individual. It is embodied in an aesthetic of existence—hence the individualization of cultural practices—and in emancipation from tradition and authority—hence the individualization of social mores. The same change can also be seen in the professional sphere in the, at least, partial individualization of practices, remunerations, and careers. The individual is no freer today than he was yesterday, for it is not in his power to choose to be less free or to be free in another fashion, as shown by a psychic economy in which the price of refusal to make commitments or of powerlessness to exercise personal "sovereignty" is mental depression.

The contemporary individual is defined by a goal and, equally, by the means chosen to achieve it.[3] "Personal" self-fulfillment means that models and guarantees are no longer to be sought in the past, in heritage, and in tradition. On the contrary, the individual must work to free himself from these collective legacies. This "self-invention" is evident in the loosening of the statistical relationship between professional positions and social attitudes—although what remains must not be underrated—and, more spectacularly, in a crisis of transmission: rarely have successive generations felt closer while being culturally more distant from each other.

Self-fulfillment and indifference to the outside world do not imply closing oneself off, though: the individual is a relational being. His or her

[2] The following developments are justified by the available data on the increasing freedom of social mores: the decline of traditional morality, the authority crisis in the private sphere, the declining influence of belonging in general, and of class belonging in particular, the decline of major ideologies, and the extension of interpersonal sociability. These are conveniently gathered and analyzed in the collective work edited by P. Bréchon, *Les valeurs des Français: Evolution de 1980 à 2000* (Paris: Armand Colin, 2000). See also E. Maurin, *L'égalité des possibles* (Paris: Editions du Seuil, 2002), p. 56.

[3] "to choose by themselves and uniquely by themselves what is good or bad for them." O. Galland, "Individualisaiton des moeurs et choix culturels," in O. Donnat and P. Tolila (eds.), *Le(s) public(s) de la culture* (Paris: Presses de Sciences-Po, 2003), pp. 83–100.

sociability is invested first and foremost in interpersonal relationships—
first and foremost, but with variations; first and foremost, but not exclusively. The restrictions are sizable. The past three or four decades have
been characterized by the growing presence of an egalitarian individualism by virtue of which everyone has not only the possibility but the moral
duty to respect his autonomy, to construct her life, to make moral and
cultural choices in the respect of his or her own values. Such an individual knows others through network ties.

Whatever the strength of this general representation, other interpretations have to be taken into account which show that individualism breaks
down into several figures. One is the moral obligation of personal self-
fulfillment, the affirmation of the individual's originality, an aesthetics of
existence;[4] another stresses the primacy of a personal autonomy defined
by opposition to tradition, authority, and rules; yet another highlights the
loss of collective guidelines,[5] the "fatigue of being,"[6] the slide into victim-
hood, fragility, and powerlessness.[7] Individualism is thus also pluralistic.
Therefore, nothing authorizes linking this diversity to a single cultural
configuration. On the contrary, everything—especially history—pleads
for the diversity of collective orientations.

The rise of individualism has been amplified in France as elsewhere by
economic mutations, by the collapse of traditional industries, and by the
disintegration of forms of collective belonging—neighborhoods, unions,
political parties—that gave meaning to social life and collective action.
The speed and magnitude of this "social disaffiliation"[8] explain the rapid
appearance and generalization of a collective representation that suddenly replaced social classes with individualism.

However significant the economic turmoil and social crisis that began
in the 1970s may have been, individualism did not spring up in response
to a social vacuum: it has been brewing for centuries.[9] In France, after its
incarnation in the May 1968 worker-student movement and its two-
pronged attempt at breaking with tradition and authority, individualism
made unremitting progress; but that does not mean that social classes

[4] C. Taylor, *The Malaise of Modernity* (Toronto: House of Anansi Press, 2003), pp. 69–70.

[5] J.-C. Kaufmann, *L'invention de soi* (Paris: A. Colin, 2004), p. 323.

[6] A. Ehrenberg, *L'individu incertain* (Paris: Calmann-Lévy, 1995).

[7] G. Lipovetsky and S. Charles, *Hypermodern Times* (Cambridge: Polity Press, 2005).

[8] R. Castel, *From Manual Workers to Wage Laborers: Transformation of the Social Question* (New Brunswick, NJ: Transaction Publishers, 2003), pp. xiii–xvii.

[9] L. Dumont, *Essays on Individualism: Modern Ideology in Anthropological Perspective*
(Chicago: University of Chicago Press, 1983, 1992); N. Elias, *The Society of Individuals*
(New York: Continuum International Publishing Group, 2001); M. Gauchet, *The Disen-
chantment of the World: A Political History of Religion* (Princeton: Princeton University
Press, 1999).

and the effects of collective belonging suddenly vanished, to be completely supplanted by individualism. If today the influence of this social force is probably predominant, it is far from being exclusive.

No demonstration sums it up better than the following statement: "Today we are not prepared to sacrifice any commitment whatsoever in our personal or even professional life. . . . There is something here having to do with our generation that is not discussed. . . . The question of the individual, on the other hand, is present. . . . If you do not take this as your point of departure and your perspective, you aren't credible. . . . We ask to be left alone so that we can get on with our life, without the [political] party allowing itself to judge us in one sense or the other."[10]

One could find no clearer way of saying that the social actor is henceforth a composite being, defined, in different proportions, by collective belonging and individual autonomy, and that the share of the latter increases with each generation. The distinction between the public and private spheres (and this is not the only distinction we could use) previously inconceivable in a labor movement that demanded the complete subordination of private life to public commitment now seems obvious and in no need of justification. The behaviors of the new being, because they must be linked simultaneously to two general principles of action, become problematic.

As social disaffiliation, propelled by a long economic and social mutation, was making itself felt in France, the "society of individuals" was gaining ground. It was able to do so only through the growing multiplication and intensification of the processes of *reaffiliation* in the market and society alike, which was accomplished by the multiplication of private and public mediations. And, paradoxically, the main consequence analysts have usually drawn from the astonishing enlargement of the universe of impersonal devices is the development of the network. It would seem that this invisible and spontaneous social structure grew so extensive and dense that it is now capable of single-handedly regulating society's information, values, and interactions. Alongside the state, so the thinking goes, a society—one that is coextensive with the grid of interpersonal relations—should connect each individual to all others.

On the scale of the market, and even more on the scale of society as a whole, there is no question of reasoning on the basis of the network in isolation, except when conditions demand it, as in the case of markets relying exclusively (or almost exclusively) on personal devices. In fact, the idea that the network covers a large territory seems shaky, except perhaps

[10] O. Besancenot, *Le Monde*, 11 August 2004. Besancenot is one of the leaders of a far left-wing party, Ligue Communiste Révolutionnaire (LCR), and calls himself a revolutionary. In 2007, he ran in the presidential election and won 4.2 percent of the total vote; in 2008 he was busy building an "anticapitalist" party.

for the upper class. For the popular classes, network means above all "relational niches", and social and territorial segregation.[11]

At the same time, as economic regulation became weaker, political regulation extended its reach. And with it, reaffiliation increased. State intervention was the answer to two—at times contradictory—demands that developed simultaneously. First, there was the call for the building of a law-and-order state, which was considered to be all the more necessary because the local collective forces that traditionally, informally, and spontaneously once ensured a certain social order had disappeared.[12] The demand for protection on the part of individuals increasingly bereft of belonging and collective mediations took the form of insistent demands for law and order, for the expansion of the criminal justice system, for the growth of a surveillance society,[13] and as a consequence, for a stronger state. Both films and TV series, in their own fashion, express this shift: while films of the 1960s–1970s enrolled the figures of the journalist and the private detective to depict the reality of the day, nowadays this task falls to the police inspector and the judge.

Second, there was the call for the development of a rule-of-law state based on public authorities and the judicial system as a result of a greater demand for diversity, autonomy, the demand for subjective rights, the extension of contractualization, and more generally, the proliferation of legal rules. The legal universe thus grew up alongside the expansion of market equipment. To be sure, judgment devices and law do not work in the same fashion, but both share the common characteristic of being mediations between the individual and his action, and these mediations are becoming increasingly numerous and detailed.

•  •  •

The multiplication of judgment devices and the development of the legal system have, separately and together, transformed relations in the market and in society at large. The spectacular inflation of impersonal media-

---

[11] Bréchon, *Les valeurs*, p. 243; and E. Maurin, *Le ghetto français* (Paris: Editions du Seuil, 2004); J.-L. Pan Ke Shon, "Isolement relationnel et mal-être," *INSEE Première* 931 (November 2003).

[12] L. Boltanski and E. Chiappello, *Le nouvel esprit du capitailsme* (Paris: Gallimard, 1999), (*The New Spirit of Capitalism* [New York: Verso, 2005]). Although the authors of this important book, after having shown the importance of networks in managerial literature and in social sciences, and after having formulated a criticism of this collective representation based on networks, nevertheless give a limited position to the impersonal devices, whatever their specific names: the representation of the society is not really modified.

[13] A. Garapon, *Les gardiens des promesses: Justice et démocratie* (Paris: Odile Jacob, 1996); M. Gauchet, *La démocratie contre elle-même* (Paris: Gallimard, 2002); L. Karpik, "Nouvelle justice, nouvelle démocratie," in H. Dalle and D. Soulez-Larivière (eds.), *Notre justice* (Paris: Robert Laffont, 2002), pp. 397–419.

tions has changed society itself, although, given the intangible nature of these shifts, all of the consequences are not yet clear. Economic and social relations have become at once more abstract, more specific, and also more complicated to decipher. For different reasons that make them all the more effective, the state and the market have cooperated in producing on a grand scale a reality that necessarily interposes itself as a condition of action between wills and achievements. This reality embodies the promise of rationality and protection, of affluence and freedom; but at the same time it changes not only the relationship between the individual and the market or the state, but also relationships between individuals. The central consequence is that the individual, even if he feels lonely, even if she does not recognize an omnipresent reality as being real, is now *part of collective action*, of several forms of collective action, sometimes as a partner, sometimes as a target, sometimes as the power reference, sometimes as a victim, and sometimes as all of these at once when all types of relations are inextricably enmeshed. Which may explain that, for long periods, such a schizophrenic situation may be eloquently expressed by a silent civil society.

## Singularities and Individualism

For singular products and "individualistic" consumers to converge on a grand scale, two tendencies had to develop, come together, and sustain each other: (1) large-scale production of some singularities at least—particularly products of the culture industry—and (2) multiplication of individuals who were more demanding, more autonomous, and more interested in originality and personalized service; individuals who in growing numbers discovered exchange products as concrete forms of self-fulfillment. Incommensurability organized the market and society in one swoop.[14] In both cases, heterogeneity predominated. Not only were there many different coordination regimes and eventually several variants, but the same was true for individualism.

Until this point, our analysis has concentrated on the capacity of the producers/sellers/professionals/public authorities to anticipate, channel, and construct demand by means of the devices and products and, as a result, to "produce" and maintain, with the help of consumers of course, the coordination regimes. Because judgment devices are tools that bring individuals to see themselves as singularities through repeated commitments in the market, we could posit that markets of singularities, by the place they now occupy in society and by the implementation of both the

[14] Taylor, *Malaise of Modernity*.

TABLE 5
Relationship Between Types of Devices and Types of Individualism

|  | Substantial Devices (absolute qualification) | Formal Devices (relative qualification) |
| --- | --- | --- |
| Active individual | 1 | 3 |
| Passive individual | 2 | 4 |

originality model and the personalization model, have the effect of reinforcing and consecrating individualism.

But, vice versa, should we not also show the influence that social forces can exert on the market? To do so, we need to identify the main cleavages that simultaneously express the transformations of the market of singularities and individuals' orientations toward self-fulfillment. There may be a diversity of solutions, but in the present case, it is the result of the will to maintain the viewpoint that has organized the whole analysis. However speculative it may appear, we have chosen to relate forms of individualism and market equipment.

We suggest dividing (1) all judgment devices into two categories: *substantial devices* (absolute qualification) and *formal devices* (relative qualification) and (2) all orientations toward personal self-fulfillment into two categories—the *active individual* (defined by self-fulfillment based on personal commitment) and the *passive individual* (self-fulfillment necessitates broad delegation of judgment to devices) (Table 5).

These two common dimensions yield a highly simplified view of reality: it is composed of four modalities of relations between (1) absolute qualification and active individuals; (2) absolute qualification and passive individuals; (3) relative qualification and active individuals; and (4) relative qualification and passive individuals.

Concrete examples would need specific studies, and therefore only general cases will be presented. The first case is the encounter between substantial devices (linked to the specific contents of the products) whose high symbolic value is expressed through the moral obligation to use them in order to make a choice and individuals whose commitment is based on an active and autonomous search for singularities as a means to personal self-realization. This encounter is a process of reinforcement—whatever the ideality that is expressed—that moves from egocentrism or commitment toward aesthetic values or the formation of a new elite. With the fourth case, the reverse is true, with the meeting between products ranked by formal devices whose often-changing positions favor cultural relativism all the more because consumers have given their consent to the delegates' action without evaluation and control. Such a form of interrelations could easily produce a common neutralization of the value of singularities and the consensual disaggregation of this universe of products.

Situations two and three are conflictual. Case two is defined by the encounter between, on the one hand, substantial devices whose continuity is maintained primarily by producers, the cultural complex, and eventually public authorities and, on the other hand, passive individuals whose consent is linked to a limited search for "good" singularities because they readily trust the devices, and their desire for autonomy is limited. This discontinuity may result in something like the Tocquevillian view of collective happiness in democracy. The third case is characterized by opposition between the ways formal devices as delegates carry out their implicit mandate and fulfill consumers' active demands for quality and convenience. Such conflicts open the way for a form of political consumerism.

Even if we do not know the external forces that intervene to modify the orientations and equilibria of the forms of individualism, it is not impossible to identify the specific effects that may follow from the dynamics operating within markets of singularities. We will mention two here. First, as has been shown, without *counterpowers*—such as learning or the engineering of judgment devices—the more vigorous the cultural complex is, the more it will requalify singularities and, in the short term at least, dequalify a large number of consumers, reduce the validity of the substantial devices, and weaken the consumer's drive for active self-realization. Second, owing to the large-scale use of new persuasion techniques, *beliefs* in the symbolic value of the singularities, identification with the cultural and human ideals developed by the cultural complex may lose their power to maintain adherence to the market. If this were to happen, the relationship between the universe of singularities and the ideal of personal self-fulfillment would be weakened.

Taking into account the tensions prevailing in the markets of singularities, analysis of the influence of the various forms of individualism allows us to explain a number of realities found there: the growth of singularization as well as the increase in desingularization, the maintenance of a universe of singular products purported to hang on the good will of the power holders, and the power struggles surrounding the definition of "good" singularities. Such an analysis thus lends intelligibility to the modalities whereby "society" alters the relative weights and modes of functioning of its coordination regimes.

• • •

Individualism and the economics of singularities not only developed concomitantly, they also penetrated and mutually transformed each other.
The new social force asserted itself through values and preferences that
favored the relative extension of certain universes of singular products
and certain coordination regimes. In exchange, the workings of the market
of singularities favored the diversification of individualistic practices. Or
more accurately, the relationship between forms of individualism, consumer practices, and product qualifications placed the social relationship
at the very center of the functioning and transformations of the market
and, vice versa, the autonomous dynamics of the market modified individualistic practices. The structuring of the market and the structuring of
individualism are, and will remain, intertwined.

●  ●  ●

What has our enlargement of the frame of analysis added? The interpretation of desingularization in the pop-music market rests basically on the
actors, the devices, the orientations, and the powers internal to the market. This specificity is indispensable, but it is not self-sufficient for that. Is
it, in effect, possible to separate the market so radically from the dynamics of social forces, especially when it comes to products and services
having such a strong symbolic value? Should we not add to the explanation the weight of social forces that are unaware of the existence and
complexity of the desingularization process and which have, by their
practices, a powerful influence in bringing about the very thing that, elsewhere, they consistently reject?

# NAME INDEX

# SUBJECT INDEX

GPSR Authorized Representative: Easy Access System Europe - Mustamäe tee
50, 10621 Tallinn, Estonia, gpsr.requests@easproject.com

www.ingramcontent.com/pod-product-compliance
Ingram Content Group UK Ltd.
Pitfield, Milton Keynes, MK11 3LW, UK
UKHW040330190325
456107UK00006B/146